Knowledge Representation:
An AI Perspective

Tutorial Monographs in Cognitive Science
Nigel Shadbolt, Series Editor

Knowledge Representation: An AI Perspective, *Han Reichgelt*

In Preparation
Processing Images of Faces, *edited by Vicki Bruce and Mike Burton*

A Developmental Cognitive Science, *David Wood*

Inference, *Peter Jackson*

Knowledge Representation:
An AI Perspective

Han Reichgelt

**Artificial Intelligence Group
Dept of Psychology
University of Nottingham, England**

**ABLEX PUBLISHING CORPORATION
NORWOOD, NEW JERSEY**

Cover design by Thomas Phon Graphics

Printed in the United States of America.

Library of Congress Cataloging-in-Publication Data

Reichgelt, Han.
    Knowledge representation: an AI perspective / Han Reichgelt.
        p.   cm. — (Tutorial monographs in cognitive science)
    Includes bibliographical references and index.
    ISBN 0-89391-590-4
    1. Knowledge representation (Information theory)   2. Artificial intelligence.   I. Title.   II. Series.
    Q387.R45   1990
    003'.54—dc20
                                                                    90-14470
                                                                        CIP

Ablex Publishing Corporation
355 Chestnut Street
Norwood, New Jersey 07648

Contents

Preface

Knowledge representation is one of the main concerns of Artificial Intelligence, and no AI course is complete without a thorough introduction to this area. It is therefore surprising that there does not seem to be a book on the market that provides such an introduction. This book is an attempt at filling this gap.

Most research in Artificial Intelligence to date has been based on the knowledge representation hypothesis, the assumption that in any AI program there is a separate module which represents the information that the program has about the world. As a result, a number of so-called knowledge representation formalisms have been developed for representing this kind of information in a computer. This book discusses the most popular knowledge representation languages, namely logic, production rules, semantics networks and frames, and also provides a short introduction to AI systems that combine various knowledge representation languages.

Recently, the knowledge representation hypothesis has been challenged by the reemergence of a new style of computing, variously called parallel distributed processing, connectionism, or neural networks. This particular approach is discussed in a separate chapter, and the arguments in favor of and against parallel distributed processing are reviewed.

The book is aimed at third-year undergraduates in computer science or psychology, as well as first-year postgraduates. Although the book takes an AI perspective to the problem of knowledge representation, in a number of places attempts have been made to relate the discussion to issues in cognitive psychology.

A number of people have been extremely helpful while I was writing this book. I particularly want to mention Mike Burton, Peter Jackson, and Nigel Shadbolt, who each read the book and provided many valuable comments. Needless to say, any remaining mistakes are entirely my responsibility. Finally, I would like to thank Nikki Reichgelt for encouraging me to finish the book, and for giving me much needed support when it looked as if the book was never going to be finished.

1
What is Knowledge Representation?

1. ARTIFICIAL INTELLIGENCE AND KNOWLEDGE REPRESENTATION

Knowledge representation is a major concern in Artificial Intelligence and its importance cannot be overestimated. There are many different definitions of AI, and there is a lot of disagreement about what AI is and is not. This is not the place to discuss them in great detail. What most definitions agree about, however, is that AI programs involve symbolic information processing: An AI program manipulates symbols that somehow represent pieces of information about the world in order to perform a task that we normally take to require intelligence, such as playing chess, diagnosing an illness in a patient, or understanding an English sentence. Given the importance of symbols to represent information about the world, the quest for formalisms that can be used to this end is essential to any worker in AI. They are the main concern of the subfield of AI called knowledge representation.

There are many areas that clearly illustrate the need for representing information about the world in an AI program. Experience has shown that vision systems, for example, need to have prior information about the kinds of things that they are going to see in order to be able to interpret a scene. Natural language understanding systems also need to have information about the topics of conversation, and about the discourse participants in order to be able to fully understand a sentence. Even learning systems are greatly helped if they have some prior knowledge about the domain that they are supposed to learn about.

Although there are in principle many different ways in which one can imagine endowing a program with information about the world, most work in AI has been based on a methodological assumption which Brian Smith (1982) has called the *knowledge representation hypothesis*. According to this assumption, any intelligent process contains structural ingredients which external observers naturally take to represent the knowledge that the process exhibits. Moreover, these structural ingredients, independent of what external observers take them to be, play an essential and causal role in engendering the behavior that manifests the knowledge. In other words, any system, whether it be human or artificial, that shows intelligent behavior, is assumed to contain as a substructure a *knowledge base*. The knowledge base is a more or less direct encoding of the knowledge that the system has available. The knowledge base is manipulated by a separate substructure, which is often called the *inference engine*. The inference engine processes the symbols in the knowledge base in order to generate intelligent behavior.

Expert systems constitute maybe the clearest illustration of the knowledge representation hypothesis. An expert system is a program whose performance is comparable to human experts in its problem-solving behavior on very specific tasks. (For an excellent introduction to expert systems, see Jackson [1986].) Examples of early expert systems are DENDRAL, a program that infers the structure of an unknown chemical compound from various data about this compound (Buchanan, Sutherland, & Feigenbaum, 1969), MYCIN, a program that diagnoses certain blood infections and prescribes courses of antibiotics (Shortliffe, 1976), and INTERNIST-1/CADUCEUS, a diagnostic program with an impressive amount of knowledge of internal medicine (Pople, 1977). The advent of expert systems was a reaction to earlier work on general purpose problem solvers. The original idea was to construct programs that had some general intelligence, whatever that was, and could be used to solve different problems in different domains. The best known of these systems was GPS (Newell & Simon, 1963; Ernst & Newell, 1969). However, it became clear from these early experiments that the dream of a generally intelligent system that could solve all kinds of problems in all kinds of domains was not realizable. The conclusion was that the crucial factor in determining the quality of a problem-solving program was the amount of knowledge it had about the domain in which it was expected to solve problems. It was therefore necessary to endow a program with lots of domain-specific knowledge in order to construct a high-quality problem solver. As a consequence, the question of knowledge representation became very important.

The knowledge representation hypothesis has recently come under attack from a relatively new approach in AI, called *connectionism*. Although connectionists also recognize the importance of knowledge in many tasks that require intelligence, they reject the knowledge representation hypothesis. In particular, they reject the notion of separate substructures for representing and manipulating knowledge. Rather, they opt for a completely different style of endowing a system with knowledge about the world, which they claim is more in accordance with the way in which information is stored in the human brain. We return to the connectionist program in Chapter 8. For the moment, let us assume, as a working hypothesis, that the knowledge representation hypothesis is correct.

When talking about knowledge representation, there are of course a number of general philosophical questions that spring to mind, such as what are representations, and what makes it possible for certain symbols to represent certain pieces of information? While these deep philosophical questions are important, they are not the main concern of this book. In this book we concentrate on the various knowledge representation languages that have been proposed in the AI literature.

We discuss their strong and weak points, and contrast them with each other. It has to be said that there is no consensus in AI as to which knowledge representation formalism is best. In fact, there is not even agreement about whether there is such a thing as a single best knowledge representation language. Many would argue that each formalism has its pros and cons, and that it depends on the particular application which knowledge representation language is to be preferred. We return to some of these issues in the concluding chapter of this book.

There is one more general remark that needs to be made. Philosophers have defined knowledge as "true justified belief." This is not the way in which it is used in AI, at least not in the context of knowledge representation. Knowledge representation languages are used to represent information without making any claims whatsoever that the expressions written down in the language are either true or justified. Thus, the fact that some piece of information has been written down in a knowledge representation language does not by itself make it true, and does not justify it. Maybe the term *information representation languages* would have been preferable to the term *knowledge representation language*.

In the remainder of this chapter we make some more general remarks about knowledge representation and knowledge representation formalisms. In particular, we argue that there are two aspects to any knowledge representation language, and that one needs to distinguish between four different levels when talking about knowledge representation formalisms.

2. TWO ASPECTS OF A KNOWLEDGE REPRESENTATION LANGUAGE

One can distinguish between two aspects of any knowledge representation language, namely a *syntactic* and an *inferential* aspect. The syntactic or notational aspect concerns the way in which one stores information in an explicit format. The inferential aspect concerns the way in which the explicitly stored information can be used to derive information that is implicit in it. We look at these different sides of a knowledge representation language in some detail.

A knowledge representation language is a formal language. The first task that one faces when one is defining a knowledge representation language, therefore, is to specify precisely what expressions are part of the language and how these expressions can be combined to construct new expressions in the language. A user needs to be told exactly what sets of symbols count as well-formed expressions in the language in order to be able to use the knowledge representation formalism to represent information about the world. For example, should one write *green(my_car)*, or is the correct way of representing this piece of information *(green my_car)*? The syntax of a knowledge representation language answers these questions.

But defining a knowledge representation language involves more than just defining some formal language. Apart from a syntax, each knowledge representation language also has an inferential aspect. Each knowledge representation language has its own preferred way of drawing inferences, that is, deriving implicit information from explicitly stored information. A knowledge base will always contain certain pieces of information, but one might be able, by doing some reasoning, to derive some information that is implicit in the stored information. For example, if I believe that all Ferraris are red, and I believe that my car is a Ferrari, then I can derive from these two explicit pieces of information the implicit piece of information that my car is red. The *interpreter* for a knowledge representation language is a computer program that automatically draws these inferences.

The interpreter for a knowledge representation language behaves according to certain abstract rules. Thus, an interpreter for some logic-based knowledge representation language may behave according to the rule of *modus ponens*, and infer from a knowledge base which contains both *if* ϕ *then* ψ and ϕ, that ψ is the case. We follow terminology used in the logical literature, and refer to such abstract rules as *inference rules* in the remainder of this book.

Before we continue, two further remarks need to be made here. First, inference rules are completely independent of the actual knowledge in the knowledge base. They are abstract rules which describe the behavior of the interpreter independently of which domain-dependent information is stored in the knowledge base. There is another sense in which the term inference rule is used in the AI literature in general, and the expert systems literature in particular. In this second sense, an inference rule is a domain-dependent rule that is stored in the knowledge base. Thus, in an expert system that gives advice on which car to buy, there might be a rule like *if you want good road holding, buy an Alfa Romeo*, and sometimes the term inference rule is used to refer to this type of rule as well. Clearly, there is a close relationship between the information in the knowledge base and the inference rules that the interpreter implements. For one thing, the interpreter's inference rules will have to be applied to the knowledge in the knowledge base. Thus, an interpreter which implements the inference rule of modus ponens may apply it to a knowledge base which contains both the rule *if you want good road holding, buy an Alfa Romeo*, and the statement *Smith wants good road holding* to infer that *Smith should buy an Alfa*. Nevertheless, it would be confusing to use the term inference rule both to refer to the domain-dependent rules in the knowledge base and the inference rules that the interpreter implements, and we therefore use the term only in the second sense.

A second remark concerning the notion of inference rule that, although it is derived from the logical literature, its use is not restricted to logic-based knowledge representation languages. The term is equally applicable to other knowledge representation languages. For example, in Chapter 6, we will see that frame-based languages use inheritance for inference, and inheritance can thus be regarded as an inference rule as well.

The syntactic and the inferential aspect are of course closely related. The syntax of every knowledge representation language will specify some primitive expressions. One can use these primitives to construct more complicated expressions for representing particular pieces of knowledge. The meanings of these primitives need not be specified any further, but have been determined by the designer of the language. The interpreter for the language has been (or should have been) constructed in accordance with the specification of these primitives. As Brachman (1979) writes in the context of a particular representation language: "The primitives are those things that the interpreter is programmed in advance to understand, and that are not usually represented in the language itself." For example, if we use logic as our knowledge representation language, then the meaning of the connective & (read: *and*) will not be represented in the language itself. Rather, the meaning of this symbol will be programmed into the interpreter. This is of course very similar to programming languages where the meanings of the primitives are determined by the interpreter and are not defined by the user. For example, in Lisp the meaning of the primitive *CAR* is given by the Lisp interpreter and is not usually specified as an explicitly defined function. The way in which the interpreter for the knowledge representation deals with the primitives determines what implicit information can be derived from explicitly stored information. For example, suppose that & is indeed a primitive of our knowledge representation language that has been programmed into the interpreter. Then, if the knowledge base contains the information *green(my_car) & red(your_car)*, the interpreter can derive the implicitly stored information *green(my_car)*, as well as *red(your_car)*. One might argue that the inference rules of a knowledge representation language in the sense in which we defined the term above can be regarded as a specification of the meanings of the primitive expressions in a knowledge representation language.

It is important to distinguish the syntactic and inferential aspects of a knowledge representation language. There are usually two types of arguments that have been put forward for preferring one knowledge representation language over another. The first type relies on the syntax. In this case, arguments usually stress the naturalness and the expressiveness of one knowledge representation language over another. It might, for example, be much easier to represent a particular piece of information in one knowledge representation language than in another, or it might indeed be impossible to represent some pieces of information. We will see examples of this later on. The second type of argument relies on the inferential aspects. Arguments of this type usually draw attention to the power of the underlying inference machinery.

There are some obvious relations between the syntactic and inferential aspect. The more primitives the knowledge representation language has, that is, the richer the syntax, the more inference rules are needed. After all, the meanings of the primitives are not specified in the language itself, but rather are hard-wired into the interpreter. Conversely, as Levesque and Brachman (1985) point out, the more powerful the inference machinery associated with a knowledge representation language the more information can be left implicit. Thus, if the interpreter of the knowledge representation language had the meaning of & hard-wired into it, and would be able to infer φ and ψ if φ & ψ was explicit stored, then we did not have to store the two pieces of information *green(my_car)* and *red(your_car)* explicitly alongside the information that *green(my_car)* & *red(your_car)*. The interpreter could derive the first two pieces of information from the last piece of information. The cost of more powerful inference rules is that it becomes much more difficult to write an efficient interpreter for that knowledge representation language. We discuss this point in section 3 of Chapter 2.

3. FOUR LEVELS OF KNOWLEDGE REPRESENTATION

Another important distinction that will be used throughout this book is a distinction between four different levels at which knowledge representation formalisms can be discussed. The distinction is based on Brachman (1979). In fact, Brachman distinguishes five levels in a discussion of a particular type of knowledge representation formalism, namely semantic networks. Brachman's fifth level, the linguistic level, concerns the way in which particular pieces of knowledge are represented in a given knowledge representation formalism. However, because we are mainly interested in knowledge representation formalisms as such, we will ignore the linguistic level here. The reader will note that in the discussion of the four levels below, we again draw the distinction between the syntactic and the inferential aspects of a knowledge representation language.

The first level is the *implementational* level. Knowledge representation languages are intended to be used to represent information on a computer, and it is therefore essential that it be possible to build a computer program underlying the knowledge representation language. This is the main concern at the implementational level. From the notational point of view, the emphasis is on data structures for representing the knowledge, while from the inferential point of view one is concerned with discovering and implementing algorithms that draw the desired inferences. Examples of questions that play a role here are "what data structures are best suited for representing expressions in the language inside the machine?" and "is this programming technique suitable for building an interpreter for this knowledge representation language?" or "would this technique lead to a more efficient/more elegant program?"

Another important question that has to be solved at the implementational level is the question of indexing mechanisms. Knowledge bases can become very large, and in these cases it is not feasible to search a knowledge base from top to bottom in order to find whether some piece of information is stored in it, or to determine whether it can be derived from the explicitly stored information. It therefore becomes important that there is some sort of index that allows the program to decide rapidly where the answer would be stored if there is one. Indexing mechanisms are intended to solve this problem. A simple example of an indexing mechanism is the way in which a dictionary is organized. Clearly, a randomly ordered list of words and their definitions is not very useful when it comes to finding the meaning of some word. It may take a very long time to determine whether a given word was in the list or not. Under such a regime, if you have not found the word yet, it is always possible that it will occur later in the list, and you will have to continue your search until you either find the word, or until you reach the end of the list. By using alphabetical ordering as an indexing mechanism, you can determine rapidly where the word could be found, if it is indeed in the dictionary. If the word cannot be found in the expected place, then you know that it does not appear in the dictionary.

The second level at which one can discuss a knowledge representation language is the *logical* level. Notationally, the main concern at the logical level is the logical properties of the knowledge representation language. As far as the syntactic aspect are concerned, there are two main questions. First, there is the question about the meanings of expressions in the formalism. For example, what does it mean to write:

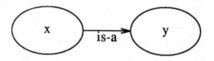

Does it mean that every x is a y, or that some x's are y's? Or does it mean that x's have all or some of the properties of y's? As we shall see later on in Chapters 5 and 6, all these interpretations have been used. Thus, one question that one is concerned with at the logical level is the meaning of the formalisms that are allowed by the knowledge representation language. A second question concerns the expressive power of the formalism. One needs to know what types of information can be represented, and what types cannot. For example, suppose you want to represent the information that "either Fred's car is red, or John's car is green." Then you obviously need a knowledge representation language that is powerful enough to represent this type of information.

From the inferential point of view, the main concern at the logical level is what one might call the logical properties of the inference procedures. An example of a question that arises here is the soundness of the inference procedure. An inference procedure is sound if whenever the input expressions are true, then the output expressions are true as well. It is obvious that one would prefer knowledge representation formalisms whose inference procedures are sound. After all, a sound inference procedure guarantees that if all the information that is explicitly stored in the knowledge base is true, then the information that can be inferred is true as well. So, you can never derive anything false from true information. We return to these questions in Chapter 3 when we discuss the use of logic as a knowledge representation formalism.

The third level at which one can discuss a knowledge representation formalism is the *epistemological* level. The main concerns here are the knowledge structuring primitives that are needed for a satisfactory knowledge representation language and the types of inference strategy that should be made available. At this level one is concerned with discovering the types of primitives that are needed for representing particular pieces of knowledge without considering which particular primitives are needed. For example, the types of primitives that are needed for representing the knowledge that is used in certain skills, such as the knowledge used by an expert pianist, are likely to be very different from those needed for representing the knowledge used by somebody trying to prove a mathematical theorem. Similarly, the types of inference strategy that are used in different tasks are likely to be very different. For example, somebody trying to diagnose a faulty electronic circuit is likely to use different inference strategies from somebody who is designing a new circuit. It should be noted that at the epistemological level, one does not make any decisions about which *actual* primitives and inference strategies are used to represent knowledge about some domain. Rather, at this level, one is exclusively concerned with the *types* of primitive expression and the *types* of inference strategy that are used.

The final level is the *conceptual* level. Whereas the epistemological level is concerned with the *types* of knowledge structuring primitives that are needed, the conceptual level concerns itself with the *actual* primitives that should be included in a knowledge representation language. Suppose, for example, that we had chosen, at the epistemological level, that knowledge was to be represented using a semantic network. That is, the decision was made that the primitive in the language would be nodes for representing objects, and arcs between these nodes for representing relationships between objects. So, in order to say that some object stood in some relationship to another object, one would write something like:

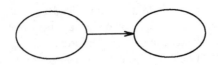

In addition, one would say that arcs were to be used to draw inferences. The decisions at the conceptual level would then concern, for example, which actual arcs there would be. Would there be an is-a arc, representing the information that the first object is an instance of the second object; would there be a part-of arc, and so on? An example of a theory that is clearly at the conceptual level is Schank's conceptual dependency theory (Schank, 1975a). Schank proposed a set of primitive arcs which he claims should be enough to represent any piece of knowledge that one would want to represent. We will discuss Schank's work in Chapter 5.

It is important to keep these four different levels distinct. A lot of the discussion in the literature is rather confused because knowledge representation formalisms that are intended to be at one level are often attacked because they are not adequate at another level. Also, in a number of knowledge representation formalisms that have been proposed in the literature, the primitives that are defined as part of the language often come from different levels. Keeping these levels separate should clear at least some of confusions surrounding the area of knowledge representation.

4. REQUIREMENTS ON KNOWLEDGE REPRESENTATION LANGUAGES

There are various criteria which one can use to assess the value of a knowledge representation language. In this section we discuss some of them. Each of the four levels at which knowledge representation formalisms can be analyzed has its own criteria of adequacy, and a completely satisfactory knowledge representation language would of course meet the criteria at all levels.

At the implementational level, the main criterion of adequacy concerns efficiency. An implementationally adequate knowledge representation language should allow one to store information in a space-efficient way, that is, without taking up too much of the computer's memory. It should also draw its inferences in a time-efficient way, that is, it should draw its inferences as quickly as possible. One way in which the latter might be achieved, of course, is by having an efficient indexing mechanism.

At the logical level, one is concerned with the logical properties of the knowledge representation language. A logically adequate knowledge representation language should ideally have a clear semantics: It should be clearly specified what the meanings are of the syntactically well-formed expressions. One principle that is often used in defining the semantics of any formal language is the principle of compositionality, or Frege's principle. The principle of compositionality states that it should be possible to completely determine the meaning of a complex expression on the basis of the meanings of the simpler expressions that make up the complex expression, and the way in which they have been syntactically combined. Thus, in a language which obeys the principle of compositionality it is possible to determine the meaning of the complex expression *red(my_car)* if you know the meanings of the simpler expressions *red* and *my _car*. We return to the principle of compositionality in section 1.1.3. of Chapter 3.

A second logical criterion of adequacy on a knowledge representation language is that its inference rules should be sound. If the information that is explicitly stored in the knowledge base is true, then the implicit information that can be retrieved using the inference rules should be true as well. A knowledge representation language that allows one to retrieve false information from true information is not satisfactory. We return to the logical criteria of adequacy in more detail in Chapter 3.

At the epistemological level, the relevant criteria of adequacy have to do with the naturalness with which representations can be constructed and understood. There are various epistemological criteria of adequacy. First, if there is a natural way to organize information about a particular domain, then an epistemologically adequate knowledge representation language will reflect this organization. For example, one of the most natural ways to look at the knowledge involved in cognitive skills might be as rules that say what action is to be performed when certain circumstances hold. An epistemologically adequate representation language would respect this.

A second important criterion of adequacy that is best analyzed as epistemological is that of the modularity of a knowledge representation language. It is likely that the information that is stored in a knowledge base will change over time, either because the domain that this information concerns changes, or because it turns out that the constructor of the knowledge base was mistaken and represented some information that is not true. An epistemologically adequate knowledge representation language would be modular so that whenever a particular piece of information changed, only a small part of the knowledge base would have to change. An example of a nonmodular knowledge representation language would be a program in which all the information was somehow buried inside the actual program code. If the information that is to be represented changes, then the whole program would have to be changed with all that that entails.

A third epistemological criterion of adequacy is closely related to the previous two. It concerns the granularity of the knowledge representation language. Knowledge has to be stored in chunks. The granularity of the knowledge representation language determines the size of the chunks in which the knowledge is organized. One may, for example, store knowledge as a set of facts, thus opting for a knowledge representation language with a relatively fine granularity, or, alternatively, one may want to organize in larger chunks corresponding to what one might call a concept, all the knowledge that there is about a particular object, or class of objects.

A final epistemological criterion of adequacy concerns the relation with the conceptual level. Obviously, an epistemologically adequate knowledge representation language should support whatever actual primitives one chooses at the conceptual level. Suppose that we decided that the best way to represent knowledge was as a set of facts, where each fact was represented as a predicate followed by a set of arguments. Then an epistemologically adequate representation language would allow the user to choose whatever predicates they liked at the conceptual level. A framework which insisted that HAS-PART was one of the required conceptual primitives would not be adequate at the epistemological level.

Conceptual criteria of adequacy have to with how concisely particular pieces of knowledge can be represented. If it is impossible to represent a simple piece of knowledge in a concise way, then it is likely that the actual primitives used at the conceptual level are wrong, and need to be changed. Similarly, if a particular simple inference can only be made in a very complicated way, then one suspects that the actual inference procedure that is used is not adequate.

5. OUTLINE OF THE BOOK

The outline of this book is as follows. Chapter 2 is a discussion of general problems in the area of knowledge representation and the construction of interpreters for knowledge representation languages. Chapter 3 discusses logic and its use as a knowledge representation language. In this chapter we also introduce certain concepts that will be relevant to most of the other chapters. As a consequence, it is somewhat longer than the other chapters. Chapter 4 introduces production rules, the knowledge representation language that has probably been most popular in the area of expert systems. In Chapter 5 we look at semantic networks. Chapter 6 contains an introduction to frame-based representations. Frame-based representations are the underlying concept of a relatively new style of AI programming called object-oriented programming, which is briefly discussed as well. Chapter 7 discusses mixed representational formalisms. This particular approach has become more popular over the past years with the advent of the large AI tool kits such as ART, KEE, and KnowledgeCraft, which combine many of the techniques and representational formalisms introduced in the previous chapters. We discuss one particular system, KRYPTON, in some detail. Chapter 8 looks at the new connectionist approach in AI. Chapter 9 is a concluding chapter, in which we discuss some of the open problems in the area of knowledge representation.

2
Some General Problems in Knowledge Representation

In this chapter, we discuss a number of general issues in the area of knowledge representation. Because these issues are very general, they will come up in some form or other when we discuss the various knowledge representation formalisms in more detail.

1. THE DECLARATIVE VERSUS PROCEDURAL CONTROVERSY

A debate that raged furiously in the early years of work on knowledge representation was the declarative versus procedural controversy. Although the debate seems to have died down a bit, and a consensus seems to have been reached, a recent paper by McDermott (1986) challenges this consensus. We discuss McDermott's paper in Chapter 3. Here we concentrate on the original discussion and the consensus that was reached.

The declarative versus procedural controversy concerns the way in which knowledge is represented in a program. According to Winograd (1975), it is the incarnation in AI of the philosophical distinction between knowing *how* and knowing *that*. The procedural position asserts that human knowledge is primarily knowing how, and that in order to capture knowledge in a computer, it is necessary to write computer programs consisting of a set of procedures, each of which represents some piece of knowledge. Thus, the knowledge that a person has, for example, about chess is identical to the procedures that he or she has for playing chess, and a procedural representation of this is a program that represents this knowledge as a set of internal procedures. The declarative position, on the other hand, believes that knowledge is primarily knowing that. People know facts about the world. Consequently, knowledge should be represented explicitly and in a declarative format, rather than embedded inside the procedures of some program. Of course one needs procedures to use knowledge, for example, in order to derive implicit knowledge from the explicitly stored knowledge. However, these procedures are assumed to be very general, and can be used for knowledge about different domains. This is in contrast to the procedures that the proceduralist uses, which are very special purpose, and can be used for one domain only.

Each position has its pros and cons. The most important argument against the procedural position is that it requires that a piece of knowledge is specified by laying down how it is used. If knowing a piece of information is essentially knowing how to use it, then representing a piece of knowledge implies specifying how it can be used. But often a given piece of information can be used in more than one way, and in ways that were possibly not envisaged when it was represented. Winograd (1975) mentions as an example the statement *all lawyers from Chicago are clever*. This piece of information can be used to derive that Fred is clever, if it is known that he is a lawyer from Chicago; or it can be used to infer that Fred is not a lawyer, if it is known that he is not clever, but comes from Chicago; or the statement can be used to conclude that Fred does not come from Chicago, if it is known that he a stupid lawyer. According to the proceduralist, each use would have to be represented separately.

A related argument in favor of declarative representations points to the fact that the inference procedures used for deriving information are very general purpose and can therefore be applied to many different knowledge bases. Not only is it possible to use the same piece of information in more than one way, the inference procedures for manipulating knowledge can also be applied to more than one piece of information. Thus, a statement like *all dentists in Edinburgh are rich* could be used in ways analogous to the ways in which the statement *all lawyers in Chicago are clever* can be used. In a procedural representation, where there is no separation between the information that has been represented and the procedures for manipulating it, it is hard to see how this generalization could be captured. In a declarative representation, with its general purpose procedures for manipulating knowledge, this poses no problems.

Another advantage of declarative representations is that it is much easier to change the information stored in a knowledge base. Suppose, for example, that one finds out that the statement *all lawyers from Chicago are clever* is no longer true. Then, in a declarative representation, all one would have to do is delete this statement from the knowledge base. However, in a procedural representation, where each use has been specified separately, this would involve some (possibly major) rewriting of the program that represented this piece of information, and the problem is that, as any programmer knows, more often than not, little changes in one part of the program may have large effects on other parts of the program. Similar arguments apply when an existing piece of information needs to be modified, for example, when one wants to change the above statement into *all lawyers from the North side of Chicago are clever*. In a declarative representation one only needs to change one statement in the knowledge base, whereas in a procedural representation the program may have to be changed in many different places. Finally, adding a piece of information is easy when the representation is declarative, but more difficult when the representation is procedural, as it involves writing procedures for each use to which this new piece of information may be put.

The arguments in favor of the procedural position point to the fact that many things that we know are more naturally seen as procedures. An example is counting and adding numbers. It is possible to specify arithmetic knowledge declaratively by means of the so-called *Peano* axioms. From these axioms, one can prove, for example, that $2 + 2 = 4$. However, it seems unlikely that you actually use these axioms whenever you add two numbers. It seems much more likely that there is a special-purpose addition procedure that you run whenever you are faced with a problem of this kind. In general, humans have a lot of knowledge about processes that take place in the world, and this type of information, although it could in principle be represented declaratively, is much more easily represented procedurally. As Winograd (1975) puts it: "We trade some degree of flexibility for a tremendous gain in the ease of representing what we know about processes."

Winograd mentions two other arguments in favor of procedural representations. The first one is that *second-order* knowledge, or *metaknowledge* as it is called these days, is more easily represented procedurally. Metaknowledge is knowledge about what we know or can know, or knowledge about how to use the knowledge that we have. For example, when you are asked the telephone number of one of your friends, then you may not be able to recall it directly, but you will know that if you made some effort you would be able to retrieve it. This is of course in sharp contrast to the situation in which you are asked the telephone number of a complete stranger, in which case you know that you do not know it. Again, although it is possible to represent metaknowledge declaratively, Winograd claims that it is simply more natural to represent it procedurally. A second additional argument that Winograd mentions is a pragmatic argument: Procedural representations work. Winograd claims that complex AI programs have a large amount of their knowledge built into their procedures. He also alleges that programs that keep the domain-specific knowledge in a declarative knowledge base are limited to the simplest of worlds and the simplest of goals.

Having made the distinction between declarative and procedural representations, Winograd then continues to propose a knowledge representation formalism that is supposed to be a synthesis between these two extremes. The representation that he proposes is very much based on Minsky's notion of a frame (Minsky, 1975). We discuss frame-based representations in Chapter 6. In the remainder of this section, we take a critical look at Winograd's arguments.

Winograd gives three arguments in favor of procedural representations: A lot of knowledge is more naturally seen as procedural, metaknowledge is more naturally represented procedurally, and procedural representations work, whereas declarative do not. The third argument is no longer valid, at least not as an argument against declarative representations. Winograd's paper was written before the advent of expert systems. In Chapter 1 we defined an expert system as a program whose performance is similar to human experts in its problem solving behavior on specific tasks. In expert systems, the domain knowledge is usually represented in a declarative format. The knowledge representation formalism most often used are production rules, discussed in Chapter 4. While it is easy to overestimate the success of expert systems, there seems little doubt that successful expert systems solve difficult problems in complicated domains. Hence, the pragmatic argument against declarative representations is no longer valid.

It is also becoming less clear whether metaknowledge is more naturally represented declaratively or procedurally. A lot of research has focused on the problem of reasoning about knowledge, and many workers have used epistemic logic to tackle this problem (see, e.g., Halpern, 1986). Logic, of course, is the declarative representation language *par excellence*. Also, the problem of knowledge about how to use knowledge has become an important research topic, and many people have built programs that use declarative representations of this type of knowledge We return to this point in section 3 of this chapter.

The arguments in favor of declarative representations concern the economy of storage (the same piece of information can be used more than once), generality (the same procedures can be used for manipulating more than one piece of information), and flexibility and maintainability (it is easy to add to, modify, or delete knowledge stored in a declarative format). It seems beyond doubt that declarative representations are essential for multiple uses of the same piece of information. Similarly, the separation of the knowledge from the procedures for manipulating it would seem impossible in non-declarative representations. However, the advantage of flexibility and maintainability is really a consequence of the modularity of representation. Each separate piece of information is represented independently of the others, and therefore it can be changed without affecting other pieces of information. However, the issue of modularity is independent of the procedural/declarative distinction. While it is no doubt true that declarative representations encourage one to represent information in modular fashion, it is certainly not impossible to do in a procedural knowledge representation language. Indeed, as Winograd (1975) points out, the idea of *structured* programming, which originated in computer science in the early 1970s, and is now common good, was a response to the complexity that arose when the programmer made use of all the power that a programming language gave. This often led to convoluted code. Within the structured programming paradigm, the programmer is encouraged to write modular code. Each module in a program performs a particular function, and the interactions between the modules are precisely specified in advance. Thus, in a procedural representation, each procedure could correspond to one particular piece of information. If this procedure is independent of the other procedures embedded in the program, then one has achieved modularity, and all the advantages that this entails. It would, of course, be advantageous if one could develop procedural knowledge representation languages that encourage such modular programming. Object-oriented programming languages, programming languages that grew out of frame-based knowledge representations languages, are a response to this need. They are discussed in Chapter 6.

A last point concerns a computational advantage of procedural representations. Often a program that embeds a procedural representation of some pieces of information will solve problems faster than a program that uses a declarative representation. The reason lies in the fact that the program with the declarative representation uses very general principles to solve the problem, whereas the program with the knowledge embedded in its procedures can use very specific shortcuts in its problem solving. Therefore, there is a tradeoff between the flexibility of the representations, and the speed of the resulting program. A program with a very flexible knowledge base will have to rely on general procedures for manipulating knowledge. As a consequence, it will be slower than a program with a less flexible knowledge base that can use very specific procedures.

The greater speed of procedural representations might also account for the fact that as humans acquire certain skills, they becomes less good at articulating the rules that they are using. Anderson (1985) discusses the example of second language learning. When you first learn a foreign language, you are particularly aware of the grammatical rules of the language, and you use them explicitly. However, as you become more fluent, you no longer need to reflect on the various rules, and you use them without any conscious awareness. One way of explaining this phenomenon would be to say that what was originally a declarative representation has become a procedural representation.

Summarizing then, there are two types of representation language, procedural and declarative. Procedural representations have two advantages. First, certain types of knowledge, especially those involving skills, seem more naturally represented as procedures. Second, programs that rely on procedural representations are computationally more efficient than programs that rely on declarative representations. Declarative representations, on the other hand, allow for one piece of information to be used in more than one way. The conclusion that many researchers have drawn from these arguments is that you need both types of representation. While one might prefer declarative representations, because they allow multiple uses of the same piece of information, there are certainly occasions where procedural representations are more appropriate, either because it is difficult to see how to represent that particular piece of knowledge declaratively, or because one is prepared to trade in some of the flexibility of a declarative representation for the speed of a procedural representation.

2. TYPES OF KNOWLEDGE

In this section we distinguish between two main types of knowledge that can always be found in a program that contains some explicitly represented information. The analysis is loosely based on Clancey (1983) and Wielinga and Breuker (1986). It is important to distinguish between different *types* of knowledge. For example, it seems likely that different kinds of knowledge are more easily represented in different knowledge representation formalisms. This kind of analysis might therefore be useful in deciding on an appropriate knowledge representation language for particular applications.

The first type of knowledge we distinguish is *domain knowledge*. Obviously, a program that manipulates information about a particular domain will have to contain information about the domain. We call this type of knowledge domain knowledge. For example, a program may contain domain knowledge about internal medicine, or about electronic circuits.

One can distinguish between two kinds of domain knowledge. The first type concerns the types of the entities that are relevant in the domain. Following Clancey (1983), we will call knowledge of this kind *structural knowledge*. Often, a domain has a very specific structure, and it might be important to represent this information explicitly. For example, if one is representing information in the domain of internal medicine, then the types of entity that one would want to talk about are things like patients, diseases, organs, drugs and so on. Often, there are hierarchical classificatory relationships between certain classes of entity in the domain which can be used in problem solving. In the internal medicine example, jaundice is a form of liver disease, which itself is a particular form of disease.

A second type of domain knowledge concerns the relations between the entities that are distinguished in the structural knowledge. One might call this *relational knowledge*. In the domain of internal medicine, typical relationships between entities are one disease causing another, or a patient suffering from a disease. Another important type of relational knowledge concerns relationships between facts in the domain. For example, one might know that if a patient looks yellow, then they probably have a liver disease.

Apart from domain knowledge, an expert often also possesses knowledge about how to use the domain knowledge to solve particular problems in the domain. Following Clancey, we call this problem-solving knowledge *strategic knowledge*. For example, one can imagine knowing everything there is to know about internal medicine without being able to use this knowledge effectively to diagnose patients. In fact, the latter stages of the training program of doctors often involves learning how to put the "textbook" knowledge into practice.

The distinction between structural, relational, and strategic knowledge is somewhat of an abstraction. Quite often, the domain knowledge that somebody has is very tightly coupled to the structural knowledge that they have. This problem is especially clear in the knowledge elicitation phase of the construction of expert systems. One of the first stages of expert system construction is the interrogation of a human expert. One tries to determine how experts solve problems in their particular area of expertise. This turns out to be a very difficult task. Experts often use rules of thumb which they have acquired through years of using their domain knowledge to solve problems. The domain knowledge therefore becomes tied up with the problem solving knowledge, and experts often find it difficult to draw an explicit distinction between the two.

3. THE PROBLEM OF CONTROL

One of the problems that arises in every knowledge representation language is the problem of control. As pointed out in section 2 of Chapter 1, there are two aspects to a knowledge representation language, a syntactic and an inferential aspect. The inferential aspect concerns the ability to make explicit information which is implicit in the knowledge stored in the knowledge base, and the term *inference rule* was introduced to describe this aspect of a knowledge representation language. A problem now arises because, when trying to determine whether something follows from the knowledge base, it is often possible to draw more than one inference. Thus, more than one of the inference rules that the interpreter implements may be used at this point. Alternatively, the interpreter may be able to apply the same inference rule to different pieces of information in the knowledge base. The problem of *control* is the problem of deciding which of these possible inferences to draw. Obviously, the problem of control is very closely related to the problem of the representation of strategic knowledge.

The problem of control is very reminiscent of the problem of search, which is another central topic in AI. (For a thorough introduction to the problem of search and the various algorithms that have been proposed to deal with this problem, the reader is referred to Nilsson [1980].) A search problem is the problem of trying to determine whether a given goal state can be achieved from a certain state of the world. Classic examples of search problems are game-playing applications, such as chess-playing programs. The initial state of the world as represented in a chess-playing program is the initial position of the chessmen on the board. The goal state is a state in which the opposition has been mated. In order to achieve the goal given the initial state, one has to apply operators which change the initial state into another state. In the chess-playing example, the operators are the legal moves that are possible in a given position. The problem is, of course, to decide which operators to apply (in the chess example, which moves to make) in order to achieve the desired goal state.

Trying to determine whether a given piece of information follows from a given knowledge base can also be analyzed as a search problem. The initial state is the state of the knowledge base. The operators are applications of the inference rules that are part of the knowledge representation formalism to the information stored in the knowledge base, and the goal is the piece of information that one is trying to derive. If more than inference rule is in principle applicable, then we face a similar problem to that in the chess-playing program, namely, which inference rule to apply? This, then, is the problem of control.

Of course, the problem of control becomes much more pressing if the knowledge representation language has a large number of inference rules. The more inferences you can drawn in a knowledge representation language, the harder it becomes to build an efficient computer program that draws the required inferences. A very powerful inference engine is very difficult to implement. In Chapter 1, we mentioned Levesque and Brachman's (1985) observation about the relationship between the expressive power of a language and the inferential power of its inference engine. A knowledge representation language which allows a lot of information to be left implicit requires a more powerful inference engine. As more powerful inference engines are more computationally intractable, Levesque and Brachman conclude that more expressive knowledge representation languages requires inference engines that are less computationally tractable. We thus see an important tradeoff between expressive power and computational tractability. As a result, knowledge representation languages either have to be limited in the amount of information that can be left implicit, or unlimited in the reasoning effort that they might need. This trade-off between expressive power and computational tractability is one of the themes throughout the book.

Because the problem of control is such an important problem, it has received a lot of attention. There are many schemes around that determine how inference rules should be applied, and in which order. These schemes are known as *control regimes*. We first discuss a number of control regimes that have been proposed. Then we discuss another approach to the problem of control, namely explicit representations of strategic knowledge.

3.1. Forward versus Backward Reasoning

A first distinction one can draw is between forward and backward reasoning. In forward reasoning, one starts from the information that is available in the knowledge base and applies all the inference rules until one has found the given piece of information, or until one has determined that the requested information does not follow. This control regime is sometimes called *data-driven* because one starts from what one knows, the data, and tries to find out whether the goal follows.

Normally, the inference rules are formulated in a forward reasoning fashion: If you know this, then you implicitly know the following pieces of information as well. Consider, for example, the rule of modus ponens: If you know that *if* ϕ *then* ψ and that ϕ, then you know that ψ as well. But it is of course entirely possible to read these rules backwards: If you want to determine whether this piece of information is implicit in the information stored in the knowledge base, then determine whether you know certain other pieces of information. For example, if you want to know whether ψ is the case and you know that *if* ϕ *then* ψ then you should try to find out whether ϕ is the case. In backward reasoning, the inference

one searches breadth-first, then one will find the shortest solution. For example, referring to the above figure, let the boxes represent nodes that can be solved while the circles represent nodes that cannot be solved directly, either because they need to be expanded further, or because they cannot be expanded and also are not in the knowledge base. Then, depth-first search will find solution 9 after applying only five inference rules. Breadth-first search will find solution 8 which is one step shorter than solution 9, but it will take eight inferences to do so.

3.3. Heuristic Search

The control regimes that we have discussed so far are all complete in the sense that each node in the search tree is visited once until a solution is found. The main differences were in the direction in which the inference rules were used, either goal-driven or data-driven, and the order in which the nodes in the tree were visited. However, in a lot of cases it is impossible, or impractical, to visit all nodes. Visiting all nodes may be impossible because there are an infinite number of inferences that can be drawn at a given stage. Interpreters for some logic-based knowledge representation languages, for example, implement the rule of universal elimination. This inference rule allows one to conclude for any individual a that it has the property p if it is known that every individual has the property p. Now, if there are an infinite number of individuals, then applying this rule to each individual would lead to an infinite number of nodes. Also, in a lot of cases where it is in principle possible to visit all nodes, it is not practically possible because there are too many nodes. An example of this case is the chess-playing program. Although for any given board position, there are only a finite number of moves, the complete search tree is so big that it is impossible to search it in finite time. The *branching factor* of the tree is too large; there are too many descendants for every node.

In order to get around this problem, you can use *heuristics* while searching a tree. Often there is information available that can be used in guiding the search. For example, a good chess player will recognize that the result of making a particular move will lead to an inferior position, and will not further consider that position. In other words, the branch in the search tree that arose by making that move in the current position need no longer be considered and can be *pruned*. The pieces of information that can be used in guiding the search of a tree are called heuristics.

Good heuristics can also be used to search trees that could in principle be searched using nonheuristic methods more efficiently. Thus, while for certain problems, heuristic search is the only possible solution, for other problems, heuristics, although not necessary, may help improve the performance of a program.

There are three areas in which heuristics can be used. The first area is in the choice of operator. Once it has been decided to work on a particular node, or to try to achieve a particular goal, you have to choose an operator to apply to this node. Often there is more than one operator applicable. The above example provides an illustration of this: When we were backward chaining on *Fred's car will probably have difficulty starting*, we could apply the inference rules of modus ponens both to rule 5 and 6. Often, there is heuristic information that can be used to guide the choice. It might, for example, be the case that applying modus ponens to one domain rule in the knowledge base will lead to a subgoal that is much easier to solve than the subgoal generated by applying modus ponens to another rule. If we are trying to solve a goal quickly, then taking the first route makes more sense. The process of deciding which operator to apply is known as *conflict resolution*.

A second choice in which heuristics can be used is in *conjunct ordering*. Often reducing a goal *G* leads not to just one subgoal. Rather, it leads to a set of subgoals each of which has to be solved in order to solve *G*. For example, when we were trying to prove *Fred's car will probably have difficulty starting* and we were backward reasoning on a domain rule such as

IF a car is Italian
   AND the weather is cold
   AND it is not stored in a garage
THEN it will probably have difficulty starting.

we ended with the following three subgoals

Fred's car is Italian
the weather is cold
Fred's car is not stored in a garage

each of which has to be solved in order to solve the original goal. When faced with a set of subgoals, one can use heuristic information to order the set. Although each of them will have to be solved in order to solve the original goal, some subgoals might be harder to solve than others, so that it should be possible to decide more quickly that the original goal cannot be solved in this way.

Note that there is an interesting difference between conflict resolution and conjunct ordering. In conflict resolution, one usually first wants to generate the subgoal that looks easiest to solve. The reason for this is that each subgoal represents an alternative way of solving the original goal, and one just wants to try the easiest looking first. In conjunct ordering on the other hand, one tends to try the most difficult goal first. After all, all the subgoals must be solved, and this particular attempt at solving the goal is going to fail if one subgoal cannot be solved. One would therefore prefer the search to fail as quickly as possible, rather than spend a lot of effort on proving one subgoal when the next subgoal fails. Therefore, it makes most sense to start with the subgoal that is most likely to lead to failure.

Applying heuristics in conflict resolution or in conjunct ordering need not result in incomplete searches of the tree. All the heuristics do in these cases is change the order in which the various nodes are visited. All the nodes would still be visited. However, the third area in which heuristics can be applied may lead to incomplete searches of the tree. Sometimes one may decide that a given node in the tree looks so bad that it is unlikely that one is ever going to be able to solve it. An example mentioned earlier was in the chess-playing program, where the position resulting from a particular move may be so bad that it does not seem worthwhile to consider that move at all. One may then decide to *prune* that particular branch. Of course, in order to decide whether a given position in a chess game looks good or bad, one needs some criteria that one can use in this decision. In a heuristic search program, there is a function that is based on these criteria, called an *evaluation function*. How good the results are of a heuristic search algorithm that prunes certain branches in tree of course depends on how good the evaluation function is. For example, in the chess program, an evaluation function that only looked at the material that each opponent had would never consider a queen sacrifice, even if it led to checkmate on the next move.

One example of a heuristic of this third kind leads to *resource-limited* search. In this type of heuristic search, one applies only a limited number of rules, say 25, when one is trying to solve a goal. If, after 25 steps, a branch still has not yielded a set of subgoals that can be solved directly, then one decides that this attempt at solving the problem will not be successful, and the branch is pruned from the search tree. The danger, of course, is that applying the 26th rule would have lead to a solution, but that of course is the danger inherent in heuristic search.

3.4. Explicit Control Knowledge

Earlier we drew a distinction between domain knowledge and strategic knowledge. Strategic knowledge concerns the way in which the domain knowledge is used to solve problems, and, as pointed out earlier, the problem of control is closely related to strategic knowledge. A control regime determines how the domain knowledge and the inference rules that are part of the knowledge representation language are used in order to solve certain problems. A control regime can thus be regarded as a procedural representation of (usually) relatively simple pieces of strategic knowledge. This then naturally led to attempts to built problem-solving systems that contained an explicit, declarative, representation of strategic knowledge, and used this to guide their problem-solving behavior. Early examples of systems that tried to achieve this were TEIRESIAS (Davis, 1980), and MECHO (Bundy, Byrd, Luger, Mellish, & Palmer, 1979). Although it still an area of active research, it is worthwhile to say a few words about it. For a more in-depth overview of the literature the reader is referred to van Harmelen (1989).

Explicit, declarative representations of the strategic knowledge have various advantages over the hardwired, procedural representations that are more common at the moment. Separate representations are clearer from an epistemological point of view: Domain knowledge and strategic knowledge are different types of knowledge and, if possible, should be represented separately. It turns out that in a lot of knowledge representation languages, knowledge bases conflate domain and strategic knowledge. Also, an explicit representation of the strategic knowledge that is used by a system makes it easier to develop, debug, and modify (Davis & Buchanan, 1977). These arguments are, of course, reminiscent of the arguments for preferring declarative representations to procedural representations.

Another important and related argument is that often there are specific domain-specific heuristics that could in principle be used in the control regime. Thus, doctors might know that in certain groups of the population disease A is more likely than disease B, and they might use that knowledge in diagnosis. They might, for example, first try to see if a patient from one such group suffered from disease A before they would try to diagnose B. If we were to use a general purpose knowledge representation language, then it would be hard to see how this domain-dependent heuristic knowledge could be used without violating the requirement of distinguishing between domain and strategic knowledge. After all, general purpose knowledge representation languages will have control regimes hardwired into them that work for the general cases. Thus, if one wants to include specific domain-dependent heuristics in a reasoning program, then it is easier to do so in systems with an explicit and declarative representation of the control regime.

A third argument follows from the fact that an expert can use the same (domain) knowledge for more than one task. Earlier we mentioned the example of engineers who might use their knowledge about electronic circuits both to troubleshoot a faulty circuit, and to design a new one. Wielinga and Breuker (1986) point out that, if one wants to build programs that have this capability as well, then one has to separate domain knowledge and strategic knowledge. After all, strategic knowledge concerns the way in which domain knowledge is used, and experts in particular domains seem to be able to use the same domain knowledge for solving different types of problems.

A fourth argument comes from the area of expert systems. One important aspect of systems of this kind is an explanation facility that allows the user to ask the program to explain its conclusions (see also Chapter 4). Now, as Swartout (1981) and Clancey (1983) point out, a satisfactory explanation not only states which pieces of domain knowledge were applied, but also why they were used. In other words, a satisfactory explanation includes not only domain knowledge but also strategic knowledge. However, if the strategic knowledge is hardwired into a program, it will not be available for explanation. Therefore, if one wants to build an expert system with a sophisticated explanation facility, it is necessary to represent the strategic knowledge declaratively.

The explicit representation of strategic knowledge, and the use of it to reason explicitly about control, is a special case of the more general concept of meta-knowledge, knowledge about knowledge. The area of reasoning about knowledge is, of course, closely related to the psychological notions of meta-cognition and meta-memory, the knowledge that individuals have about the content of their own long-term memory, and strategies for storing information and retrieving it. It is an area of growing interest in AI as well. Halpern (1986) contains a collection of papers devoted to the problem of reasoning about knowledge. Being able to reason about knowledge, or as Smith (1982) puts it, the ability to *reflect*, under-lies a lot of intelligent activities, such as mastering new skills (that is, learning), reacting to unexpected circumstances, recovering from mistakes, and so on. Although there are a lot of programs around that are capable of some reflective tasks, they are often quite *ad hoc*, and none of the systems seem capable of general reflective behavior. As one would like to construct generally intelligent programs, then one would prefer them to be capable of these introspective tasks in a more principled way. However, the problem is a very difficult one and is still very much an open research area.

The main difficulty with systems that have their strategic knowledge de-claratively represented, and then use it to reason explicitly about control, is their inefficiency. Rather than drawing an inference, systems of this kind spend a long time in what has been called a *reflect-and-act* loop. Before performing an action, in this case drawing an inference, systems of this kind first reflect on what action to take. Clearly, first thinking about an action before doing it, is slower than just doing the action. This is, of course, a special case of the tradeoff between flexibility and speed that is mentioned in section 1: Procedural representations are computationally more efficient, but less flexible than declarative representations.

The above argument needs to be qualified however. Part of the reason for spending some time before drawing an inference is to make a more intelligent choice of which goal the program should try to solve next. Hardwired control regimes often lead to silly decisions, and part of the reason for building systems with explicit representations of strategic knowledge is to make these decisions smarter. As a consequence, one would hope that the number of unsuccessful attempts at solving a particular goal will diminish. Thus, although it might take longer to draw an inference, one would hope that the inferences that are drawn are more intelligent in that they are more likely to lead to a quick solution of the goal.

4. CONCLUSION

In this chapter, we raised several points that we return to in later chapters. The first point concerned the controversy between procedural and declarative repre-sentations. Procedural representations were argued to be computationally more efficient but less flexible than declarative representations. Their main problem was that if a piece of information was to be used in more than one way, then each use had to be represented separately. However, certain pieces of information seemed to cry out for procedural representations. The second point that we raised concerned a distinction between different types of knowledge. In particular, we distinguished between domain knowledge and strategic knowledge, knowledge about how to use the domain knowledge. Finally, we discussed the problem of control in some detail. The problem of control arises because at any given state of a problem-solving process, there might be more than one way of continuing the search for a solution. We briefly discussed certain solutions that have been proposed in the literature, all of which involved procedural representations of strategic knowledge. We also briefly discussed more recent attempts at building systems with declarative representations of this type of knowledge. In the next five chapters, we discuss specific knowledge representation languages, starting with the use of logic to this end.

3
Logic-based Knowledge Representation Languages

In this chapter, we discuss logic-based knowledge representation language. In the course of the discussion, many concepts and themes are introduced that will be essential in the remainder of this book. As a consequence, this chapter is somewhat longer than the other chapters.

As Israel and Brachman (1981) point out, there is a considerable amount of confusion in cognitive science and AI about what exactly a logic is. It is therefore necessary to define the term *logic* precisely. We do so in this section 1. In section 2, we look at the use of logic as a knowledge representation language. Section 3 reviews the arguments in favor of logic, while section 4 will point to some of the problems that arise from the use of logic as a knowledge representation language, and some of the solutions that have been proposed to deal with them. Section 5 is a summary.

1. WHAT IS A LOGIC?

Logic can be defined as the study of correct inference, of what follows from what (see, e.g., Robinson, 1979, p. 1). Although there might be some disagreement about exactly what makes an inference correct, there can be little doubt that minimally it should be impossible for the assumptions on which the argument rests, the premises, to be true while the conclusion is false. Minimally, a correct inference is *truth preserving*: If the premises are true, then the conclusion must be true as well. There might be many other conditions that have to be met for an inference to be called correct from an intuitive point of view. However, logicians have taken truth preservation as their only criterion. Thus, logic is the study of truth preserving inference.

To illustrate these ideas, compare the following two arguments.

> If it is cold, my car will not start.
> It is cold.
> Therefore, my car will not start.

If it is cold, my car will not start.
My car will not start.
Therefore, it is cold.

The first argument is truth preserving. If it is true that whenever it is cold, then my car will not start, and if it is true that it is cold, then it must be true that my car will not start. The second argument, on the other hand, is not truth preserving. It might well be true than whenever it is cold, my car will not start, and that my car will not start, without it necessarily being true that it is cold. There might be many other reasons why my car will not start.

Logicians construct systems that formalize the notion of a correct inference. The first step in constructing such a system is the exact definition of a formal language. Inference is a relationship between sentences and, in order to specify a system that formalizes the notion of correct inference, you first have to specify which strings of symbols are the well-formed expressions of the language. The usual way of doing this is by defining a set of basic expressions and a set of recursive grammatical rules for forming complex expressions out of other expressions, be they basic or themselves complex. One set of well-formed expressions that is defined for every logical language, is the set of sentences. The term *syntax* is commonly used for this aspect of a logic. The syntax of a logical language corresponds of course to the notational aspect of a knowledge representation language.

However, merely defining the language is clearly not enough. We are interested in the notion of truth preserving inference, and in order to make this notion precise, you have to define exactly under what conditions a sentence of the language would be true. Now, the notion of truth is a semantic notion; it concerns the meaning of a sentence. The second step in defining a logic is therefore a precise specification of the meanings of the well-formed expressions of the logical language. This is done in the *semantics*, or *model-theory*, of the logic. You usually start by defining the meanings of the basic expressions in terms of some *interpretation*, that is, a possible state of affairs in the world. Corresponding to each syntactic rule, that is, each rule that tells you how to combine primitive expressions to form complex expressions, there is a semantic rule which tells you how to combine the meanings of the primitive expressions to form the meanings of the complex expressions. The meaning of a sentence in an interpretation is the truth value of the sentence, that is, whether the sentence is true or false. Thus, given a possible state of affairs in the world, the semantics enables you to determine whether a sentence is true or not.

In order to define the notion of a correct inference precisely, you have to abstract away from particular interpretations. After all, an inference is correct if, whenever all its premises are true, the conclusion is true as well. The notion of a correct inference is made precise in the notion of *valid consequence*: A sentence ϕ is a valid consequence of a set of sentences S if and only if for all interpretations whenever all the sentences of S are true in an interpretation, then ϕ is true in that interpretation as well. Thus, if a sentence ϕ is a valid consequence of a set of sentences S, then there is no conceivable state of affairs in which ϕ is false and all the sentences in S true. Sentences that are true in all interpretations are called valid as well.

In addition to the syntax and the semantics, a logic often also has a *proof theory*. Whereas the notion of valid consequence provides a semantic character-ization of the notion of correct inference, in the proof theory you define a purely formal specification of this notion. A proof theory consists of a set of axioms and a set of inference rules. Axioms are sentences that can always be assumed, while inference rules are rules that take as input one or more sentences and return as output another sentence. A proof of a sentence ϕ from a set of sentences S then is simply a list of sentences, such that ϕ is the last sentence in this list, and each sentence in this list (including ϕ) is either an axiom, or a sentence from S, or obtained from previous sentences by applying an inference rule. This process of derivation is completely formal in that you look only at the form of the sentences without taking into account their meanings.

An adequate proof theory usually corresponds closely to the semantics of the logical language. First, you make sure that every sentence ϕ that can be derived from a set of sentences S is also a valid consequence of S. A proof theory that has this property is called *sound*. Soundness can be achieved by making sure that the axioms are valid sentences and hence always true. Also, the inference rules have to be truth preserving: You ensure that if a sentence ϕ can be derived from one or more given sentences by applying an inference rule, then it is also a valid consequence of these sentences. Thus, if ϕ can be derived from S in a logic with a sound proof theory, then ϕ is also a valid consequence of S.

For certain logics, it is also possible to define proof theories that have the converse property of soundness: Every sentence ϕ that is a valid consequence of a set of sentences S can also be formally derived. A proof theory with this property is called *complete*. Two remarks are in order here. First, completeness is true only for some logics. It is by no means true for all, and for some logics it can be proved that it is impossible ever to formulate a complete proof theory. Second, unlike soundness, which is usually very easy to prove, completeness is often very hard to prove.

In a sense, the proof theory can be regarded as an abstract specification of a computer program for finding the valid consequences of a set of sentences. It could thus be seen as an abstract specification for an interpreter for a logic-based knowledge representation language. It is, of course, essential that the proof theory be sound. Otherwise, the sentences that would be generated could be false even if the input sentences in the knowledge base were true.

Before we discuss an example of a logic, it is worth stressing that there are a great many different logics available (cf. Haack, 1974, for a discussion of some of these). When people in AI talk about logic, what they often seem to mean is one particular logic, namely classical first-order predicate calculus. We will *not* follow this example and we will *not* use the terms "logic" and "classical first-order predicate calculus" interchangeably.

1.1. An example logic: Classical first-order predicate calculus

In order to make the above abstract introduction to logic more concrete, we briefly introduce classical first-order predicate calculus. We use the abbreviation FOPC to refer to this logic. This has the added advantage of defining the logic that is most widely used in AI. This book is not an introduction to logic, and the discussion here is rather terse. There are many introductory texts, and interested readers are referred to, for example, Allwood, Andersson, and Dahl (1977). It is impossible to understand this brief introduction without some understanding of set theory. In order to make the discussion self-contained we first very briefly introduce those parts of set-theory that are relevant to this book. Readers familiar with set theory, or logic, may want to skip this section.

1.1.1. Set theory

A *set* is a collection of items. A set is completely determined by the items, called *elements*, that it contains. Thus, two sets with exactly the same elements are identical. A set can contain any type of element, including sets themselves. In the examples in this section we use numbers. We use the notation $\{1, 2\}$ for the set containing the elements 1 and 2. $1 \in \{1, 2\}$ is the notation that is used for saying that 1 is an element of the set $\{1, 2\}$. The order in which the elements are listed in a set is unimportant. Thus, $\{1, 2\} = \{2, 1\}$. Also, listing the same element more than once does not make any difference to the set. Thus, $\{1, 1, 2\} = \{1, 2\}$.

An important notion in set theory is that of a *subset*. A set S is a subset of a set T if every element in S is also an element of T. We write $S \subseteq T$. For example, $\{1\} \subseteq \{1,2\}$. Note also that $\{1, 2\} \subseteq \{1, 2\}$. If $S \subseteq T$, and $T \subseteq S$, then S and T are identical. Thus, S and T can only be different if T contains elements that are not in S, or vice versa.

There are a number of operations that can be applied to sets. The first operation is constructing an ordered n-tuple: given n elements $e_1, \ldots, e_n$ of some set S, you can form an ordered n-tuple $\langle e_1, \ldots, e_n \rangle$. Unlike sets, the order of the elements in an n-tuple is relevant, and $\langle 1, 2 \rangle$ is *not* equal to $\langle 2, 1 \rangle$. Thus, an ordered n-tuple is a sequence of elements.

The second important operation is forming a new set from a number of available elements. In particular, once you have formed some n-tuples by combining some elements from a set S, you can collect these n-tuples in a new set R. Thus, suppose that we start with the set $\{1, 2, 3\}$. Then, we can for example form the ordered 2-tuples, or ordered pairs, $\langle 1, 2 \rangle$, $\langle 2, 3 \rangle$ and $\langle 1, 3 \rangle$. We can then collect these ordered pairs into a new set $\{\langle 1, 2\rangle, \langle 2, 3\rangle, \langle 1, 3\rangle\}$. The set R is then called an *n-ary relation over S*. Note that as a limit case, a unary relation over S is simply a set of elements of S, that is, a subset of S.

1.1.2. The syntax of FOPC

The first aspect of the definition of a logic is the definition of the logical language. In this section, we define the syntax of the language of FOPC.

The first step in defining the syntax of a logical language is defining the set of primitive expressions, or the *vocabulary*. The following definition defines the vocabulary for FOPC.

Definition 1
The vocabulary consists of
1. a set of constants, $\{a_1, a_2, \ldots\}$
2. a set of individual variables, $\{x_1, x_2, \ldots\}$
3. for each number $n > 0$, a set of n-ary predicates, $\{P_1^n, P_2^n, \ldots\}$

The second step in defining a syntax for a logical language consists in defining the *formation rules*. The formation rules state how simpler expressions can be combined to form more complex expressions. Below we give the formation rules for the language of the FOPC. Note that in FOPC the only complex expressions that can be formed out of simpler expressions, are sentences.

1.   if $a_i, \ldots, a_m$ are n constants, and P_j^n is an n-ary predicate,
     then $P_j^n(a_i, \ldots, a_m)$ is a sentence.

2.   if ϕ is a sentence, then $(\neg\phi)$ is a sentence (read: *not* ϕ)

3.   if ϕ and ψ are sentences, then $(\phi \,\&\, \psi)$, $(\phi \lor \psi)$, $(\phi \rightarrow \psi)$ are sentences
     (read: ϕ *and* ψ, ϕ *or* ψ, and *if* ϕ *then* ψ respectively).
     ($\neg$, $\&$, $\lor$ and $\rightarrow$ are called *connectives*)

4.   if $\phi[a_i]$ is a sentence containing the constant a_i, and x_j is a variable,
     then $(\forall x_j)[\phi[a_i/x_j]]$ and $(\exists x_j)[\phi[a_i/x_j]]$ are sentences,
     where $\phi[a_i/x_j]$ is obtained from $\phi[a_i]$ by replacing all occurrences of a_i by x_j
     (read: *for all* x_j, $\phi[a_i/x_j]$, and *there exists an* x_j, $\phi[a_i/x_j]$,
     $\forall$ and $\exists$ are called the *universal* and *existential quantifier* respectively,
     the formula $\phi[a_i/x_j]$ is called the *matrix* formula.)

There are a few remarks that need to be made about the above definitions. First, note that we have not really defined just one language. Rather, the above definition defines a family of languages. For every choice of constants, predicates, and variables, that is, for every choice of vocabulary, the above definitions define a new language. Thus, the above definition insists only that there be sets of constants, variables, and predicates without actually defining one particular set. In order to instantiate the above definition, and define an actual language, you would have to decide on a vocabulary. In a sense, the definitions above operate at the epistemological level as defined in Chapter 1: you specify the kind of primitive expressions that are needed. The choice of vocabulary for a particular logical language concerns the actual constants and predicates that are used to represent the knowledge about the domain. This choice is at the conceptual level as it does not concern the kind of primitives but the actual primitives that are to be used.

A second point concerns the notion of *scope*. This notion will be used later on, and it is best to define it now. Rules 2, 3, and 4 all assume that there already are some sentences available to which they can be applied. A new sentence can then be formed by placing connectives in front, or between, the original formulas or by putting a quantifier in front of it. The original formula, and all the subexpressions that it contains, such as predicates and variables or constants, are then said to be in the *scope* of the connective or quantifier in the new more complicated formula. For example, in the formula $(\forall x)[P(x) \rightarrow Q(x)]$, P(x) occurs in the scope of both the universal quantifier as in the scope of the connective $\rightarrow$, as do the predicate P and the variable x.

Third, although the above definitions follow the standard notational conventions for defining a logical language, there is nothing that forces you to define a logical language as a string of symbols. If you wanted, you could define the language just as well as a configuration of arcs and nodes, with each arc for example representing a predicate and each node representing a variable or a constant.

Finally, it is customary to omit brackets when this can be done without the risk of ambiguity. In particular, outermost brackets are usually left out. We do the same. Thus, rather than writing $(\phi \, \& \, \psi)$, we usually write $\phi \, \& \, \psi$.

In order to make the above definitions more concrete, we define a very small logical language. We also use this language below to illustrate the semantics and the proof theory. Our little language LL contains three constants c, d, and e. LL has two 1-place (or unary) predicates, P and Q, and one 2-place (or binary) predicate, R. The following sentences are examples of sentences in LL.

$P(c)$
$P(d)$
$Q(e)$
$R(c,d)$
$P(e) \rightarrow R(d,e)$
$(\exists x)[P(x)]$
$(\forall x)[\neg R(x,d) \lor P(x)]$
$(P(c) \, \& \, (\forall x)[P(x) \rightarrow (\exists y)(R(x,y))]) \rightarrow (R(c,z))$
etc.

1.1.3. The semantics of FOPC

The second aspect of a logic is a definition of the meanings of the expressions in the logical language. These meanings can then be used to define the notion of valid consequence, which is intended as the formalization of the notion of a correct inference.

Defining the meanings of the expressions is a two-stage procedure. The first stage is the definition of an *interpretation*. An interpretation consists of two parts. The first part usually consists of one or more sets of primitive entities, called the *domain(s) of discourse*. The primitive entities are the things in the world about which you can express information in the logical language. Different logics have different sets of primitive entities. In FOPC, the assumption is that the world consists solely of individuals. As Moore (1982) points out, the restriction to individuals is not as bad as it looks because many things can be regarded as logical individuals. Moore specifically mentions times, events, kinds, sentences, and so on.

The second part of an interpretation is the *interpretation function*. The interpretation function is a function which assigns to each primitive expression in the language a meaning. The meanings for primitive expressions are either entities in the domain of discourse, or entities that can be constructed from the domain(s) of discourse by purely set-theoretical operations. An example of the latter would be a 2-place relation over the set of entities in the domain of discourse.

The second stage of defining the meanings of a logical language consists of using the interpretation function to define the meanings of the complex expressions of the logical language. As mentioned before, for each syntactic rule there is a semantic rule. Whereas the syntactic rule defines how expressions can be combined to form a new more complicated expression, the semantic rule defines how the meaning of the complex expression can be determined on the basis of the meanings of the simpler expressions. The assumption that the meaning of a complex expression can be determined from the meanings of its constituent expressions and the way in which the constituent expressions are syntactically put together to form the complex expression is called the *principle of compositionality*.

The following is a definition of the semantics for the language that we defined in the previous section. We first define an interpretation.

An interpretation for FOPC is an ordered pair $\langle M, f \rangle$,
where M is a non-empty set (the set of individuals),
and f is an interpretation function, such that
    if a_i is a constant, then $f(a_i) \in M$.
    if P_j^n is an n-ary predicate, then $f(P_j^n)$ is an n-ary relation over M.

Two things have to be noted about this definition. First, the interpretation function can assign any individual to any constant. It is therefore possible that the same individual is assigned to different constants. Thus, it is entirely possible for the same individual to be assigned to both the constant *Mary* and the constant *my head of Department*.

Second, the meaning of an n-ary predicate is an *n*-ary relation over M. This means for example that the meaning of a unary predicate such as *red* is a set of individuals from M. In other words, the meaning of *red* is given as the set of all red things. Similarly, the meaning of a binary predicate such as *is-married-to* is the set of all married couples. This analysis is known as an *extensional* analysis using terminology derived from Carnap (1947). Carnap also proposes an *intensional* analysis according to which the meaning of a predicate can be seen as a function that determines from every possible state of affairs (possible world) what its extension is in that state of affairs. (The distinction between what Carnap calls extension and intension goes back to Frege [1893].) You can define logics, so-called intensional logics, that use an intensional analysis of meaning. An example of the need for an intensional analysis of meaning is provided by the sentence *Frank believes my head of Department to be a man*. Now, suppose that Mary happens to be my head of the Department. Then a purely extensional analysis of *believes to be a man* as a 2-place relationship between individuals would give this sentence exactly the same truth value as *Frank believes Mary to be a man*. But this is clearly wrong. Observations such as these led to the development of intensional logics. Montague (1973) used intensional logic in an analysis of natural language, which has proved popular with a good many philosophers. For an introduction to intensional logic, and Montague's work, see Dowty, Wall, and Peters (1981).

When an interpretation has been dei..ed, the meanings of the complex expressions can be given. In the language that we defined in the previous section, there was only one kind of complex expression, namely sentences. In order to define the meaning of a sentence we have to say, given an interpretation, whether it is true or not. There were various ways in which you could construct a sentence, and there is a semantic rule corresponding to each one.

Let $I = \langle M,f \rangle$ be an interpretation for FOPC, let ϕ be a sentence in the language of this logic, then we define

$$\phi \text{ is true in } I, \text{ (symbolically } I \vDash \phi)$$

1. if ϕ is of the form $P^n_j(a_i, \ldots, a_k)$, then $I \vDash \phi$
   if and only if $\langle f(a_i), \ldots, f(a_k) \rangle \in f(P^n_j)$
2. if ϕ is of the form $\neg\psi$, then $I \vDash \phi$
   if and only if it is not the case th $I \vDash \psi$ (symbolically $I \nvDash \psi$)
3. if ϕ is of the form $(\psi \, \& \, \chi)$, then $I \vDash \phi$
   if and only if $I \vDash \psi$ and $I \vDash \chi$
4. if ϕ is of the form $(\psi \lor \chi)$, then $I \vDash \phi$
   if and only if either, $I \vDash \psi$, or $I \vDash \chi$, or both.

5. if ϕ is of the form $(\psi \rightarrow \chi)$, then $I \models \phi$
    if and only if either, $I \nvDash \psi$, or $I \models \chi$, or both.

For the next two rules, let a be a constant not occurring in ϕ

6. if ϕ is of the form $(\forall x)\psi$, then $I \models \phi$
    if and only if for all interpretations I' which are exactly like I, with the possible exception of the individual assigned to a, $I' \models \psi[x/a]$, where $\psi[x/a]$ is as defined before.

7. if ϕ is of the form $(\exists x)\psi$, then $I \models \phi$
    if and only if there is an interpretation I' which is exactly like I, with the possible exception of the individual assigned to a, $I' \models \psi[x/a]$.

The only clauses in the above definition that might give problems are clause 6 and 7 in which the meanings of quantified sentences are defined. The basic idea is that we replace the quantified variable by a constant that does not occur in the sentence. We then systematically vary the individual the constant stands for. If the variable was universally quantified, then the sentence with the constant substituted in it should be true for every individual in the set M; if the variable was existentionally quantified, then the sentence needs to be true of only one individual. The qualification "with the possible exception of the individual assigned to a" is necessary because the interpretation function f will assign an individual to a. For a universally quantified sentence to be true, the property must also be true of this individual, while for existentially quantified sentences it is possible that the individual assigned to a has the property in the interpretation I that we are considering.

The above definition defines the truth of a sentence with respect to a given interpretation. However, in logic you are interested in truth preserving inferences. You therefore want to abstract from a given interpretation. The following definition does so:

A sentence ϕ is *valid* (symbolically $\models \phi$)
if and only if for all interpretations I, $I \models \phi$

We can then generalize the above definition to define the notion of *valid consequence* as follows:

A sentence ϕ is a *valid consequence* of a set of sentences S (symbolically $S \models \phi$)
if and only if for all interpretations I, if $I \models \psi$ for all sentences $\psi \in S$, then $I \models \phi$.

If we call the sentences in S the *premises*, and the sentence ϕ the *conclusion*, then the definition of valid consequence can be paraphrased as saying that it is impossible for the premises to be true and the conclusion to be false. The notion of valid consequence then is the formalization of the intuitive notion of correct inference.

In order to illustrate these ideas, let us return to the language LL defined in the previous section. An interpretation for LL consists of a domain of individuals, and an interpretation function. Consider the following set {Madonna,Sean Penn,Prince} and the interpretation function f such that

f(c) = Madonna
f(d) = Sean Penn
f(e) = Prince
f(P) = {Madonna}
F(Q) = (Prince, Sean Penn}
f(R) = {⟨Madonna, Sean Penn⟩, ⟨Sean Penn, Madonna⟩}

Then the pair ⟨{Madonna,Sean Penn,Prince}, f⟩ is an interpretation for LL. The intuitive meaning of the predicates P, Q and R could be female, male and has _been_married_to respectively. The reader can check that the following sentences

P(c)
R(c,d)
P(e) → R(d,e)
(∃x)[P(x)]
(∀x)[¬R(x,d) v Q(x)]
(P(c) & (∀x)[P(x) → (∃y)[R(x,y)]]) → (∃z)[R(c,z)]

are all true in this interpretation. Note that, with the exception of the last sentence, it is possible to change the interpretation in such a way that each of the sentences is no longer true. We could for example change the individual assigned to the constant c, or change the set of individuals that have the property P. However, it turns out to be impossible to find an interpretation that makes the last sentence false. The last sentence is therefore valid.

1.1.4. A proof theory for FOPC

In the introduction to this section, we said that many logics also had a proof theory. A proof theory can be regarded as an abstract specification of an inference machine that determines valid consequences of a set of sentences. This is obviously very useful when you want to use logic as a knowledge representation language. The knowledge base is a set of explicitly stored sentences, and the proof theory can be used to determine which sentences are implicitly stored as well.

There are many styles of giving proof theories. Most proof theories consist of a set of axioms, and a set of inference rules. A sentence φ can be proven from a set of sentences S (symbolically S ⊢ φ) if there is a proof of φ from S. The exact definition of a proof depends on the particular style of proof theory. We define a tableau style proof theory. Proof theories of this type are due to Beth (1959). However, Smullyan (1968) proposed a more readable notation which we use as well.

Tableau style proof theories are slightly out of the ordinary because there are no axioms. They only have inference rules. Before the notion of a proof in a system of this kind can be defined, another definition is necessary, namely that of a *signed sentence*. If ϕ is a sentence, then Tϕ and Fϕ are signed sentences. The intuitive readings of signed sentences are "ϕ is true" and "ϕ is false" respectively. A proof of a sentence ϕ from a set of sentences S is defined as a sequence of sets of signed sentences, such that the first set contains Fϕ and, for all $\psi \in$ S, Tψ; every other set of signed sentences is obtained from an earlier one by applying an inference rule; and each final set, each set to which no other inference rules are applied, is closed, that is, there is a sentence χ such that both Tχ and Fχ occur in it.

Intuitively, a proof in a tableau-type proof theory is a *reductio ad absurdum* argument. The first step in the search for a proof consists of signing all the premises with a T and the conclusion that one would like to reach with an F. This, of course, amounts to assuming that all the premises are true, and that the conclusion is false. If there is a proof, then each final sequent will contain both Tχ and Fχ for some proposition χ. But, χ cannot be both true and false at the same time. Therefore, our initial assumption has shown to lead to false consequences and, therefore, must itself be false as well. Hence, if all the premises are true, then the conclusion must be true too.

Which inference rules are used depends on the logic for which we are formulating a proof theory. For FOPC, we use the following inference rules. The notation S[p] means a set of signed sentences S containing the signed sentence p. S[p] is a shorthand notation for S $\cup$ {P}.

S[T$\phi \rightarrow \psi$]	S[F$\phi \rightarrow \psi$]	S[Tϕ & ψ]	S[Fϕ & ψ]
Fϕ, S ∣ Tψ, S	Sϕ, Fψ, S	Tϕ, Tψ, S	Fϕ, S ∣ Fψ, S
S[Tϕ v ψ]	S[Fϕ v ψ]	S[T$\neg\phi$]	[F$\neg\phi$]
Tϕ, S ∣ Tψ, S	Fϕ, Fψ, S	Fϕ, S	Tϕ, S
S[T$(\forall x)\phi x$]	S[F$(\forall x)\phi x$]	S[T$(\exists x)\phi x$]	S[F$\exists x\phi x$]
Tϕa, S	Fϕa, S	Tϕa, S	Tϕa, S

with the restriction on the rules f-$\forall$ and t-$\exists$ that a is a constant not appearing in the sentence ϕ, or in any of the signed sentences in S.

The intuitive interpretation of a rule like T-&, the rule that has S[Tϕ & ψ] at the top is that if ϕ & ψ is true then ϕ is true and ψ is true. Certain rules (e.g., F-& and T-v) introduce splits. There are two ways in which the tableau should be extended. Take F-& as an example. Intuitively, the split is introduced because there are two ways in which a sentence like ϕ & ψ could be false: Either ϕ might be false, or ψ might be false. These two possibilities therefore need to be kept in mind. The splitting rules are, of course, responsible for the fact that there might be more than one final set of signed sentences.

The rules for the quantifiers are in fact schematic. You can choose any constant as the instantiation of a provided that for F-$\forall$ and T-$\exists$ the restriction is met, and *a* is a constant not used in S or ɸ. The rule is therefore not restricted to one constant only. This fact will be important in the next section.

In order to illustrate the above proof theory, we prove that

(∃z)[R(c,z)]

from the premise

(P(c) & (∀x)[P(x) → (∃y)[R(x,y)]])

Using the informal interpretation that we used earlier, this amounts to trying to prove that there is somebody that Madonna has been married to, from the premise that Madonna is female and that every female has been married to somebody.

The first step in the search for a proof involves signing the premise with a T and the conclusion with an F.

T(P(c) & (∀x)[P(x) → (∃y)[R(x,y)]]), F(∃z)[R(c,z)]

Now there is a choice: There are two inference rules that could be applied, namely T-& and F-∃. If you were to implement this proof theory directly, then this would be one of the control decisions you would have to make. In the remainder we just assume that whenever there is a choice, the first applicable inference rule will be used. So, we apply T-& and we get

TP(c), T(∀x)[P(x) → (∃y)[R(x,y)]], F(∃z)[R(c,z)]

Officially, we should copy the signed sentence to which we applied the rule as well, but for reasons of space this has not been done. We now apply the rule T-∀. We choose the constant *c* as the instantiation.

TP(c), TP(c) → (∃y)[R(c,y)], F(∃z)[R(c,z)]

We now apply the rule T-→, which of course introduces a split.

TP(c), FP(c), F(∃z)[R(c,z)] | FP(c), T(∃y)[R(c,y)], F(∃z)[R(c,z)]

The first branch in this tree is closed because P(c) is signed both T and F. Although it is not a final set of signed sentences (we could still apply the rule F-∃), this would make little sense, because once a branch has been closed, it will remain closed. We therefore concentrate on the second branch. We first apply T-∃, which means that we have to introduce a new constant that does not occur in the sentence itself or in another sentence in that branch. We choose *b*. This results in

FP(c), TR(c,b), F($\exists$z)[R(c,z)]

We now apply F-$\exists$, and because we have a free choice, we take *b* again as the instantiation. This gives

FP(c), TR(c,b), FR(c,b)

and this branch is closed as well because R(c,b) is signed both T and F. We have thus constructed a proof of ($\exists$z)[R(c,z)] from P(c) & ($\forall$x)[P(x) $\rightarrow$ ($\exists$y)(R(x,y)]].

1.1.5. Soundness, completeness, and decidability

The above logic has some desirable and some undesirable properties. The nice properties are that the proof theory that we defined can be shown to be sound and complete: If S $\vdash$ ϕ, then S $\models$ ϕ, and if S $\models$ ϕ, then S $\vdash$ ϕ. These results are important because they guarantee that if we implemented an interpreter according to the abstract specification that the proof theory provides, then all the inferences that we could draw would be truth preserving.

However, the logic has some undesirable properties as well. In particular, it is only *semidecidable*. A property is decidable if there is a decision procedure, a computational routine, or an effective procedure, which, when applied to any object of the appropriate sort, will, after a finite number of steps, classify this object as a positive or a negative instance of that property (Boolos & Jeffrey, 1980, p. 112). The decision problem for a logic is the question of whether there is a decision procedure which, given any set of sentences S, and given a sentence ϕ, determines whether S $\models$ ϕ. The problem is that it can be shown that there is no such routine for FOPC. There is a routine that given any set of sentences S, and given a sentence ϕ, will answer "yes" if S $\models$ ϕ after a finite number of steps. However, there is no routine that will answer "no" after a finite time if S $\not\models$ ϕ. Thus, FOPC is semidecidable.

You can get an idea of why there can be no decision procedure for FOPC by looking at the proof theory defined above. If S $\models$ ϕ, then the branches will close after a finite number of steps, thus proving that S $\vdash$ ϕ. Because the proof theory is sound, you can conclude that S $\models$ ϕ. However, if S $\not\models$ ϕ, then the branches will never close. However, rules like T-$\forall$ and F-$\exists$ can in principle be applied an infinite number of times. Therefore, when you are searching for a proof of ϕ from S and the branches in the proof tree are not yet closed, then you never know whether this is because ϕ can indeed not be proved from S or because you have not applied enough rules yet. It might well be the case that if you apply say F-$\exists$ a few more times, you will get the closure that you were looking for, or it might just be the case that closure will never be obtained. (For a rigorous proof of the undecidability of FOPC, the reader is referred to Boolos & Jeffrey, 1980.) We return to the problem of the undecidability of FOPC below.

1.2. Conclusion

In this section, we introduced many new concepts. The main aim of the section was to give some feeling for what logic is, and to dispel some of the misconceptions that some people in AI and cognitive science have about logic. In particular, we distinguished between three aspects of any logic: A syntax, which defines the logical language, a semantics, which gives the meanings of the expressions in the logical language, and a proof theory, which provides a purely formal system of deriving sentences. Also, we pointed out that there are many different logics, and that the term *logic* should not be equated with one particular logic, namely first-order predicate calculus. A lot of the terms that were introduced will be used throughout the book. In the next section, we turn to proposals that logics should be used for knowledge representation.

2. LOGIC-BASED KNOWLEDGE REPRESENTATION LANGUAGES

The career of logic in AI has been somewhat varied. In the mid-1960s, FOPC was one of the most widely used knowledge representation languages. The search was on for general problem solvers. Such problem solvers would be able to tackle a wide range of problems, where problems were formulated along the following lines. First, you describe the initial situation. Second, you describe which actions can be performed together with restrictions on when the actions are applicable. Finally, you pose the actual problem to be solved by describing the goal you would like to achieve. A classic example of such a well-specified problem is the missionaries and cannibals puzzle. Three missionaries and three cannibals are standing on one bank of a river. There is a rowing boat there that can maximally hold two people. To get across the river, there should be at least one person in the boat. However, in no situation should there be more cannibals than missionaries on either bank, because otherwise the cannibals would eat the missionaries. (There are no such fears about there being more missionaries than cannibals, even though there might be a danger of missionaries trying to convert the cannibals.) The problem then is, given this description of the situation, is it possible to get the missionaries and cannibals safely across the river?

In the mid-1960s, Robinson (1965) proposed a particular proof theory, called *resolution*, for FOPC. (We discuss resolution below.) Because of the elegance and simplicity of Robinson's system, it was thought that a general problem solver could be constructed simply by implementing Robinson's proposals. You simply had to describe the initial situation and the actions and their various restrictions in FOPC. In order to solve a problem, one would then try to prove the goal by using Robinson's resolution theorem prover.

Although this research program was widely adopted, and led to important technical advances in the area of resolution-based theorem proving techniques, within five years it became clear that this idea was not going to work. The general logic-based problem solver was simply too undirected to be usable. As a consequence, the tide then shifted against logic, and a lot of other formalisms, many of which were first proposed in the context of cognitive psychology, were taken up by AI people and turned into knowledge representation languages. As Newell (1980) points out, the failure of the research program also led to the conclusion that logic was a bad thing for AI. Uniform proof techniques for FOPC had proven too inefficient, and this was interpreted as a failure of logic-based knowledge representation languages.

In recent years, partly due to the advent of the Prolog (Clocksin & Mellish, 1981; Bratko, 1986) a logic-based programming language, the standing of FOPC, and other logics, as knowledge representation languages has substantially improved. The Japanese adopted Prolog as the main implementation language for their fifth-generation research project, and there is some research into using different logics as knowledge representation languages for expert systems (e.g., Jackson, Reichgelt, & van Harmelen, 1989). It therefore seems fair to conclude that logic is once again a fundamental part of AI, and the recent textbook by Genesereth and Nilsson (1987) reflects this trend.

In order to give the reader a flavor of how an interpreter for a logic-based knowledge representation language can be implemented, we briefly discuss Robinson's theorem prover. Then we discuss the various arguments that have been put forward in favor of using logic-based knowledge representation languages. We also discuss certain problems with the use of logic as a knowledge representation language, and the way in which people have proposed to solve them.

2.1. Building a logic-based inference engine

In order to be able to use a logic as a knowledge representation language, you need to implement an automated logic-based inference machine. This problem has been extensively studied in a subfield of AI called *theorem proving*. Various different styles of theorem prover have been proposed. We discuss a particular type of theorem prover called a *resolution refutation theorem prover*. (The discussion is to a large extent based on Robinson, 1979, and Nilsson, 1980.) Although there are resolution theorem provers for many different logics, the discussion will be restricted to theorem provers for FOPC. Thus, in what follows, the term *theorem prover* should always be read as *theorem prover for FOPC*, unless otherwise indicated.

There are three reasons for discussing resolution refutation theorem provers in preference to other styles of theorem prover. First, resolution refutation theorem provers were among the first to be developed. Robinson's original theorem prover for FOPC is a resolution refutation system. Second, many of the techniques that Robinson pioneered in his theorem prover are still used in many other theorem provers, even for other logics. Third, resolution theorem provers are today the most widely used today. The logic programming language Prolog for example is a resolution refutation theorem prover. There are disadvantages associated with using a resolution theorem prover but as this is not primarily a text on theorem proving, we ignore them here. The interested reader is referred to Bledsoe (1977).

Robinson's theorem prover is based on refutation. This means that in order to prove a sentence ϕ from a set of sentences S, you assume $\neg\phi$ and try to derive a contradiction from S and $\neg\phi$. In this sense Robinson's theorem prover is similar to the proof theory that we discussed in section 1.1.4. That too started with assuming that the premises were true, and the conclusion false, and then tried to derive a contradiction from this assumption.

One of the main insights in Robinson's work was the fact that he distinguished between two different mechanisms for dealing with different types of reasoning, namely propositional and quantificational reasoning. Propositional reasoning relies completely on the meaning of the logical connectives such as $\neg$, $\rightarrow$, & and v. Thus, inferring ψ from ϕ and $\phi \rightarrow \psi$ is an example of propositional reasoning. Robinson used *resolution* for this type of reasoning. Quantificational reasoning on the other hand concerns reasoning about the terms, the variables and constants, in a proposition. An example of quantificational reasoning is the inference ϕa from the premise $(\forall x)\phi x$. Robinson used *unification* for this type of reasoning. Most theorem provers today still use different techniques for propositional and quantificational reasoning. While many do not use resolution for propositional reasoning, almost all modern theorem provers use unification for quantificational reasoning.

We illustrate a resolution refutation theorem prover on the following example. We will try to prove the formula $(\exists x)[P(x)]$ from the set of formulas

$(\forall x)[(\exists y)[Q(x,y) \lor R(x)] \rightarrow P(x)]$
$P(a) \lor (\forall x)(\exists y)[\neg S(x,y)]$
$(\forall x)[S(b,x)]$

P, Q, R, and S could be intuitively interpreted as poor_investment, worth_less, volatile, and rising_less_fast. If we then interpret "a" as referring to the company "smart investements ltd", and "b" as referring to "silly investements ltd", then we can give the following English gloss of the premises:

> All companies which are worth less than some other company, or which are volatile, are poor investments
> Either smart investments ltd is a poor investment, or for all companies there is an other company that rises less fast.
> Silly investments ltd rises less fast than all companies.

The goal can be glossed as:

Some company is a poor investment.

As said, the first step in the search for a proof is the addition of the negation of the formula to be proved to the set of premises and then trying to establish whether the resulting set of sentences leads to a contradiction. Thus, the set of sentences from which the contradiction should follow is:

$\neg(\exists x)[P(x)]$
$(\forall x)[(\exists y)[Q(x,y) \lor R(x)] \to P(x)]$
$P(a) \lor (\forall x)(\exists y)[\neg S(x,y)]$
$(\forall x)[S(b,x)]$

2.1.1. Skolemization

The first step in any resolution refutation theorem prover is to transform the sentences that are to be used in the proof. This process is called *skolemization*. The basic idea behind skolemization is to rewrite the sentence in such a form that the inference rules of resolution and unification can be applied to it. This implies rewriting it into a formula that contains no implications and no quantifiers. This process consists of 9 different steps.

The first step is simply making sure that the various formulas in S and ϕ do not contain the same variables anywhere. Thus, if S has two formulas which both contain the variable x, then this variable needs to be replaced by another in one of these formulas. It is easy enough to verify that this does not change the truth value of the various sentences. After all, the particular variable that is used in a formula is completely irrelevant when it comes to determining the truth value of a sentence. The result of the first step in our example would be something like:

$\neg(\exists x)[P(x)]$
$(\forall z)[(\exists y)[Q(z,y) \lor R(z)] \to P(z)]$
$P(a) \lor (\forall x')(\exists y')[\neg S(x',y')]$
$(\forall w)[S(b,w)]$

The second step is the elimination of implication symbols. As the reader can easily check from the semantics defined in section 1 of this chapter, at least in FOPC, $\phi \to \psi$ is equivalent to $\neg\phi \lor \psi$. We can therefore replace every occurrence of an implication by a disjunction. In our example, this means that the second sentence is replaced by

$(\forall z)[\neg(\exists y)[Q(z,y) \lor R(z)] \lor P(z)]$

The third step is a reduction in the scope of negation symbols. Negation symbols should end up in front of atomic formulas. There are a few rules that allow us to do this. It is left as an exercise to the reader to establish that these equivalences holds in FOPC, although proofs can be found in any introductory logic text. The symbol ↔ is a shorthand notation: φ ↔ ψ is an abbreviation for (φ → ψ) & (ψ → φ). First, we have what are known as de Morgan's laws:

¬(φ v ψ) ↔ (¬φ & ¬ψ)
¬(φ & ψ) ↔ (¬φ v ¬ψ)

Second, we have a rule known as double negation elimination:

¬¬φ ↔ φ

Thirdly, the existential and the universal quantifier are what are known as *duals* of each other:

(∃x)φ ↔ ¬(∀x)¬φ
(∀x)φ ↔ ¬(∃x)¬φ

This means that you can push negations inwards over quantifiers provided you change the quantifier from existential to universal, or vice versa. Applying these rules to our example gives:

(∀x)[¬P(x)]
(∀z)[(∀y)[¬Q(z,y) & ¬R(z)] v P(z)]
P(a) v (∀x')(∃y')[¬S(x',y')]
(∀w)[S(b,w)]

The fourth step is the elimination of existential quantifiers. This step is the most difficult to understand. An existential quantifier gives you the assurance that there is an individual somewhere that has the relevant property. The intuition behind the elimination of existential quantifiers is that we give these individuals a name, and use these names to reason about them. Thus, if we have an existential quantifier that does not occur in the scope of any other quantifiers, we can simply replace the existentially quantified variable by a *skolem constant*. A skolem constant is a new constant that has not been used in any of the other formulas. After all, when we use an existential quantifier, we only know that there is an individual with the relevant property; we do not know anything about whether it is identical to any of the individuals that we have information about. Therefore, if we use a new constant, we will never unwittingly identify this object with one we already know about. Because the interpretation function in an interpretation can assign the same individual to two constants, we also have not ruled out the possibility that the individual identified by the new constant is identical to another individual we already have some knowledge about.

The treatment of existential quantifiers inside the scope of a universal quantifier is more complicated. In this case we cannot simply replace the existentially quantified variable by a constant. To illustrate this consider the sentence

(∀x)(∃y)[mother(x,y)]

which says that everybody has a mother. Suppose we simply replace the existentially quantified variable by a constant, yielding:

(∀x)[mother(x,a)]

This would mean that there is an individual, called *a*, who is the mother of everybody. This, of course, is false. The problem is that the individual that makes the existential quantifier true depends on the choice of individual for the universal quantifier. Thus, you can only determine which individual is the mother if you know which individual is chosen for the universal quantifier. There is a particular type of expression in logic that can be used for encoding this sort of dependency, namely a *function symbol*. Function symbols are symbols that, given names of one or more individuals, return a name for (or a description of) another individual. Thus, *mother-of* can be regarded as a function, because given a name for an individual, say *john*, it returns a description of another individual, namely a description of John's mother. Function symbols can also take the name of more than one individual. Take, for example, the function *eldest-child-of* which takes the names of the father and the mother, and returns a description of their eldest child. Semantically, function symbols are treated as functions. A function is an entity that takes as input a number of individuals and returns as output another individual. Thus, the interpretation of the 2-place function symbol *eldest-child-of* is a function which given two individuals will return the eldest child of these two individuals.

We can use function symbols to eliminate existential quantifiers that occur within the scope of universally quantified variables. The variables corresponding to such quantifiers are replaced by new function symbols, called *skolem functions*. The arguments of this skolem function are the variables in the universal quantifiers in whose scope the existential quantifier occurs. In this way the dependency of the existential quantifier on the universal quantifier is encoded in the expression used to eliminate the existential quantifier. In our example, there is only one existential quantifier. The result of applying the rule to this formula yields:

P(a) v (∀x')[¬S(x',f(x'))]

As an aside, there is no real real difference between the treatment of existential quantifiers inside and outside the scope of universal quantifiers. You use a 1-place skolem function when the choice of individual depends on one other choice, a 2-place when the choice depends on two other choices, and so on. In the case of an existential quantifier that does not occur inside the scope of any universal quantifiers, the choice of individual depends on the choice of no other individuals. Therefore, if you regard a skolem constant as a 0-place skolem function, then the treatment of all existential quantifiers is identical.

The fifth step in the procedure for converting propositions into a form that is suitable for resolution involves putting the formula in *prenex* form. A formula is in prenex form if it consists of a string of quantifiers followed by a quantifier-free formula. Because we have already eliminated existential quantifiers, all we have to do is move the universal quantifiers to the front of the sentence. Because we also have eliminated implication signs, and because no universal quantifiers can occur in the scope of a negation symbol, we can simply move the universal quantifiers to the front of the formula. The resulting formulas are

$(\forall x)\neg[P(x)]$
$(\forall z)(\forall y)[(\neg Q(z,y)$ & $\neg R(z))$ v $P(z)]$
$(\forall x')[P(a)$ v $\neg S(x',f(x'))]$
$(\forall w)[S(b,w)]$

The sixth step simply means dropping the universal quantifiers. Because we know that the formulas contain no existentially quantified variables any more, we might as well drop the quantifiers and use the convention that every variable is universally quantified. This results in:

$\neg P(x)$
$(\neg Q(z,y)$ & $\neg R(z))$ v $P(z)$
$P(a)$ v $\neg S(x',f(x'))$
$S(b,w)$

The seventh step involves converting the formulas into *conjunctive normal form*. A formula is in conjunctive normal form if it is a conjunction of disjunctions such that each disjunct is either an atomic formula or a negation of an atomic formula. For the purposes of this definition a single disjunct of this form is also considered to be a disjunct. We can transform formulas into conjunctive normal form because we have the following equivalence:

$((\phi$ & $\psi)$ v $\pi) \leftrightarrow ((\phi$ v $\pi)$ & $(\psi$ v $\pi))$

In our example only the second formula is changed:

$(\neg Q(z,y)$ v $P(z))$ & $(\neg R(z)$ v $P(z))$

The eight step is simply to represent the different conjuncts separately. Since the whole set of formulas is already implicitly treated as a conjunction, we therefore might as well represent the separate conjuncts in a formula separately. Thus, the second formula gives rise to two new formulas:

$\neg Q(z,y)$ v $P(z)$
$\neg R(z)$ v $P(z)$

The ninth and final step is known as *standardizing the variables apart*. The idea is to make sure that none of the different formulas contain the same variables. The rationale behind this step is that if two formulas φ and ψ contain the same variable x then at some stage the set of formulas must have contained a formula of the form:

(∀x)[φ(x) & ψ(x)]

But from this formula you can conclude:

(∀x)[φ(x)] & (∀y)[ψ(y)]

This inference is captured by standardizing the variables apart. For our example this gives the final set of sentences:

¬P(x)
¬Q(z,y) v P(z)
¬R(z′) v P(z′)
P(a) v ¬S(x′,f(x′))
S(b,w)

The formulas that are obtained by applying this procedure are obviously all disjunctions of atomic propositions or negations of atomic propositions. The disjuncts that make up these formulas are called *literals*. Thus, a literal is either an atomic formula or a negation of one. We can treat such a disjunction of literals simply as a set with as members each literal in the disjunction. Such a set of literals is called a *clause*. A clause is then true if at least one formula in it is true. Thus, we end up with the following clauses

{¬P(x)}
{¬Q(z,y), P(z)}
{¬R(z′), P(z′)}
{P(a), ¬S(x′,f(x′))}
{S(b,w)}

We call the clause which contains no formulas at all the *empty* clause. The empty clause is always false. After all, a clause was deemed to be true if at least one formula in it was true. The empty clause contains no formulas, and therefore it is never the case that at least one formula in it is true. Hence, it is always false. The way in which you try to derive a contradiction in a resolution refutation theorem prover is by attempting to derive the empty clause.

2.1.2. Unification

As mentioned above, in a resolution refutation theorem prover quantificational reasoning is handled by means of unification. However, the use of unification is by no means restricted to theorem prover of this type. It is also widely used in other types of theorem prover.

The purpose of a unification algorithm is to determine whether two literals can be made identical. The algorithm returns a representation of the conditions under which this can be achieved. Such a representation is called a *substitution*. A substitution is a list of *bindings*, pairs of variables and values for these variables. These values can themselves be either variables, or constants, or functional expressions. If a variable is bound to a constant or a functional expression then there can be no other binding for that variable to another constant or functional expression. No second element of the pair may contain the first element of the pair. Thus, $\{x/a,y/g(z)\}$ is a correct substitution, while $\{x/a,x/g(z)\}$ and $\{x/a,y/g(y)\}$ are not.

If σ is a substitution and ϕ is a formula, then $\phi\sigma$ is the result of applying σ to ϕ. It is another formula in which all the variables of ϕ, if they also occur in σ, have been replaced by their values. Thus if $\sigma = \{x/a,y/g(z)\}$, then $P(x,f(x),y)\sigma = P(a,f(a),g(z))$. We can now define unification as follows:

A substitution σ is a *unification* of two formulas ϕ and ψ if and only if $\phi\sigma = \psi\sigma$.

The following are some examples of unifications.

		Resulting unification
P(x,x)	P(a,a)	$\{x/a\}$
P(x,x)	P(a,b)	fail
P(x,y)	P(a,b)	$\{x/a,y/b\}$
P(x,y)	P(a,a)	$\{x/a,y/a\}$
P(f(x),b)	P(f(c),z)	$\{x/c,z/b\}$
P(x,f(x))	P(y,z)	$\{x/y,z/f(y)\}$
P(x,f(x))	P(y,y)	fail

2.1.3. Resolution

Whereas unification was the way of dealing with quantification reasoning, resolution refutation theorem provers use *resolution* as their only inference rule. The inputs to a resolution theorem prover are always clauses, that is, sets of literals, where a literal was defined as an atomic formula or a negation of one. We can then define the following inference rule:

Let $R = \{\phi, \ldots, \neg\phi_i, \ldots, \phi_n\}$
and $Q = \{\psi, \ldots, \psi_j, \ldots \psi_m\}$ be clauses
and let ϕ_i and ψ_j unify with unification σ,
then resolve(R,Q) is the clause which contains as elements the literals
    $\phi_l\sigma$ for all l not equal to i, with
    $\psi_k\sigma$ for all k not equal to j.
resolve(R,Q) is called a *resolvent* of R and Q.

The intuitive motivation behind resolution can be illustrated by considering a simple example. Suppose that we have the clauses $\{P(x,a), Q(x,y)\}$ and $\{\neg P(b,y),$

R(z)}. Clearly, P(x,a) and P(b,y) unify with the unification {x/b, y/a}. This unification describes a situation which P(x,a) and ¬P(b,y) cannot be true at the same time. Now assume that P(b,a) is not true. Then obviously the clause {P(b,a), Q(b,a)} can only be true if Q(b,a) is true. Alternatively, assume that ¬ ¸P(b,a) is not true, then {¬P(b,a), R(z)} can be true only if R(z) is true. Since either P(b,a) or ¬P(b,a) must be true, we therefore know that either Q(b,a) or R(z) must be true. Hence, the resulting clause {Q(b,a), R(z)} must be true as well.

Now that we have defined resolution, we can return to our original example. The reader will recall that rewriting the example gave the following clauses, which for convenience have been numbered:

1. {¬P(x)}
2. {¬Q(z,y), P(z)}
3. {¬R(z′), P(z′)}
4. {P(a), ¬S(x′,f(x′))}
5. {S(b,w)}

Because P(x) and P(z) unify, we can resolve 1. and 2. against each other. This yields the following resolvent:

{¬Q(z,y)}

Unfortunately, this does not get us very far because this clause cannot be resolved against any other clause. We therefore go back and discover that because P(x) also unifies with P(z′) we can resolve 1. and 3. to give:

{¬R(z′)}

Again, this does not lead us very far, as the resulting clause also cannot be resolved against any other proposition. We therefore go back once more, and discover that because P(x) unifies with P(a) we can resolve 1. and 4. to give

{¬S(x′,f(x′))}

This is more successful, because S(x′,f(x′)) unifies with S(b,w) with unification {x′/b, w/f(b)}. We can therefore resolve the new clause with 5. and thus derive the empty clause and a contradiction. Since we have been able to derive the contradiction, we have therefore proved that (∃x)[P(x)] follows from

(∀x)[(∃y)[Q(x,y) v R(x)] → P(x)]
P(a) v (∀x)(∃y)[¬S(x,y)]
(∀x)[S(b,w)]

2.1.4. The problem of control again

The reader will have noticed that the first two resolvents that we obtained in the previous section could not be used themselves to construct any further resolvents. We had three possibilities to form the first resolvent and the first two options quickly led to dead ends. This, of course, is yet another illustration of the control problem. There are many different ways in which you can build resolution refutation theorem provers, and one of the crucial choices that you have to make concerns the control regime (see Chang & Lee, 1973, and Stickel, 1987, for a discussion of some of the options). However, no matter how good the control regime, it is almost always the case that at some stage the theorem prover will make a choice that will lead to a dead end. In these cases, it will *backtrack* to a previous choice point and take another option.

One way of coping with the control problem is by making the language less expressive. Prolog does this by restricting the language to *Horn Clauses*. Horn clauses are clauses in which there is at most one nonnegated literal. All the other literals have to be negated. Although this obviously restricts the expressive power, it makes it possible to write a faster theorem prover. First, you always make sure that the nonnegated literal is the first literal in a clause. Second, the goal that you are trying to prove is always negated. The top goal is always negated because the theorem prover is a refutation theorem prover, and a refutation theorem prover starts off by negating the goal that you are trying to prove. The subgoals are always negated because every clause contains only one nonnegated formula and that must have been resolved against a previous goal. It therefore follows that in order to find a proof of a goal you only have to try to resolve it against the first literal in a clause. You know that if this fails, then it is impossible for the goal to resolve against any other literal in the clause. Thus, by restricting the language, it becomes easier to write a faster theorem prover.

Even in resolution refutation theorem provers that are not restricted to using Horn clauses, the control problem is usually solved by choosing a particular control regime, and hardwiring this into the theorem prover. This of course leads to all the disadvantages of procedural representations in terms of rigidity. First, it becomes hard to see how you could make use of domain-specific heuristics. Second, different tasks require different control regimes. But if the interpreter has a hardwired control regime, then it becomes virtually impossible to change it. Third, if the code of the interpreter determines in which way a particular statement is to be used, it becomes less clear whether the same logical sentence can be used in more than one way. In Chapter 2, we discussed Winograd's example *every lawyer from Chicago is clever*, which could be used in at least three different ways. If the interpreter has a hardwired control regime, then this piece of knowledge can be used in only one way.

There are many different ways of trying to deal with these problems. In Chapter 2, we mentioned the idea of explicit declarative representations of the control regime. However, we saw that this still has important disadvantages in terms of efficiency. A second approach is the one taken by MRS (Genesereth & Smith, 1982; Genesereth, Greiner, & Smith, 1980). MRS allows the user to associate with every sentence two pieces of Lisp code (the language in which MRS is implemented) which tell the interpreter what to do when the sentence is asserted or retrieved. Because the interpreter also knows what to do when there are no such pieces of code associated with a sentence, it still has a hardwired control regime. However, the in-built control regime can be overwritten for particular sentences in the knowledge base. It might be the case that this way of solving the control problem actually combines the efficiency and the flexibility that are both required.

3. THE ARGUMENTS IN FAVOR

In this section we review some of the arguments that have been put forward in favor of using logic for knowledge representation. A logical language is a declarative knowledge representation language. It therefore has all the advantages in terms of economy of storage, generality, and flexibility and maintainability, as discussed in Chapter 2. We will not review these here any further. Instead we concentrate on the specific arguments in favor of choosing logic from the set of available declarative representational formalisms. There are two arguments specific to logic. The first argument is that satisfactory logics have a semantics. The second argument concerns the greater expressive power of logic.

3.1. Logics have a semantics

The first argument in favor of using logic as a knowledge representation language is probably most eloquently expressed by Hayes (1977). It concerns the fact that logics usually have a semantics. There are various arguments about why a semantics is important. First, a semantics enables you to determine exactly what the expressions in the language mean. This allows you to find out whether a given piece of information that you wanted to represent in a formalism is indeed adequately represented by the formal expression that is used. Thus, we know exactly what

$(\forall x)[man(x) \rightarrow animal(x)]$

means, and what its consequences are in the sense that you know how it can be used by the inference engine. On the other hand, it is often not entirely clear what something like

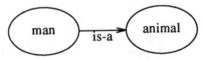

means, and what its consequences are. For example, does it mean that every man is an animal, and therefore has all the properties that an animal has? Or does it have a weaker sense and mean that men have only some of the properties that animals have? Without a semantics, these questions simply cannot be answered.

A second reason for preferring systems with a clear semantics is that it enables you to check whether the inference procedure used by the system is sound. An inference procedure is sound if, whenever the input sentences are true, the output sentence is true as well. Clearly, soundness is essential as you want to make sure that you never derive false information from true information. In order to check whether an inference procedure is sound, however, you have to have a precise specification of the conditions under which sentences are true, and a semantics provides this.

However, even given the need for semantics, the question arises why you should prefer the type of formal treatment of meaning, and truth, that is part of a logic over other possible accounts of meaning. Surely, there are alternatives, and maybe some of the alternatives are as good as the model-theoretic account of meaning given in logic.

A first alternative is what Hayes (1977) calls the "pretend-it's-English" account of meaning. You could simply pretend that the knowledge representation formalism was some kind of English. As speakers of that language we know the meanings of English sentences. Therefore, pretending that the expressions in the knowledge representation language were just formal representations of English, this would be just as good as defining the semantics in the formal way that logicians prefer.

There are a few arguments against this "pretend-it's-English" account of meaning. The first one is that this account of meaning is rather vague. An account of the meaning of a knowledge representation language should at least enable you to decide whether two different expressions in the formalism have the same meaning. But, as Hayes points out, it is not always clear whether two English sentences have the same meaning. It depends on the sense of meaning that you use. For example, under a very strict definition of meaning the sentences *John is easy to please* and *It is easy to please John* may not have the same meaning. Second, a knowledge representation formalism also has an inferential aspect, and you would like the semantics of the formalism to give an account of the inferences that can be drawn. But again it is very difficult to determine exactly what other English sentences follow from a given set of sentences, and there is often disagreement between speakers of the language about what a set of sentences actually implies. An example might be the sentence *Everyone in the room knows two languages*. Given these problems in determining the meanings of English sentences then, the "pretend-it's-English" account of meaning is not satisfactory.

Another alternative way of specifying the semantics of a knowledge representation language is similar to the way in which the semantics of a programming language is specified. In accounts of this kind, you define the meaning of a primitive procedure of the language in terms of what it returns when an argument is passed into it. Thus, in Lisp, a semantic account of the primitive procedure *car* would mention the fact that it takes a list as its argument and returns the first element of this list. This account of meaning is often called a *procedural account of meaning*. A procedural semantics of a knowledge representation language would specify what inferences could be drawn from a given expression in the language. The semantics of the language would thus be defined in terms of its behavior in reply to certain queries. For example, a procedural account of the meaning of

$(\forall x)[man(x) \rightarrow animal(x)]$

might specify that whenever the system was asked the query $(\exists y)[animal(y)]$ is might try to establish whether $(\exists z)[man(z)]$.

The main problem with the procedural account is that it cannot be used to prove soundness. To prove soundness, you have to be able to determine whether input and output expressions of the inference procedure are true, independently of the inference procedure of the language. Clearly, a procedural account of meaning, because it defines the meanings of expressions in terms of the way the inference procedure deals with them, does not provide the required independent account of the truth conditions of expressions in the language, and it can therefore not be used to prove soundness. Given that one of the main arguments for a semantic account was that it enabled you to construct soundness proofs, this is a serious problem. It has also led to a lot of research in computer science where attempts have been made to define a logical semantics for programming languages so that they may be placed on a sound footing (see, e.g., Stoy, 1979).

A second problem with procedural semantics is that the control regime used in the implementation of a knowledge representation language becomes part of the definition of the meaning of the language. Thus, in the example given above, the fact that we used a backward chaining control regime became important in determining the meaning of the expression. The problem is that it seems to involve a confusion of the logical and the implementational level. Concepts belonging to the logical level, such as the semantics, are partly explained in terms of implementational concepts, such as control regimes.

The conclusion that can be drawn from the difficulties with the "pretend-it's-English" and the procedural account of meaning is that you really want a semantics that is nonlinguistic and independent of the implementation of an interpreter for the language. Such an account will clearly define the meanings of the expressions of the language, and can be used to prove soundness of the inference procedure. Logic provides such an account.

The fact that logics have a semantics also makes them a very useful analytic tool in AI. In Chapter 1, we listed a number of criteria of adequacy that a satisfactory knowledge representation language should meet. Some of these criteria were at the logical level, and had to do with the semantics of the formalism, the soundness of the inference procedure, and the expressive power of the language. It should be clear that these questions involve logical concepts which can only be analyzed in terms of logic. Logic can thus be used to analyze other knowledge representation languages at the logical level.

The role of logic as an analytic tool is also embraced by Newell (1980), although he explicitly rejects the view that logic should also be used as a knowledge representation language. Newell introduces a new level at which a computer system can be regarded, which he calls the *knowledge level*. At this level, the computer should be regarded as an agent which is capable of interacting with its environment. It has a body of knowledge and a set of goals. Its behavior is governed by a principle of rationality according to which it will always select those actions that will lead to the attainment of one or more of its goals. Newell distinguishes the knowledge level from the *symbol level*. At the symbol level you are concerned with implementing the knowledge level. The symbol level is thus very similar to the implementational level, while the knowledge level is reminiscent of the logical level. Newell claims that the only appropriate analytic tool at the knowledge level is logic. Determining exactly what the knowledge formalized in some knowledge representation language is requires the use of logic. However, Newell also says that logic is often not the appropriate formalism at the symbol level. He reaches this conclusion because of the efficiency problems that led to the failure of the early experiments with the use of logic for knowledge representation. Newell claims that logic has been tried at the symbol level, and has failed. However, there are other possible interpretations of the failure of these early experiments, a point to which we return below.

3.2. Expressiveness

A second argument in favor of using logic is that logics are very expressive. This argument really has two parts: the ability of logic to express incomplete knowledge, and the fact that there are many different logics to choose from.

The first part of the argument draws attention to the fact that it is very easy to express in logic what you might call *incomplete* knowledge, or information about incompletely known situations (Moore, 1982). The expressive power of classical first-order predicate calculus, or FOPC as it was called earlier, "determines not so much what can be said, but what can be left unsaid" (Levesque & Brachman, 1985). As a result, you do not have to represent details that are not (yet) known. A few examples may clarify this point. In FOPC, you can use existentially quantified sentences to express the knowledge that some object has a given property without knowing the identity of the object. Or you can express disjunctive knowledge, such as *either my car is red or your car is green*. Finally, you can draw a distinction between something not being known, that is, ϕ not appearing in the knowledge base, and something being known to be false, that is, $\neg\phi$ appearing in the knowledge base.

An example of the need for this greater expressive power can be found in Moore (1982). He discusses the following situation: Suppose there are three blocks A, B, and C lined up from left to right. A is blue, C is green, and the color of B is not known. The question then is whether there a nongreen block to the left of a green block. A little thought will show that this is indeed the case: If B is green, then there is a nongreen block (A) to the left of a green block (B), and if B is nongreen, then B is the nongreen block to the left of a green block (C). When you analyze this informal piece of reasoning, you see that the reasoner has to be able to understand that an existentially quantified sentence is true, even if he or she does not know which object in the world makes the sentence true. Also, the reasoner needs to be able to see that either a sentence or its negation must be true. Thirdly, the reasoner has to be able to see that if something follows from ϕ and also from $\neg \phi$, then it must always be true. No other knowledge representation language allows you to express these types of incomplete information.

A second way in which logic gives greater expressive power is because there are a large number of logics, each of which allow the formulation of a special type of knowledge. For example, there are temporal logics that allow you to represent and reason with information about time. (For a technical discussion, see van Benthem, 1982.) In logics of this kind, you can express not only the information that Harry is bald now, but also that Harry had curly hair in the past, thus increasing the range of information that can be expressed in the formalism. There are also epistemic logics, logics that allow you to represent and reason with information about knowledge and belief (Hintikka, 1962). Thus, in an epistemic logic, you can express not only the information that Harry is bald but also that Fred believes that Harry is bald. It must be said, however, that the problem of finding implementations for interpreters for these extended logics is still very much a research issue. Many AI researchers have dealt with the problem of reasoning about time or knowledge and belief has been by formulating propositions in FOPC that describe temporal and epistemic reasoning, and using a theorem prover for FOPC. (Examples are McDermott, 1979, and Allen, 1981, 1983, for temporal logic, and McCarthy, 1979, and Moore, 1985a, for epistemic logic; see also Shoham, 1986, and Reichgelt, 1987, for a discussion of the temporal approach.) The situation calculus, discussed in section 4.4.1., is an illustration of this approach. However, more recently, there have been a few attempts at building a theorem prover for other logics directly (e.g., Abadi & Manna, 1986; Konolige, 1986; Wallen, 1987; Jackson & Reichgelt, 1989).

3.3. Conclusion

There are two specific arguments in favor of using logic as a knowledge representation language. Apart from the general advantages that logic has because of its declarative nature, they are first the fact that a satisfactory logic has a semantics with all the benefits that this brings, and, second, its greater expressive power. Not surprisingly perhaps, the arguments in favor of using logic as a knowledge representation language are mainly at the logical level. They concern such things as the semantics of the formalism, the soundness of the inference procedure, and the expressive power of the language. It will be interesting to contrast these with the arguments that have been put forward in support of other knowledge representation languages.

4. PROBLEMS AND SOLUTIONS

In this section we discuss the arguments that have been used against logic. There are five main problems. The first problem is an implementational problem and concerns the efficiency of logic as a knowledge representation language. A second problem is at the logical level, and concerns the undecidability of certain logics. The other three problems are all at the epistemological level, and concern important types of knowledge and reasoning that are not straightforward to deal with in logic, namely procedural knowledge, default reasoning, and abductive reasoning.

4.1. Logic is too inefficient

When Robinson discovered his resolution refutation proof theory (Robinson, 1965), various people were tempted to use a theorem prover of this kind as a general problem solver. However, within five years, it became clear that the resulting programs were much too slow to be useful. Even simple problems took a very long time to solve. People took these efficiency problems to imply that logic was not suitable as a knowledge representation language.

However, Moore (1982) argues that the conclusion that logic cannot be used as a knowledge representation language is a misinterpretation of the failure of the early experiments. When you look at the early implementation of resolution refutation theorem provers, it soon becomes obvious that they used inefficient control regimes. It turns out that the way in which the control regimes dealt with the different clauses is equivalent to using every implication in a knowledge base both in a forward and a backward reasoning fashion. This obviously leads to highly redundant search spaces. Further research pinpointed this weakness, and more sophisticated control regimes were developed which overcame some of the efficiency problems that bedeviled early theorem provers. One can thus argue that the early failures of logic-based knowledge representation languages were due to inappropriate control regimes, and that use of more appropriate control regimes has led to efficient logic-based inference engines. Support for this argu-

with certain predicates, then you may be in danger of losing this advantage. The meaning of these predicates is determined by the pieces of code associated with them.

4.4. Default reasoning

Another argument against logic-based knowledge representation languages is the claim that there are particular types of reasoning which, although very important, cannot be readily captured in such a language. If you use logic as a knowledge representation language, then you are committed to the use of a logical style of reasoning, usually called *deduction*, as the main inference procedure. McDermott, a researcher who spent most of his career arguing for logic as a knowledge representation language, published a paper in 1986 in which he drew attention to two important types of allegedly nondeductive reasoning, namely *default reasoning* and *abduction*. Clearly, if McDermott's claim that these types of reasoning are nondeductive is correct, then logic-based knowledge representation languages are unsatisfactory as they would not allow one to represent important types of inference. In this section we concentrate on default reasoning. In the next section we turn to abduction. Because default reasoning is very important in commonsense reasoning, it will be one of the themes of this book.

Moore (1985b) defines default reasoning as "the drawing of plausible inferences on the basis of less than conclusive evidence in the absence of information to the contrary." A frequently used example is the following: If Tweety is a bird, then in the absence of evidence to the contrary, you are probably willing to draw the plausible inference that Tweety can fly. After all, typically birds can fly, and you are inclined to assume that if Tweety is bird, then Tweety is a typical bird. One of the features of default reasoning is that you draw a certain inference about the world from the fact that negative information about the world is not available at the time the inference is drawn.

The main problem that default reasoning poses for logic is its nonmonotonic character. In all standard logics, inference is *monotonic*: If ϕ is a valid consequence from a set of sentences S (or can be proved from it using the proof theory), then ϕ also follows (can be derived) from the set S plus the sentence ψ. In other words, in normal logics, you can add to the set of premises without making any previously drawn conclusions invalid: If ϕ is true, whenever all the sentences in S are true, then ϕ will also be true whenever all the sentences in S plus the sentence ψ are true. After all, if S and ψ are true then S will certainly be true as well, and we know that if this is the case, then ϕ is true.

In nonmonotonic inference systems adding premises may make previously derived sentences no longer derivable. The nonmonotonicity of default reasoning can easily be illustrated in our example. Suppose that you have indeed drawn the default conclusion that Tweety can fly. If you then later learn that Tweety is a penguin, then because penguins cannot fly, you have to give up the default inference. The reason for the nonmonotonicity of default reasoning is clear:

Default inferences are drawn because of an absence of evidence to the contrary. If you then add more information to the initial set of premises, this new information might constitute the evidence to the contrary that was absent when the original default inference was drawn. As a result, the initial inference will have to be withdrawn.

Default reasoning is problematic for those who maintain that one should use FOPC as one's knowledge representation language as FOPC is monotonic. The problem becomes more pressing once it is realized how much of our everyday reasoning is a form of default reasoning, and how important it is in AI (see, e.g., Reiter, 1978). Therefore, the conclusion would seem warranted that a knowledge representation language that cannot deal with default reasoning is not satisfactory.

Of course, there are ways of trying to cope with this problem in the context of logic. One obvious possible reply to this problem would be to try to construct a logic that can cope with default reasoning. Various attempts have been made (see, for example, McCarthy, 1980; McDermott & Doyle, 1980; Reiter, 1980; and McDermott, 1982), and there is now a large literature on this topic. Ginsberg (1987) is a collection of many of the most important papers in this area. It is impossible to do complete justice to all the proposals in the literature, and the following section is therefore merely an illustration of the type of approach that one may use to solve these issues.

4.4.1. Default and nonmonotonic logics

As said above, there are many different attempts to extend FOPC to enable it to cope with default reasoning. In this section, we discuss two examples, namely default logic and circumscription. We also sketch some of the objections that have been raised against default and nonmonotonic logics.

Default logic was first proposed by Reiter (1980). He analyzes defaults as inference rules, more or less on a par with *modus ponens*. The default sentence that typically birds can fly, for example, would be formalized as an inference rule of the following form:

bird(x) | flies(x) ⊢ flies(x)

The informal reading of this statement is: For any x, if it can be deduced that x is a bird, and it is consistent with the theory that x can fly, then infer that x can fly. Note that this is really a sort of schematic rule because it can be instantiated for every constant a in the language.

In the rephrasing of the above sentence, we used the word *consistent*. A sentence ϕ is consistent with a theory S if it is possible for ϕ to be true in an interpretation in which all the sentences in S are true as well. A little thought will show that this definition is equivalent to saying that $\neg\phi$ should not be a valid consequence of S. After all, if $\neg\phi$ is a valid consequence of S, then it is impossible for all the sentences in S to be true, while $\neg\phi$ is false. It would therefore be impossible for all the sentences in S to be true, and for ϕ to be true at the same time, and hence ϕ would not be consistent with S.

The following examples illustrate Reiter's default logic. Suppose that we have the following theory S:

bird(tweety)
$(\forall x)[\text{penguin}(x) \rightarrow \text{bird}(x)]$
$(\forall x)[\text{penguin}(x) \rightarrow \neg\text{flies}(x)]$

S also contains the default inference rule

bird(x) | flies(x) ⊢ flies(x)

while the only nondefault inference rules that are used are:

$\phi, \phi \rightarrow \psi \vdash \psi$
$(\forall x)[\phi(x)] \vdash \phi(a)$
for any constant a.

The only way in which one can prove that Tweety can fly is by applying the inference rule to the default sentence, and in order to be able to do that, you have to determine whether *bird(tweety)* is true and *flies(tweety)* is consistent with the theory. *bird(tweety)* is a sentence in S, and therefore certainly follows from it. Also, it is easy to establish that *flies(tweety)* is consistent with S because you cannot prove ¬*flies(tweety)* from S.

The situation changes dramatically however if you add the sentence *penguin(tweety)* to S. In that case, you can no longer apply the default inference rule because *flies(tweety)* is no longer consistent. After all, you can derive ¬*flies(tweety)*. As a consequence, the default inference rule cannot be applied.

Another proposal for coping with default reasoning is due to McCarthy (1980). McCarthy introduced the notion of *circumscription*. Circumscription is a rule of conjecture that allows you to jump to the conclusion that the objects that you can show to have a certain property ϕ are in fact *all* the objects that have this property. In subsequent work, people discovered other forms of circumscription (see, e.g., McCarthy, 1986; Lifschitz, 1987). However, rather than discuss the different forms of circumscription, we simply illustrate the basic ideas by showing how the system deals with the Tweety example.

Suppose that we know

bird(tweety)
$(\forall x)[\text{penguin}(x) \rightarrow \text{bird}(x)]$
$(\forall x)[\text{penguin}(x) \rightarrow \neg\text{flies}(x)]$

McCarthy's analysis of the default sentence *typically, birds fly* is based on the paraphrase of this sentence as *a bird will fly if it is not abnormal*. Thus, we can introduce another predicate called *ab* (for *abnormal*), and formalize the default sentence as

$$(\forall x)[(bird(x) \& \neg ab(x)) \rightarrow flies(x)]$$

Nota that unlike Reiter who analyzed defaults as additional inference rules, McCarthy analyzes defaults as sentences in the language itself.

In itself, adding this formalization of the default sentence to the original theory is not enough. After all, we cannot use it to conclude *flies(tweety)* simply because we cannot prove that ¬*ab(tweety)*. But we now use circumscription on the predicate *ab*, or, to use the technical term, we now circumscribe *ab*, and assume that those things that can shown to be *ab* are the only things that are *ab*. We can rewrite the default sentence to

$$(\forall x)[(bird(x) \& \neg flies(x)) \rightarrow ab(x)]$$

We can now see that there is nothing that can be shown to be *ab*, and we therefore can add the following sentence to our theory

$$(\forall x)[\neg ab(x)]$$

Clearly, we can use this extension to the theory to conclude ¬*ab(tweety)* and hence *flies(tweety)*.

Circumscription also gives the right results for the following theory:

penguin(tweety)
$(\forall x)[penguin(x) \rightarrow bird(x)]$
$(\forall x)[penguin(x) \rightarrow \neg flies(x)]$
$(\forall x)[(bird(x) \& \neg ab(x)) \rightarrow flies(x)]$

Clearly, we can now prove that *ab(tweety)*. If we now circumscribe *ab*, we add the sentence that Tweety is the only individual who is *ab*:

$$(\forall x)[ab(x) \leftrightarrow (x = tweety)]$$

In this extended theory we can then no longer draw the inference *flies(tweety)*.

Although default logic and circumscription might seem attractive ways of dealing with the problem of default reasoning, neither they, nor any of the other default and nonmonotonic logics that have been proposed, are entirely without their problems. There are four problems that can be raised.

A first problem with default and nonmonotonic logic follows from the semi-decidability of FOPC. As said earlier, it can be shown that it is impossible to design a procedure what will always return "no" if a sentence φ does not follow from a set of sentences *S*. This problem is important here because default rules can only be applied if a given piece of information is consistent with the information in the knowledge base. As we saw earlier, in order to make sure that a given piece of information is consistent, you have to prove that its negation cannot be derived. But this is undecidable. Thus, in order to be able to use default or nonmonotonic logic as a knowledge representation language its inference procedure needs to include a subroutine which will not return for certain queries. As a result, these logics are not even semidecidable.

Earlier, we argued that for standard FOPC the undecidability problem could be solved by the use of heuristics to stop the search for a proof, for example, after the same inference rule had been applied a number of times to the same formula. We argued that this use of heuristics was acceptable because although we might loose completeness, and not be able to derive everything that follows from the knowledge base, we would retain soundness, and derive information that would have to be true if the information in the knowledge base was true. However, in the context of default and nonmonotonic logic, this argument does not apply. Default rules can only be used if some piece of information cannot be derived. If we use heuristics to decide that something cannot be derived, then for some pieces of information we might mistakenly decide that they are not derivable. Thus, some pieces of information will be regarded as consistent, even when they are not. As a result, we might apply default rules because heuristics told us that we could do so, even when in reality we could not. As a result, we would loose soundness and be able to derive false information from a true knowledge base. It would seem that it is impossible to write a completely satisfactory theorem prover based on default logic.

While this first problem for default and nonmonotonic logics is simply a fact, and therefore not controversial, the following three arguments are very controversial. Nevertheless, we present them here as they will give the reader some flavor of the research that is going on in this area, and the type of arguments that are used in this context.

It is still an open question to what extent the various default and nonmonotonic logics can be given an entirely adequate semantics. For example, Reiter's default logic was originally characterized purely proof theoretically with no attempt at providing a semantics. Given the fact that one of the reasons for preferring logic as a knowledge representation language was the fact that a logic comes with a semantics, this is of course a serious problem.

In recent years, a lot of work has gone into supplying nonmonotonic and default logics with a semantics. For example, Moore (1985b) provides a semantics for one particular type of nonmonotonic logic, called autoepistemic logic, which Konolige (1987) shows to be equivalent to Reiter's default logic. Other interesting, recent, proposals include Ginsberg (1986) and Etherington (1987a). Finally, Shoham (1987) contains a very elegant proposal which can be used to give a semantics to a large class of default and nonmonotonic logics. Because of its generality and elegance, we discuss Shoham's proposal in some more detail.

Shoham's semantics is based on a preference relation $<$ between interpretations. Thus, if I and I' are interpretations, then I $<$ I' means that I is preferred to I'. Using this relation, Shoham then defines a preferential model M for a sentence ϕ as an interpretation such that M $\vDash$ ϕ, and moreover, there is no M' such that M' $\vDash$ ϕ and M' $<$ M. Shoham then defines the notion of minimal entailment as follows: A sentence ϕ minimally entails a sentence ψ if every preferential model for ϕ is also a model for ψ. The notion of minimal entailment is indeed nonmonotonic because a minimal model for ϕ & π is not always a minimal model for ϕ as well. Thus, while ψ might be true in every minimal model for ϕ, ψ may not to be true in every minimal model for ϕ & π. Therefore, ϕ can preferentially entail ψ without ϕ & π preferentially entailing ψ as well.

Shoham claims that the various nonmonotonic and default logics can be analyzed as using different preference relations. For example, circumscribing a predicate ϕ can be seen as a preference relation which states that an interpretation I is to be preferred to an interpretation I' if I and I' are exactly the same except that all individuals with the property ϕ in I also have the property ϕ in I', where there are some individuals with ϕ in I' but not in I. Shoham's proposal is very recent, and, as Shoham admits, needs further work. Nevertheless, it seems an interesting way forward and might provide a uniform semantics for the various default and nonmonotonic logics.

A third objection to default and nonmonotonic logics can be found in Hanks and McDermott (1986, 1987). Hanks and McDermott observe that there has been a lot of technical work on default and nonmonotonic logics. There are also a number of applications in which default rules would seem to be of use. Howeverm, there have been very few attempts at determining whether these logics give the intuitively correct results for problems that seem to involve default reasoning. If default logic is an adequate account of default reasoning, then the conclusions that can be derived in default logic should agree with one's intuition. Hanks and McDermott present an informal argument, which has become known as the *Yale shooting* problem, together with the intuitively desired consequence. Hanks and McDermott then formalize this problem in various nonmonotonic and default logics, and show that the derived conclusion is too weak.

The Yale shooting problem is a special instance of the *frame* problem. McCarthy and Hayes (1969) proposed an account of temporal reasoning, known as the *situation calculus*, which has become very popular. The basic idea of the situation calculus is to represent temporal information by having a special two-place predicate *true*, whose first argument is a *fact* while its second argument is a *situation*. Thus something like

true(happy(j), s_j)

would represent the information that John is happy in situation s_j. Actions can then be represented as functions from situations to situations, and their effects can be represented by special axioms. Thus, waking up is an action, which results in a situation in which John, who was asleep before, is no longer asleep:

true(asleep(j),s$_1$) → true(awake(j),result(wake-up(j),s$_1$)

One of the problems in situation calculus is the question of what information stays true from one situation to the next. Thus, you would expect the action of John waking up to have no effect on the color of his bed: If it was red before John woke up, then it will still be red immediately after he wakes up. But, in the formalization given thus far, you are not able to infer *true(color(johns-bed,red),result(wake-up(j,s$_1$)))* from *true(color(johns-bed,red),s$_1$)*. The problem of deciding what facts remain true when a certain action is performed is known as the *frame* problem.

One way of dealing with the frame problem might be to add a large number of so-called *frame* axioms that state which facts are not affected by some action. Thus, you would include in the formalization of the problem an axioms which asserts that John waking up does not change the color of his bed. The problem with this solution is of course that most facts are unaffected by a certain action, and you would have to specify an enormous number of these frame axioms.

A more natural way of dealing with the frame problem might be to add a default rule. Most facts are not changed when a certain action is performed. Thus, an action which does change the truth value of a fact is abnormal with respect to this fact. Hanks and McDermott formalize this intuition in default logic by introducing a 3-place abnormality predicate *ab*. *ab(f,a,s)* means that action *a* performed in situation *s* is abnormal with respect to fact *f* and will change its truth value. We can then add by the following *ab axiom*.

(∀f)(∀a)(∀s)[(true(f,s) & ¬ab(f,a,s)) → true(f,result(a,s))]

Using circumscription as our nonmonotonic logic, we then want to circumscribe on the predicate *ab*, and make sure that we add as few triples of facts, actions and situations with the property *ab* as possible.

We now return to the Yale shooting problem. Initially, some person called Fred is alive. As time goes by, three actions take place. First, a gun is loaded. Then, we wait a while. And finally the gun is fired. We have the axiom that if Fred is alive, and the gun is loaded, and the gun is shot, then Fred is dead. In other words, if the gun is loaded, then shooting is abnormal with respect to Fred being alive. Hanks and McDermott argue that given this problem the intuitively correct conclusion is that Fred should no longer be alive in the final situation. Apart from the *ab* axiom give earlier, we specify the initial situation, the loading axiom, and the shooting axioms:

The initial situation:
    true(alive(fred), s$_1$)

The loading axioms:
($\forall$s)[true(loaded, result(load,s))]
The shooting axiom:
($\forall$s)[true(loaded,s) → (ab(alive(fred),shoot,s)) & true(dead(fred),result(shoot,s)))]

The problem then is what is true if the following situations occur:

s_1
s_2 = result(load, s_1)
s_3 = result(wait, s_2)
s_4 = result(shoot, s_3)

In all nonmonotonic and default logics the prediction made is that there are two possibilities. Either Fred is dead in situation s_4 (which is the intuitively correct conclusion), or somehow during the waiting action, the gun becomes magically unloaded. The first conclusion can be reached by reasoning forward in time, the second conclusion can be reached by reasoning backward in time, using the following versions of the *ab* axiom, and the *shooting* axiom. (The reader can check that these formulations are equivalent to the original formulations.)

($\forall$f)($\forall$a)($\forall$s)[(true(f,s) & ¬true(f,result(a,s))) → ab(f,a,s)]
($\forall$s)[(¬ab(alive(fred),shoot,s) v ¬true(dead,result(shoot,s))) → ¬true(loaded,s)]

In both cases, we have only one triple that is *ab*. When we reason forward in time, then we have *ab(alive(fred),shoot,s_3)*. When we reason backward in time, we have *ab(loaded,wait,s_4)*. We leave it as an exercise to the reader to check that both possibilities can indeed be obtained by circumscribing *ab*.

It thus appears that the type of default reasoning that Hanks and McDermott try to formalize cannot be adequately dealt with by circumscription. Moreover Hanks and McDermott demonstrate that the same result can be achieved in other default and nonmonotonic logics. Given the intention of nonmonotonic logic to model default reasoning, Hanks and McDermott argue that this casts severe doubt on systems of this type.

Since Hanks and McDermott first published their Yale shooting problem in 1986, there have been various reactions to the paper. It must be said that Hanks and McDermott's conclusion about the failure of nonmonotonic and default reasoning is very controversial. Ginsberg (1987) and Brown (1987) contain a number of replies to Hanks and McDermott's points as well as references to other papers. These replies range from completely new nonmonotonic logics, to arguments that Hanks and McDermott's formulation is not the correct one. Hanks and McDermott (1987) is a reponse. Whatever the final outcome of the debate, Hanks and McDermott have at least shown that the most straightforward formalizations in default and nonmonotonic logic of problems which involve default reasoning do not always lead to the required solutions.

A further argument against default and nonmonotonic logics is raised by Perlis (1986), who extends and generalizes earlier arguments in Israel (1980,1987). Perlis distinguishes between two different approaches to the problem of reasoning in general, and default reasoning in particular. The first approach, which he calls the *spec* approach, is to try to specify the formal relations that holds between the premises of some argument, and its conclusion. The default and nonmonotonic logics are obvious examples of the spec approach. The second approach, which Perlis calls the *process* approach, tries to identify specific actions that constitute the drawing of default conclusions. Thus, rather than concentrating on the formal relations between premises and conclusions, the process approach concentrates on the process of drawing conclusions from premises. Perlis acknowledges that there is a close relationship between the two approaches, in that the first can be seen as a more abstract study of the second. Nevertheless, he argues that some of the central properties of default reasoning derive from their process nature. and that by ignoring these process properties default and nonmonotonic logics do not give a satisfactory account of default reasoning.

Perlis argues that any commonsense reasoner will have to be able to jump to conclusions. For example, in circumscription we jump to the conclusion that the things which we can now show to be *ab* are all the things that are *ab*. Similarly, in Reiter's default logic, we jump to the conclusion *flies(tweety)* from *bird(tweety)* and our inability to show ¬*(flies(tweety)*. But, a commonsense reasoner should also be what Perlis calls *Socratic* and *recollective*. A reasoner is Socratic if it believes that it can make mistakes, and it is recollective if it can recall its past conclusions. Now, Perlis shows that various default and nonmonotonic logics, including Reiter's default logic and McCarthy's circumscription become inconsistent if we allow for Socratic and recollective commonsense reasoners.

Perlis' analysis is rather technical and is therefore beyond this book. Nevertheless, the reader can get a feel for why this results holds by considering the following piece of reasoning in Reiter's default logic. Consider again the following theory S

bird(tweety)
$(\forall x)[penguin(x) \rightarrow bird(x)]$
$(\forall x)[penguin(x) \rightarrow \neg flies(x)]$

together with the default inference rule

bird(x) | flies(x) ⊢ flies(x)

If we apply the default rule at this point in time, then we can obviously derive *flies(tweety)*. A recollective reasoner might now add this conclusion to the theory S to obtain the new theory S':

bird(tweety)
(∀x)[penguin(x) → bird(x)]
(∀x)[penguin(x) → ¬flies(x)]
flies(tweety)

But if the reasoner now also learns *penguin(tweety)* then it can also derive ¬*flies(tweety)*. We now have an inconsistency because S' contains both *flies(tweety)* and ¬*flies(tweety)*. Inconsistency in a knowledge base however, should be avoided at all costs. First, φ and ¬φ can never be true at the same time, and you would like a knowledge base to reflect the state of affairs in the world. Second, an inconsistent knowledge base implies every sentence in the language. This can easily be checked: φ is a valid consequence of the set of sentences S if, whenever all the sentences in S are true, then φ is true as well. But if S is inconsistent, then the sentences in it can never be all true, and therefore any sentence is a valid consequence.

Partly based on these conclusions, a number of authors have tried to give process accounts of default reasoning. Perlis (1984), Elgot-Drapkin, Miller, and Perlis (1987), and Reichgelt (1988) are examples. One type of tool that has proven useful in this strategy are the so-called reason maintenance systems which we discuss in the next section. Before we do so, it should be noted that Perlis' conclusion about the inconsistency of the various default and nonmonotonic systems relies crucially on the assumption that the reasoner be recollective. As we shall see in the next section there are good reasons for making a reasoning system recollective, but it is less clear whether these arguments also apply to those, like default and nonmonotonic logicians, who take a spec approach to default reasoning and are primarily interested in the formal relations between premises and conclusions.

4.4.2. Reason maintenance systems

The main problem with default reasoning is that inferences drawn from an initial set of premises might turn out to be false when more premises are added. As a consequence, a recollective reasoner, that is, a reasoner that stores sentences derived from a default sentence in its knowledge base, may end up with a contradictory set of sentences. We saw an example of this above.

The inconsistency problem arises not only in default reasoning. The problem is more general and arises in all cases where the information in the knowledge base can change. Another example is a knowledge base containing information about a changing domain. Thus, as time goes by, some of the sentences in the knowledge base that were true at one stage may no longer be true later on. Systems of this kind have difficulties that are very similar to the problems posed by default reasoning. The main difference is that the problem arises here because the world changes and some of the initial information in the knowledge base will therefore have to be withdrawn, whereas in the case of default reasoning, the problem arises because the system learns more about the world, and therefore can no longer rely on derivations that were made because certain things were not known at the time at which the derivation was made.

At first sight, the most obvious way of coping with the problem might be not to make the reasoning system recollective. The problem seems to arise only if you store previously derived sentences. So, if the system does not store derived sentences, then the problem disappears. Also, storing derived sentences, even when they do not lead to any further difficulties, seems redundant, as the system could derive them again if it needed them a second time. Note incidentally that this might be the line of argument that default and nonmonotonic logicians would take to avoid inconsistencies in their logics.

Although the above argument is theoretically correct, there might be practical reasons for storing derived sentences. For example, it may be a long and costly process to derive a certain sentence. If such a sentence is likely to have to be used more than once, then the efficiency of the system would obviously be improved if you stored the derived sentence the first time that the system derived it. It is interesting to point out that these arguments are all practical arguments and therefore presuppose a process approach to reasoning, that is, an approach which concentrates on the process of deriving conclusions from premises. As a result, these arguments do not really affect the default and nonmonotonic logicians who are taking the spec approach. They are interested only in the formal relations between premises and conclusions, independent of the processes by which these conclusions are reached.

A second possible solution that might seem attractive at first sight is simply to retract one of the contradictory sentences. Thus, if the knowledge base contains both *Tweety can fly* and *Tweety cannot fly*, then you simply retract one of them.

There are two problems with this suggestion. First, if the sentence that you withdraw had been included because it had been derived from other sentences in the knowledge base, then merely retracting the offending sentence is not sufficient. If the sentences from which it had been derived remain in the knowledge base, then the system would still be able to re-derive the sentence in question. Thus, when you withdraw a sentence that was included because it could be derived from other sentences, then you will have to withdraw at least one of the sentences used in its derivations as well. Second, it is entirely possible that the sentence that you retract has itself been used to derive other sentences. When you withdraw it, then you will probably want to retract these derived sentences as well. You usually only want to include information in the knowledge base if you have a reason for believing it.

There has been a lot of work on systems that can cope with changing knowledge bases without falling foul of any of the problems mentioned above. Systems of this kind are known as *reason maintenance* systems (RMS), also called *truth maintenance*, or *belief revision* systems. An RMS stores with every sentence in the knowledge base the reason for its inclusion. This information is then used whenever a contradiction is discovered. There are quite a few RMSs around. One of the earliest systems that had some reason maintenance facilities was AMORD (de Kleer, Doyle, Steele, & Sussman, 1977). Later systems include Doyle (1979) and McAllester (1980). Recently, de Kleer (1986) proposed a more sophisticated RMS. However, we describe the earlier and simpler systems.

To reiterate, an RMS records for every sentence in the knowledge the reason why the sentence was included. This piece of information is called a *justification*. Just as there are many types of reason for including a sentence in the knowledge base, there are many types of justification. The reasoner may, for example, accept a sentence as true without needing any further support. In this case the justification will be empty, and is called a *premise justification*. Or a reasoner may accept a sentence because it could be derived from other sentences in the knowledge base. The justification in this case will consist of the sentences that were used in its derivation. We call these sentences the *justifying sentences*.

Justifications are used whenever the system discovers a contradiction and has to change the information in the knowledge base to get rid of it. Whenever a contradiction arises, one of the contradictory sentences will have to be withdrawn. If the system retracts a sentence that does not have a premise justification, and hence was included because it could be derived from a set of justifying sentences, then at least one of the justifying sentences will have to be withdrawn as well. Thus, suppose that the system has included ϕ in the knowledge base because it could derive it from ψ and $\psi \rightarrow \phi$. Thus, if the system discovered a contradiction between ϕ and $\neg\phi$, and decided to withdraw ϕ, then either ψ or $\psi \rightarrow \phi$ will have to be withdrawn as well. We call this process *backward belief revision*.

However, in addition to backward belief revision, we also need what you might call *forward belief revision*. If a sentence has to be withdrawn from the knowledge base, then the system is no longer justified in believing any sentences that were derived from it, unless of course they can be proved in some other way. For example, suppose that the knowledge base contains the sentences ϕ and $\phi \rightarrow \psi$. The interpreter might then use these sentence to derive ψ, and store this sentence as well. If it then subsequently found out that ϕ was false, and had to be retracted, then ψ would have to be withdrawn as well, unless the system could prove ψ from alternative premises. Of course, if the system can find no other way of deriving ψ, then the sentences derived on the basis ψ will have to be reproved or retracted as well.

In order to make the above ideas more concrete, we discuss a simple example. We start off with the following knowledge base, containing three sentences, each of which has a premise justification and was therefore included in the knowledge base without relying on other sentences.

1. ϕ $\langle \rangle$
2. $\phi \rightarrow \psi \; \langle \rangle$
3. $\psi \rightarrow \chi \; \langle \rangle$

When the system starts reasoning, it can derive ψ and χ and add the following:

4. ψ $\langle 1,2 \rangle$
5. χ $\langle 3,4 \rangle$

$\langle 1,2 \rangle$ is the justification of ψ and expresses the information that ψ was added because it could be derived from sentences 1 (ϕ) and 2 ($\phi \rightarrow \psi$). Similarly, χ was derived from sentences 3 and 4.

Now suppose that the system finds out for example from an outside sensor that $\neg \psi$, and adds it to its knowledge base.

6. $\neg \psi$ $\langle \rangle$

The knowledge base now obviously contains a contradiction, and the systems needs to decide which sentence ($\neg \psi$ or ψ) to withdraw. It must be said that the decision which sentence to withdraw is often left to the user of an RMS. An exception is the system of McAllester (1980). McAllester proposes to divide the sentences in a knowledge base into likelihood classes. Whenever a contradiction arises, then the sentence in the lowest likelihood class is retracted first. Using this idea, suppose then that ψ is in a lower likelihood class than $\neg \psi$ and therefore has to be withdrawn. Assuming that the RMS will first do forward belief revision on ψ, it will first try to prove the sentences that have ψ in their justification in some other way. Thus, because χ contains ψ in its justification, it will have to try to prove it in some other way. Fortunately, this can be done because one can derive the following:

7. $\phi \rightarrow \chi$ $\langle 2,3 \rangle$

and use this to find the new justification for χ. Therefore, the system will change the justification for χ.

After the forward belief revision has been done, the system will then have to engage in backward belief revision in ψ, and decide which sentence in ψ's justification has to be withdrawn as well. The choice is between ϕ and $\phi \rightarrow \psi$. Assuming that ϕ is in the lower likelihood class, ϕ is withdrawn and the system engages in forward belief revision on ϕ. (Because ϕ has a premise justification, it is not necessary to do backward belief revision.) Because the new justification for χ ($\langle 1,7 \rangle$) mentions ϕ, and because there is no other way of proving it, it will have to be withdrawn as well. The resulting knowledge base therefore looks like

2. $\phi \rightarrow \psi$ $\langle \rangle$
3. $\psi \rightarrow \chi$ $\langle \rangle$
6. $\neg \psi$ $\langle \rangle$
7. $\phi \rightarrow \chi$ $\langle \rangle$

There are some severe efficiency problems with this basic RMS. They can be illustrated in the above example. Suppose that at some later stage the systems finds out that ϕ was true after all. The earlier work to find the valid consequences of ϕ, namely the derivation of ψ and χ, has been lost because the forward and backward belief revision mean that ψ and χ have disappeared out of the knowledge base altogether. So, if ϕ was reasserted, the earlier inferences would have to be rederived. This problem has been called the *unouting* problem (de Kleer, 1986).

Doyle (1979) proposes a solution to the unouting problem which involves complicating the way in which a sentence is stored in the knowledge base. In addition to storing with a sentence its justification, Doyle's system also stores a *support status* with a sentence. There are two choices for the support status: a sentence is either *in* or *out*. If a sentence is *in*, then the system believes that it is true; if a sentence is *out*, then the system does not believe that it is true. Note that a sentence being out does not mean that the system believes the negation of the sentence. Doyle explicitly distinguishes between a sentence ϕ not being believed (i.e., having the support status *out*), and ϕ being believed to be false (i.e., $\neg \phi$ having the support status *in*).

In Doyle's system, retracting a sentence becomes a matter of changing its support status, rather than deleting it from the knowledge base. Thus, in the above example, the final knowledge base would have the form

	Sentence	Support Status	Justification
1.	ϕ	out	$\langle \rangle$
2.	$\phi \rightarrow \psi$	in	$\langle \rangle$
3.	$\psi \rightarrow \chi$	in	$\langle \rangle$
4.	ψ	out	$\langle 1,2 \rangle$
5.	χ	out	$\langle 3,4 \rangle, \langle 1,7 \rangle$
6.	$\neg \psi$	in	$\langle \rangle$
7.	$\phi \rightarrow \chi$	in	$\langle 2,3 \rangle$

Note that χ has two different justifications, corresponding to the fact that the system was able to derive this sentence in two different ways. With this addition, the task of an RMS now changes from maintaining the consistency of a knowledge base to calculating the support status of the sentences in the knowledge base. Clearly, the support status of a sentence is *in* if every sentence in one of its justifications is *in*.

Doyle extends the basic RMS in a second way. This second extension is directly relevant to the treatment of default inferences. Recall that a default inference can be drawn because of the failure to prove another sentence. Thus, to use the Tweety example again, you can draw the default inference that Tweety can fly from the fact that Tweety is a bird, and the inability to draw the inference that Tweety cannot fly. In terms of support status: the sentence *Tweety can fly* is *in* because *Tweety is a bird* is *in*, and *Tweety cannot fly* is *out*. Thus, it seems that a justification for default inferences should mention not only sentences that should be *in*, but also sentences that must be *out*. Doyle indeed follows this line, and proposes that a justification consists of an *in-list* and an *out-list*. In order for a sentence ϕ to be *in*, the RMS then has to make sure that there is a justification for ϕ such that all the sentences in the in-list are *in*, and all the sentences in the out-list are *out*. Given this complication, you can then reformulate default rules, which, it will be remembered were formulated as,

$$\phi \mid \psi \vdash \chi$$

as follows:

sentence	support status	justification	
		in-list	out-list
χ	?	ϕ	$\neg\psi$

A justification with a nonempty out-lists is nonmonotonic: As more sentences are added to a knowledge base, it is possible that some of the sentences mentioned in the out-list are added as well. When this happens, the sentence with such a nonmonotonic justification will have to be withdrawn itself. Adding out-lists to justifications then seem to provide a relatively natural way of dealing default reasoning in an RMS.

4.4.3. Default reasoning and RMSs

The previous paragraph sketches how you could use RMSs to deal with default reasoning. Because of the brevity of the discussion many details have been left unexplained. There are also many difficulties with a simple RMS, some of which are dealt with in de Kleer's so-called assumption-based truth maintenance system (de Kleer, 1986).

The question that this treatment of default reasoning raises is how much of logic is maintained. Are RMSs simply an implementation of a theorem prover for default and nonmonotonic logics, as Doyle (1979, p. 268) suggests, or is the relation more complex? The fact that RMSs allow one to make a reasoning system recollective without becoming inconsistent, something which was impossible for default and nonmonotonic logics, suggests the latter.

Another view about the relationship between logic and reasoning maintenance systems can be found in de Kleer (1986). According to de Kleer, a general reasoning system consists of two parts: A problem solver and an RMS. The problem solver is usually based on classical first-order predicate calculus (FOPC), and includes all domain knowledge and inference rules. It will communicate all the inferences that it has drawn to the RMS, whose task it then is to determine which sentences should be *in* and which should be *out* given the justifications that the problem solver has found. Under this view, the problem solver could then be purely logic-based, with the RMS bolted on, so to speak, for dealing with the problems that arise when sentences have to be withdrawn. The problem with this view from the present standpoint is, of course, where to deal with default sentences. On the one hand, default rules seem to be domain-dependent and should therefore be handled in the problem solver. On the other hand, default rules cannot be formulated in FOPC, and therefore cannot be part of the problem solver.

It should be clear by now that RMSs, although they seem to provide a promising way of dealing with default inference, constitute an extension to a pure logic-based inference engine. It is therefore not entirely clear to what extent using an RMS is an essential departure from the use of logic alone for knowledge representation.

4.5. Abduction

McDermott's criticism of logic as a knowledge representation language (McDermott, 1986) mentions a second type of reasoning that he claims cannot be dealt with in a purely logical knowledge representation language. This type of reasoning is called *inference to the best explanation*, or, to use the term introduced by the philosopher Peirce, *abduction*. An example of an inference to the best explanation is the following: If you see that the streets are wet, then you may draw the inference that it has rained. You know that if it has rained, then the streets are wet. You then use this piece of knowledge to infer that the best explanation for my observation that the streets are wet is the assumption that it has rained. Clearly, this is not a deductive inference. After all, it is entirely possible for the streets to be wet even if it has not rained. The inference is abductive: The assumption that it has rained seems to provide the best explanation.

There is a distinction between abductive inference and backward chaining use of inference rules. In abduction, you conclude the truth of the antecedent of the implication on the basis of the fact that the consequent has been found to be true. If the system uses inference rules in a backward chaining fashion on the other hand, then it reduces a sentence ϕ that it is trying to prove to other sentences that might be easier to prove. Only if and when the system manages to prove the other sentences will it conclude that ϕ is true as well. Thus, while both might look like inferences from ψ and $\phi \rightarrow \psi$ to ϕ, in the abductive case ϕ is concluded to be true, whereas in the backward chaining case it is set up as a new goal to prove.

Abduction is an important type of inferencing. Medical diagnostic reasoning, for example, is likely to be abductive, rather than deductive. A doctor observes that the patient has certain symptoms and concludes from these observations that the patient is probably suffering from a particular disease. This inference is not deductive because sometimes a patient with symptom A, does not necessarily suffer from disease B. The same symptom can be caused by more than one disease. The implication is the other way around: If a patient suffers from disease B, then they have symptom A. A medical diagnostician thus concludes the presence of a disease because they have observed the symptom, and thus engage in abductive reasoning.

Although abduction is not itself a form of logical inference, Pople (1973) presents a way in which abduction can be seen as essentially involving deduction. Pople observes that in deduction you try to determine *whether* a sentence is true, whereas in abduction you try to establish *why* a certain sentence, such as a particular observation, is true. Now, answering the "why" question involves answering the "whether" question. If sentence φ follows deductively from a set of sentences S, then it can be argued that the question why φ is true, is answered by the proof that has just been given. Abduction can be seen as the process of finding hypotheses from which the fact that is to be explained follows deductively. There is an important link between abduction and deduction. In order to enable a logic-based inference engine to engage in abductive reasoning, you need to add a component which generates possible hypotheses. The logic-based interpreter can then be used to determine whether the hypothesis actually explains the sentence in question by establishing whether adding the hypothesis to the knowledge base would make derivation of the sentence possible. Poole, Goebel, and Aleliunas (1987) present a system along these lines.

Although the above might be an acceptable explanation of abduction, a similar criticism can be voiced here to the one that we raised in connection with the use of an RMS to deal with the problem of default reasoning. In particular, the problem that abduction poses for a logic-based knowledge representation language, is "solved" by positing a particular component that will generate hypotheses. The problem is how far this hypothesis generator violates the spirit of a logic-based knowledge representation language. Since any sentence can be derived from an infinite number of other sentences, there are an infinite number of ways in which a particular sentence could be explained. The task of the hypothesis generator is to generate the most plausible one. The question is how much knowledge the hypothesis generator must have in order for it to generate the best hypothesis, and how much of this knowledge can be explained logically.

5. CONCLUSION

In this chapter, we discussed logic-based knowledge representation languages. We first explained what a logic is, and introduced some terminology that will be relevant throughout the book. Then we discussed the arguments in favor of using logic. They were the fact that logics often have a clear semantics, and their greater expressive power. However, there were also a number of problems with using logic as a knowledge representation language. There is, of course, the big theoretical problem of the semidecidability of any sufficiently expressive logic. Other problems concerned two important, but nonlogical, forms of inference, namely default reasoning and abduction. We sketched ways in which one might extend the logical framework to deal with these types of reasoning. The problem, however, was that in order to do so, you needed to extend the logical framework in nonlogical ways, and the question might be raised whether you are not giving up logic, and its advantages, by adding such nonlogical components to a reasoning system. There are also other objections that can be raised against logic. However, it will be easier to discuss these in the context of other knowledge representation languages, because some of the advantages of these other systems can actually be seen as (implicit) criticism of a logic-based approach.

4
Production Rules

In this chapter we discuss production rules. Production rules are one of the most popular and widely used knowledge representation languages. Their popularity is partly due to the fact that they have turned out to be very useful in the construction of expert systems. Early expert systems such as DENDRAL (Buchanan, Sutherland, & Feigenbaum, 1969), and MYCIN (Shortliffe, 1976), used production rules as their main knowledge representation language, and many of the systems that have been developed since also represent knowledge in this format. However, the use of production rules has certainly not been confined to expert systems. Newell and Simon (1972) argue on psychological grounds for the use of production rules in modeling human problem solving, and Young and O'Shea (1981) present a program that uses production rules for modeling the errors that children make when they are learning subtraction.

1. PRODUCTION RULE SYSTEMS

Production rules are a knowledge representation language that is particularly suited for modeling what has been called "pattern-directed inference" (Waterman & Hayes-Roth, 1978). Any pattern-directed inference system consists of three components.

The first component is usually called *working memory* and contains a set of *working memory elements*. Working memory elements are intended as representations of the knowledge that the system has acquired about the particular problem it is trying to solve. Thus, imagine a system that is trying to determine why a car will not start. The working memory then contains working memory elements representing facts that are potentially relevant to the problem at hand. For example, the facts that the battery is flat, or that the gasoline tank is empty may be represented in working memory.

The second component in a pattern-directed inference system is a set of *pattern-directed modules*. Each module consists of a triggering pattern and an instruction to be executed. When the triggering pattern matches working memory, then the instruction may be carried out. The result of performing an action is a change in working memory. An action may add new elements to working memory. Alternatively, it may delete or modify existing ones. In the car example, one of the modules might have the instruction to add the piece of information that the gasoline pump is working whenever working memory contains the information that gasoline is reaching the engine. In a production rule system a pattern-directed module is usually called a *rule*, and the component that contains the pattern-directed modules is accordingly called the *rule base*.

The third component in a pattern-directed inference system is the *interpreter*. The interpreter is there to solve the control problem. The control problem arises in the context of pattern-directed inference systems because working memory may match the triggering pattern in more than one production rule. One therefore has to decide which instruction should actually be executed. The task of the interpreter is to make this decision. Consequently, the interpreter goes through three distinct stages: retrieval, refinement, and execution (Davis, 1980). During the retrieval stage, the interpreter retrieves all those rules whose triggering pattern matches working memory. The result of this stage is a set of potentially applicable rules. Because the rules in this set are competing for execution, this set has been called the *conflict set*. During the refinement stage, the conflict set is pruned and possibly reordered. The interpreter decides which of the potentially applicable rules should indeed be applied. Refinement is also known as *conflict resolution*. During the final execution stage, the interpreter then executes the selected rules. This results in a different state of working memory, and the cycle is repeated again. The behavior of the interpreter has also been described as a *select-execute* loop (Davis & King, 1977), because the first two stages, retrieval and refinement, effectively select a (set of) rule(s) to be executed. Other terms that are used include *recognize-act* loop, and *situation-action* loop.

In the next three subsections we discuss these components in more detail.

1.1 Working memory

Working memory contains the information that the system has gained about the problem thus far. In general, the information in working memory comes from two sources. A first source of information is the reasoning that the system has performed so far. Production rule systems often draw intermediate conclusions which they then store in working memory. The second source is the user of the system. Production rule systems often include a facility for users to volunteer information about the problem that they want solved. Also, production rule systems usually treat users as a kind of external database that can be interrogated when the need arises. Thus, a production rule system may ask the user for a particular piece of information that is needed to solve a particular problem, and store the answer in working memory.

Although the precise syntax of various production rule languages varies greatly, most of them store the information in working memory in the form of *object-attribute-value triples*. The intuitive reading of an object-attribute-value triple $\langle A, B, C \rangle$ is that the B of A has the value C. Thus, a typical object-attribute-value triple would be ⟨MY_CAR, COLOR, RED⟩ representing the piece of information that the color of my car is red. Certain production rule language slightly extend this. In OPS5 (Brownston, Farrell, Kant, & Martin, 1985), for example, you can associate any number of attributes and values with an object, thus slightly expanding the expressiveness of the language. MYCIN, on the other hand, stores its basic information in the form of object-attribute-value triples, but adds a certainty value which is intended to express the degree of certainty that the system has about the information expressed in the object-attribute-value triple. We return to certainty values in section 2.

Another syntactic format that is often used can be described as *attribute-relation-value* triples. An example of an attribute-relation-value triple is something like ⟨TEMPERATURE, GREATER-THAN, 20⟩, which represents the information that the temperature is greater than 20.

1.2. The rule base

The second component in a production rule system is the rule-base. Whereas working memory is used for storing "temporary" information, that is, information that only concerns the problem the system is currently trying to solve, the rule-base contains "permanent" information, that is, information that applies to all the problems that the system may be asked to solve.

Production rules are generally of the following form:

IF $cond_1$,
   AND $cond_2$, . . ,
   AND $cond_n$
THEN $action_1$,
   AND $action_2$, . . ,
   AND $action_m$

Production rules are also called *IF-THEN rules*. The IF-part of the rule is called the *antecedent*, or the *left-hand side*. The THEN-part is called the *consequent*, or the *right-hand side*.

Again, there are many differences between different production rule systems in the detailed format of the actual rules. Three differences in particular come to mind. They are the actions that are allowed in the execution part of a rule, the possibility of allowing variables both in the antecedent and the consequent, and the number of statements that are allowed in the left-hand side of a rule.

Production rule systems draw inferences by executing certain instructions if the triggering pattern associated with the rule matches the current state of working memory. Various production rule systems differ in the types of action that they allow. In the most simple systems, the only actions allowed are the addition of working memory elements to working memory, or the replacement of those working memory elements that matched the rule, by the patterns in the other part of the rule. More complicated production-rule languages, such as OPS5, allow other actions as well, such as the deletion of working memory elements, or the modification of existing ones, or even the execution of some arbitrary piece of code, typically written in whatever programming language the production rule system has been implemented in.

As an aside, it is often claimed that production rules are nothing more that implications in first-order predicate calculus (FOPC). At the very least, this is at least misleading. Although implications in FOPC can certainly be seen as one form of production rule, the action part of a rule might specify all sorts of actions whose logical status is less than clear. In OPS5, for example, you can also remove working memory elements, or modify them, and it is not clear how you would model this using FOPC implications.

A second difference between production rule systems is related to the process of matching one part of the rule against working memory. The simplest production rule languages do not allow variables to occur either on the left-hand side nor the right-hand side. Thus, the statements in the triggering pattern in a rule must be identical to an element in working memory. Production rule systems of this kind are not very expressive. For example, it would be impossible to express the piece of information that, for *any* car, if its battery is flat, then it will not start. The situation is, of course, reminiscent of the difference between propositional logic, and full first-order predicate logic. Most production rule systems, however, allow variables in both left-hand sides and right-hand sides of rules. Matching one side of a rule against working memory will then usually result in bindings for variables, which are substituted into the other side, before the instruction associated with it is executed. Thus, suppose that we have the following rule, where $x denotes a variable

IF (car $x)
   AND (lights $x faint)
THEN (check battery $x)

Suppose that we use the left-hand side to match against working memory. Then, if working memory contains the following

(car d550ttv)
(lights d550ttv faint)

then the result of matching this is the new task of checking the battery of the car denoted by d550ttv. Of course, production rule systems that allow variables on both sides are less efficient than production rule system that do not allow this. Matching with variables takes more time than simply checking whether two object-attribute-value triples are identical. However, the gain is greater expressiveness. This is yet another example of the tradeoff between expressiveness and computational tractability (Levesque & Brachman, 1985), mentioned in Chapter 2.

A final difference between the various production rule systems concerns the number of statements that they allow on the left-hand side of a rule. Because this problem is closely related to the behavior of the interpreter, we discuss it in the next section.

1.3. The interpreter

The main task of the interpreter is to solve the control problem: It has to decide which rule to execute on each selection-execute cycle. One can distinguish between two aspects of the control problem.

The first aspect is whether the system tries to match the left-hand side of a production rule against working memory, or the right-hand side. Following Jackson (1986), we use the term *global* control for this problem.

Matching against right-hand sides can most easily be done for systems that allow only one statement on the right-hand side. Systems whose interpreter matches right-hand sides against working memory therefore often have this restriction. It might seem a little strange to match right-hand sides of production rules against working memory. After all, working memory contains information about the problem that the system is currently trying to solve, whereas right-hand sides of production rules describe actions that can be performed.

However, this problem can be solved if we interpret the statement in the right-hand side as a goal-statement, that is, as an instruction to attempt to establish the truth of a certain proposition. The left-hand side can then be regarded as a set of subgoals that have to be fulfilled in order to prove the goal. Working memory in these cases will contain not only information about the world, but also special goal-statements that indicate the goal that the system is presently pursuing. Whenever a right-hand side matches against such a goal-statement, the goal-statement can be retracted, and replaced by sub-goals corresponding to various statements in the left-hand side of the rule. MYCIN uses this control regime. The overall problem-solving behavior of a system that uses this global control regime can be described as goal reduction: A goal is reduced to a set of subgoals which it is hoped are easier to solve. Matching of the right-hand side against working memory results in backward chaining behavior. Because the reasoning process is dependent on the goal that the system is currently trying to prove systems that use this global control regime are often also called *goal-driven*.

Another possible control regime is matching of the left-hand side against working memory. This type of matching results in forward chaining behavior. When production rules are used in a forward chaining fashion, then they are also called *condition-action* or *situation-action* rules. Because the reasoning process in forward chaining production systems is dependent on the data that are available in working memory, systems of this kind are also called *data-driven*.

As an aside, it can be argued that the most natural global control regime for production rule systems is forward chaining. If the system is backward chaining, then the interpretation of the entities in working memory becomes problematic. Working memory contains information about the current state of the world, as well as information about the goals that the system is pursuing. This leads to a potential confusion between domain knowledge, knowledge about the state of the world, and control knowledge, knowledge about the state of the problem-solving process. For reasons of epistemological clarity, it seems preferable to separate these two types of knowledge.

Apart from the global control decision of forward versus backward chaining, there are other control decisions that the interpreter has to make. During a recognize part of a recognize-act cycle, it may be the case that the condition part of more than one rule matches working memory. Thus, at any stage of the problem solving process there may be more than one rule that could be executed. Earlier we used the term conflict set to refer to the set of rules that are potentially applicable. The interpreter has to engage in conflict resolution, that is, it has to decide which rule(s) to execute. Jackson (1986) uses the term *local control* to refer to this aspect of the behavior of the interpreter.

Various strategies that have been used for local control. A simple strategy is to rely on *textual order*: Simply take the first rule in the rule-base that matches. Thus, the interpreter goes through the rule-base trying each condition against working memory, and as soon as one of them matches, it performs the associated action. If you use this strategy, then the next control decision that has to be taken is where the next select-execute cycle starts: You can go back to the top, and try the first rule first, and so on, or you can continue with the rule that was immediately below the one that was executed. In the former case, the nearer the rule is to the top of the rule base, the greater the chance that it will be executed. In the latter case, the interpreter keeps cycling through the entire rule base and on each cycle through the rule base, executes every rule whose condition matches the current state of working memory. One advantage of the textual order strategy is that it may lead to a considerable speed-up of the entire system. Since the interpreter can just execute the first rule that matches working memory, there is no need to generate a conflict set first and to select one rule from it. The interpreter can just execute a rule whenever it finds one that matches working memory.

A second strategy is called *refractoriness*. It states that the same rule should not be applied twice to the same data. Thus, after a rule has been executed once, it should not be executed again. The situation is in fact slightly more complicated for systems that allow variables in the rules. In systems of this kind, an antecedent may match more than one working memory element. If this is indeed the case, then we say that the rule has been instantiated more than once. For systems of this kind, refractoriness states that the same rule instantiation cannot be executed more than once.

The rationale behind the refractoriness is to prevent looping of those rules that do not delete or modify any of their own conditions. Suppose that a rule matched against working memory on the first cycle, and was executed. If in the action part of the rule none of the working memory elements that its condition part matched against are deleted or modified, then the condition part will still match working memory after the rule has been executed. The rule would once again be included in the conflict set on the next recognize-act cycle as well, and it would be possible to execute it again. This could, of course, continue indefinitely. Refractoriness prevents this looping behavior.

Another strategy that has proved popular is *recency*. The idea is to prefer rules that match against the most recent working memory elements. When working elements are added to working memory, or when existing working elements are modified, then you can record the execution cycle at which this happened. During conflict resolution the interpreter inspects these time tags, and executes the rule that matches the most recent working memory element. The effect of the recency strategy is that the system tends to pursue one line of reasoning first, and only tries other solutions when the present line of reasoning fails.

A final strategy that is worth mentioning is *specificity*: Prefer the more specific rules. There are various ways in which a rule can be more specific than another. First, if two rules have the same conditions, but in the first rule more variables have been instantiated during the matching process, then the first rule is more specific than the second. Second, suppose that we have two rules that both contain p and q in their condition part, but the first rule contains r as well, whereas the second does not. Then the first rule is more specific than the second. The specificity strategy can be used to make sure that exceptions to general rules are caught before the general rule is applied. This may be especially useful in dealing with default reasoning. To return to the perennial Tweety example, we may have the rules:

IF (bird tweety)
THEN ADD(can_fly tweety)

IF (bird tweety)
    AND (penguin tweety)
THEN ADD(cannot_fly tweety)

The specificity strategy leads to the second rule being preferred, thus making sure that the correct conclusion is drawn.

There are many more possible strategies but the above ones are the most widely used. Obviously, the various strategies can be combined to give a more powerful strategy for conflict resolution.

2. THE REPRESENTATION OF UNCERTAIN KNOWLEDGE

Production rules have been used extensively in expert systems. However, in many domains, experts do not use hard and fast rules. Often the rules only allow the conclusion to be drawn with some degree of uncertainty. As a result, a lot of work has been done in the area of expert systems on how to deal with uncertain knowledge, and various proposals have been made to enable production rule systems to reason with uncertainty. In this section, we briefly discuss some of the proposals that have been made. For more extensive discussions, interested readers are referred to Frost (1986), Spiegelhalter (1986), and Saffiotti (1987).

We already dealt with one type of uncertain knowledge in the previous chapter when we discussed default reasoning. One can see the default *typically, birds fly* as a more uncertain version of the stronger *all birds fly*. However, the way in which uncertainty has typically been handled in the context of production rule systems is different in two respects. First, uncertainy is dealt with *quantitatively*. One assigns to each working memory element and to each rule a quantitative measure which expresses the degree of confidence that the system has in this particular piece of information. Second, uncertainty is usually dealt with in this context by what Cohen (1985) calls "a parallel uncertainty inference process." By this he means that the basic inference machinery of a production rule system remains the same. As far as inference is concerned, knowledge is treated as if it were absolute and uncertainty is ignored. Uncertainty is dealt with by adding a separate uncertainty inference process to the basic architecture. For each new working element, the uncertainty handler computes a certainty value based on the certainty values associated with the production rule and the working memory elements that were used in deriving this new fact. This is, of course, different from, for example, default logics where changes are made to the basic inference machinery that was used for, for example, first-order predicate calculus.

MYCIN was one of the first system to tackle the problem of uncertain reasoning in a quantitative way. MYCIN's uncertainty handling process is loosely based on probability theory. In probability theory you associate with each proposition in the language a probability measure between 0 and 1. If a proposition ϕ has probability $p(\phi) = .1$, then this is interpreted to mean that in 1 out of 10 cases, ϕ will be true. Clearly, the probability of some proposition ϕ may change on the basis of other evidence. Thus, the probability that some patient is suffering from pneumonia will increase when it is known that the patient has a chest pain. Probability theory then gives a number of rules for calculating the conditional probability $p(\phi|e)$ of some proposition ϕ on the basis of some evidence e. $p(\phi|e)$ is interpreted as the proportion of cases in which ϕ is true given that e is known to be true. An example of such a rule is Bayes' theorem which allows one to calculate $p(\phi|e)$ given $p(\phi)$, $p(e|\phi)$ and $p(e)$ through the following formula:

$$p(\phi|e) = \frac{p(\phi)p(e|\phi)}{p(e)}$$

Probability theory has a number of disadvantages which make it less suitable as a uncertainty handling mechanism in AI. First, Bayes' theorem can only be used if one has a lot of data so that one can determine all the probabilities that are necessary. Second, probability theory has the following axiom:

$$p(\phi|e) + p(\neg\phi|e) = 1$$

Thus, the probability of some hypothesis and its negation given some evidence e always add up to 1. As Shortliffe and Buchanan (1975) point out, this is counterintuitive. An expert may well agree to the fact that the observation of chest pain increases the probability of pneumonia to .7, but would be reluctant to agree that this changes the probability of the patient *not* having pneumonia to .3.

Partly because of these reasons, MYCIN uncertainty handling mechanism, which is also known as the CF model, departed from standard probability theory. MYCIN associated with each working memory element a *certainty factor* which reflects the degree of belief or disbelief that the system has in it. Certainty factors combine a measure of the degree of belief in some working memory element with a measure of the degree of disbelief. If ϕ is a working memory element, then the degree of belief in ϕ is denoted by MB(ϕ), the measure of disbelief is denoted by MD(ϕ), and the certainty factor is denoted by CF(ϕ). CF(ϕ) = MB(ϕ) − MD(ϕ). MB(ϕ) and MD(ϕ) are real numbers between 0 and −1, and CF(ϕ) is therefore a real number between −1 and 1. CF(ϕ) = −1 indicates that the system is sure that ϕ is false, whereas CF(ϕ) = 1 indicates that the system is sure that ϕ is true.

The calculation of CF(ϕ) for a working memory element ϕ in the CF model depends on ϕ's derivation. As mentioned above, many production rule systems treat the user as an external database. Whenever they come across a condition that they cannot prove themselves, they ask the user. In many systems that use the CF model, users are also given the opportunity to specify a certainty factor which reflects their confidence in the answer.

Other working memory elements are added as the result of the execution of a production rule. In the CF model, the certainty factor of these working memory elements is computed as follows. Each rule R has a tally associated with it, which is also denoted by CF(R). CF(R) indicates how strongly the system believes the consequent of R to be true if it has evidence that R's antecedent is true. The certainty factor of the consequent can now be computed by calculating the certainty factor of the antecedent and multiplying it with the tally associated with the rule. Thus, if we conclude ϕ on the base of rule R with antecedent A, then CF(ϕ) = CF(R) * CF(A).

In order to apply the above rule, we of course need to be able to compute CF(A). Sometimes A will be a single condition. In this case, CF(A) equals the certainty factor of the working memory element that it matched. However, A will often be a conjunction of conditions, each of which matches some working memory element. In this case, the CF(A) is the minimum of the certainty factors associated with the various conditions. The underlying intuition is that the degree of confidence that we can have in a conjunction is bounded by the degree of confidence in the weakest conjunct.

The following is a very simple example of the way in which one can compute the certainty factor associated with a working memory element. Suppose that we have the following rule:

IF (country-of-origin ?car Italy)
   AND (weather-condition wet)
THEN (difficulty-starting ?car) with CF = .7

Also, we have the following conditions in working memory

(country-of-origin d550ttv Italy) with CF = 1
(weather-condition wet) with CF = .5

We can now use the rule to conclude

(difficulty-starting d550ttv)

using the standard production rule architecture. But, our parallel uncertainty inference process will then try to combine the various certainty factors to arrive at a certainty factor for the conclusion. It first combines the certainty factors of the working memory elements to arrive at a certain factor of .5 (the minimum of 1 and .5) for the antecedent of the rule. This is then combined with the certainty factor of the rule itself to arrive at a certainty factor of .7 * .5 = .35 for the conclusion.

The CF model has been criticized for a number of reasons. A first criticism that it is very *ad hoc*, and lacks a firm mathematical foundation. A related criticism is that although the CF model is loosely based on probability theory, one can show that under certain circumstances the results are different from the ones that one would expect from probability theory (Adams, 1976). Another criticism is that the single certainty factor is too coarse a measure. For example, $CF(\phi) = 0$ can both indicate that there is no evidence that allows one to conclude anything about ϕ ($MB(\phi) = MD(\phi) = 0$), or it can indicate that we have contradictory evidence ($MB(\phi) = MD(\phi) \neq 0$). Similarly, there often is some "metauncertainty." An expert may not be able to associate a single certainty factor with a rule. Rather, they may want to say that if the antecedent of R is true, then there is a chance of between 40 and 60% that the consequent is true as well. In MYCIN, this can only be represented in the single tally .5. A related criticism, to which we return below, is the fact that a single certainty value makes it difficult to represent ignorance.

An alternative model of dealing with uncertainty that partly avoids these problems is the Dempster-Shafer approach. It starts out with a so-called *frame of discernment*. The frame of discernment is a set of mutually exclusive and exhaustive hypotheses. Given a frame of discerment Θ, you can form the power set of Θ, $P(\Theta)$, that is, the set of all subsets of Θ. Each element α of $P(\Theta)$ is to be read as a disjunction of hypotheses.

Unlike the CF model, which assigns a certainty measure only to single hypotheses (i.e., elements of Θ), Dempster-Shafer assigns certainty measures to sets of hypotheses (i.e., elements of $P(\Theta)$). Such an assignment is called a *basic probability assignment*. So, a basic probability assignment m assigns a value $m(\alpha)$ to each element α of $P(\Theta)$. The sum of $m(\alpha)$ for all $\alpha \in P(\Theta)$ is 1. With each piece of evidence, you associate a different basic probability assignment. To compute the combined effect of different pieces of evidence, different basic probability assignments then have to be combined into a new basic probability assignment. Rather than discuss the combination functions in abstract, we illustrate them through an example.

Suppose that we have a simple animal classication expert system. The only animals that we classify are elephants, giraffes, and zebras. Our frame of discerment Θ therefore is {elephant, giraffe, zebra}. Initially, no hypothesis is more likely than any other. We therefore assign 1 to Θ and 0 to any of the other element of $P(\Theta)$. We denote the hypothesis that the animal is either an elephant, a giraffe or a zebra by EGZ, the hypothesis that it is an elephant or a giraffe by EG, and so on. Thus, our initial basic probability assignment m_0 is

Hypothesis α	$m_0(\alpha)$
EGZ	1
EG	0
EZ	0
GZ	0
E	0
G	0
Z	0

Above we mentioned that CF models have been criticized because ignorance is difficult to represent. The above example illustrates this. In the CF model, or any other uncertainty handling mechanism which assigns certainty measures to single hypotheses, absence of any information would have to be modeled, for example, by assigning an equal certainty value to each single hypothesis. In the CF model, ignorance would be modeled by setting CF(zebra) to .33. But CF(zebra) = .33 can also mean that there is positive evidence that gives a .33 likelihood to the zebra hypothesis. In the CF model, the certainty value of .33 can therefore mean a number of different things. Because Dempster-Shafer allows one to assign certainty measures to disjunctions of hypotheses, at least some of this ambiguity disappears.

Suppose that we now observe that the animal is large. This supports EG, the hypothesis that the animal is either an elephant or a giraffe. However, there may be some noise in the data. For example, we may be looking at an unclear picture. So, the basic probability assignment may assign a value of .8 to EG. The remaining .2 accounts for the noise in the evidence. Since it does not support any specific hypothesis, the basic probability assignment assigns this to EGZ. So, the basic probability assignment m_1 associated with the noisy evidence that the animal is large is (from now on, we only give non 0 values):

Hypothesis α	$m_1(\alpha)$
EGZ	.2
EG	.8

The combination of basic probability assignments involves building a matrix. The rows correspond to one basic probability assignment, the columns to the other. We calculate the cells in the matrix by taking the intersection of the sets of hypotheses represented in the row and the column, and multiplying the corresponding certainty values. The new basic probability assignment for some set of hypotheses can then be computed by adding the values in all cells with that set of hypotheses. The following matrix illustrates this for m_0 and m_1, where where egz is the set {elephant, giraffe, zebra}, eg the set {elephant, giraffe}, and so on.

egz 1.0

eg .8	eg .8
egz .2	egz .2

The result basic probability assignment is

Hypothesis α	$m(\alpha)$
EGZ	.2
EG	.8

The new basic probability assignment is identical to m_1. Given that m_0 denotes complete ignorance, this is, of course, as expected.

A more interesting combination will result if we try to combine the evidence in m_1 with evidence that we obtain when we discover that the animal has two different colours. This makes the hypothesis that the animal is either a giraffe or a zebra more likely. Again we assume that the data are noisy, and we assume that this observation gives rise to the following basic probability assignment m_2

Hypothesis α	$m_2(\alpha)$
EGZ	.3
GZ	.7

When we try to combine m_1 and m_2, we get the following matrix.

	egz .2	eg .8
egz .3	egz .06	eg .24
gz .7	gz .14	g .56

This results in the following basic probability assignment:

Hypothesis α	$m_2(\alpha)$
EGZ	.06
EG	.24
GZ	.14
G	.56

The above should give the reader some idea about the way in which one can combine different pieces of evidence. The calculation of the resulting basic probability assignment needs to be complicated when the set of hypotheses associated with a cell in a matrix is empty, but we will ignore this complication here. The reader is referred to Gordon and Shortliffe (1984) for further details.

One can use basic probability assignments to determine limits on the probability of some set of hypotheses. The lower limit of the probability of some set of hypotheses S is determined by the sum of the values assigned to the subsets of S. Thus, on the basis of m_3, the lower limit of the probability of the hypothesis that the animal is either is giraffe or a zebra is .7, the sum of the value assigned to the hypothesis that the animal is a giraffe (.56) and the value assigned to the hypothesis that the animal is either a giraffe or a zebra .14. The upper limit is obtained by subtracting the lower limit of the hypothesis that the animal is not a giraffe or a zebra from 1. The hypothesis that the animal is not a giraffe or a zebra is, of course, the hypothesis that the animal is an elephant. m_3 assigns the value 0 to this hypothesis, reflecting the fact that there is no direct evidence for this hypothesis. We, therefore, arrive at an upper limit of 1 for the hypothesis that we are dealing with either a giraffe or a zebra. Thus, the probability that this hypothesis is true is between .7 and 1.0.

The Dempster-Shafer approach to uncertain reasoning has a number of advantages over the CF model. From a theoretical point of view its main advantage is that it has a sound mathematical foundation (Shafer, 1976). From a practical point of view, its main advantages are that it allows you to assign uncertainty measures at the right level. If the evidence supports the hypothesis that the animal is either a giraffe or a zebra, then there is no need to somehow distribute this evidence over the hypothesis that the animal is a giraffe and the hypothesis that the animal is a zebra, as one would be forced to do in the CF model. Also, one is not forced to assign a precise certainty value to each hypothesis. Basic probability assignments can be used to calculate upper and lower limits on the probability of some hypothesis. Dempster-Shafer thus allows one to represent "metauncertainty."

Apart from the CF model and Dempster-Shafer, there are a number of other numerical calculi for dealing with uncertainty, such as fuzzy logic (Zadeh, 1975, 1987). However, numerical uncertainty calculi have recently come under attack. Three arguments in particular have been used against numerical uncertainty calculi. First, uncertainty concerns knowledge about knowledge, and is a meta-level concept. The use of parallel uncertainty inference mechanisms obscures this aspect of uncertainty. For example, the various uncertainty mechanisms do not distinguish between different types of uncertainty.

A second argument against numerical uncertainty calculi is that humans do not naturally use numerical values. As Fox (1986) points out, we usually express uncertainty through such qualitative terms as *plausible, possible,* and *probable.* Fox then gives a precise definition of these terms, and gives a qualitative uncertainty calculus based on these concepts.

A final argument is that humans are simply not very good at dealing with probability measures of the kind that underlie most numerical uncertainty calculi. Tversky and Kahneman (1974) review a number of results from experimental psychology about judgment under uncertainty. It turns out that people tend to use heuristics for dealing with uncertain information. While these heuristics often give the right results, they also lead to a number of biases with people systematically over- or underestimating the occurrence of certain events. Experts are vulnerable to the same biases. But in the majority of cases, there is no objective evidence about the frequency with which some event occurs, and one has to rely on experts to assign the right certainty factors to rules, or the right basic probability assignments to pieces of evidence. Given the biases discussed by Tversky and Kahneman, this throws doubt on the use of numerical uncertainty calculi.

These problems have led a number of people to design nonnumerical ways of dealing with uncertainty. We already mentioned Fox' qualitative uncertainty calculus. Another example is the work of Cohen (1985), who associates with each statement a so-called *endorsement,* a representation of the reasons for believing or disbelieving the statement. For the moment it seems fair to say that, although there are many difficulties attached to numerical uncertainty calculi, many tools for constructing expert systems deal with uncertainty in a numerical way with a certain amount of success. Further research is needed to determine whether nonnumerical uncertainty handlers can be used with the same success.

3. AN EXAMPLE

In this section we discuss an example of a production system. The example is based on work by Young and O'Shea (1981). Young and O'Shea were interested in errors that 10-year-old children make when they subtract one two-digit number from another. (The number to be subtracted is called the *subtrahend,* whereas the number from which the subtrahend is to be subtracted is called the *minuend.*)

Young and O'Shea analyzed some 1,500 occurrences of errors and came up with a classification of 8 errors. We look at only two of those.

A first type of error that children made was that in every column they always subtracted the smallest number from the biggest. The following mistaken subtraction is an example.

$$
\begin{array}{r}
75 \\
59 \\
\hline
24
\end{array}
$$

Another error was that children borrowed under the right conditions but that the way in which they borrowed was wrong. Rather than subtracting 1 from the first digit in the minuend, they would add 1 to it, as they would have to do when carrying in addition. Thus, they would make the following error:

$$
\begin{array}{r}
75 \\
59 \\
\hline
36
\end{array}
$$

Young and O'Shea showed that each of these errors could be obtained by relatively small changes to a production rule system that performed subtraction correctly. We first formulate the correct rules. (The rules used here are different in detail from the ones used proposed by Young and O'Shea but for the present purposes this is not important.)

Because we are dealing with subtraction of two-digit numbers, we can use a simplified representation of the problem. Rather than use attribute-value pairs, or object-attribute-value triples, we use object-value pairs. Each object-value pair will represent one position in a subtraction problem together with its value. We use $\langle m_1, Val \rangle$ to represent the first digit in the minuend, and $\langle m_2, Val \rangle$ to represent the second digit in the minuend. Similarly, $\langle s_1, Val \rangle$ and $\langle s_2, Val \rangle$, and $\langle a_1, Val \rangle$ and $\langle a_2, Val \rangle$ will represent the first and the second digit in the subtrahend and in the answer respectively. In each of the rules below terms starting with a capital letter are variables. We will also assume, as did Young and O'Shea, that the subtrahend is always smaller than the minuend. Let us moreover assume that there is an input routine called *read* which sets the appropriate values for the minuend and the subtrahend and adds the appropriate object-value pairs to working memory. We can now formulate the rules. For convenience the rules have been numbered.

1. start
    ==>
    execute(read),
    add(right-column),
    delete(start).

This rule simply sets the problem and starts work on the rightmost column. There are a number of built-in key words. For example, *execute* is a key word that takes a number of arguments. The first argument is a routine written in some programming language. The other arguments are optional and are the input arguments to the routine and its output argument. The effect is that the routine is run with the input arguments as input and that the output argument is set to the return value of this procedure call. The routine *read* takes no input or output arguments. Its effect is that the user is asked for the numbers to be subtracted and that four object-value pairs to working memory, representing the first and second digits in the subtrahend and minuend. The key word *add* denotes an action that adds working memory elements. The second action in the rule thus adds the token *right-column* to working memory. Similarly, *delete* denotes an action which deletes certain elements from working memory. Deleting the working element that made execution of the rule possible (*start* in the case of rule 1) is considered a matter of good housekeeping. It prevents rules from matching under the wrong circumstances, and it also ensures that working memory is not cluttered up with obsolete working memory elements. Note incidentally that rule 1 will only fire if somehow one has put the token *start* into working memory.

2. right-column,
    $\langle m_2, \text{Val}_a \rangle$,
    $\langle s_2, \text{Val}_b \rangle$,
    $\text{Val}_b < \text{Val}_a$
    $==>$
    execute(abs-diff, Val_a, Val_b, Val_c),
    add($\langle a_2, \text{Val}_c \rangle$),
    add(left-column),
    delete(right-column)

Rule 2 is a rule which will fire if the last digit in the minuend is bigger than the last digit in the subtrahend. It will then take the absolute difference between the two, and set the second digit in the answer to the result. It will then add the token *left-column* to working memory to enable the following rule to fire, and delete the token *right-column*.

3. right-column,
    $\langle m_2, \text{Val}_a \rangle$,
    $\langle s_2, \text{Val}_b \rangle$,
    $\text{Val}_b > \text{Val}_a$
    $==>$
    add(borrow1),
    add(borrow2)

Rule 3 fires when the second digit in the subtrahend is larger than the second digit in the minuend. Borrowing consists of two different operations, namely adding ten to the second digit in the minuend, and taking 1 from the first digit in the subtrahend. To have sufficient detail in the rules to model the errors that children make, we use two rules corresponding to these two operations.

4. borrow1,
    $\langle m_2, \text{Val} \rangle$
    ==>
    delete($\langle m_2, \text{Val} \rangle$),
    execute(sum, 10, Val, Val'),
    add($\langle m_2, \text{Val}' \rangle$),
    delete(borrow1)

5. borrow2,
    $\langle m_1, \text{Val} \rangle$
    ==>
    delete($\langle m_1, \text{Val} \rangle$),
    execute(subtract, Val1, Val')
    add($\langle m_1, \text{Val}' \rangle$)
    delete(borrow2)

The final rule that we need is one for dealing with the left column:

6. left-column,
    $\langle s_1, \text{Val}_a \rangle$,
    $\langle m_1, \text{Val}_b \rangle$
    ==>
    execute(abs-diff, Val_a, Val_b, Val_c),
    add($\langle a_1, \text{Val}_b \rangle$),
    delete(left-column),
    execute(write)

In rule 6 we assume that there is a procedure *write* which will simply print out the answer.

In order to illustrate the above rule-set, considering the following problem: 75 − 59. Assuming that *start* is in working memory, rule 1. will fire, the procedure *read* will be executed and the token *right-column* will be added to working memory. Working memory therefore looks as follows:

$\langle m_1, 7 \rangle$
$\langle m_2, 5 \rangle$
$\langle s_1, 5 \rangle$
$\langle s_2, 9 \rangle$
right-column

Now rule 3 will be the only one that matches working memory. Rule 2 does not match because the value of the second digit in the subtrahend is not smaller than the value of the second digit in the minuend. Rule 3 will therefore execute and working memory contains the following elements:

$\langle m_1,7\rangle$
$\langle m_2,5\rangle$
$\langle s_1,5\rangle$
$\langle s_2,9\rangle$
right-column
borrow1
borrow2

In the next select-execute cycle, rules 3, rule 4, and rule 5 match. However, if we use recency as a conflict resolution strategy, then because *borrow2* is the working memory element most recently added, rule 5 will fire first. As a result, working memory contains:

$\langle m_1,7\rangle$
$\langle m_2,5\rangle$
$\langle s_1,6\rangle$
$\langle s_2,9\rangle$
right-column
borrow1

Rule 3 and rule 4 still match, but, again because of recency, rule 4 will fire, giving the following state of working memory:

$\langle m_1,7\rangle$
$\langle m_2,15\rangle$
$\langle s_1,6\rangle$
$\langle s_2,9\rangle$
right-column

Rule 3 will then fire giving

$\langle m_1,7\rangle$
$\langle m_2,15\rangle$
$\langle s_1,6\rangle$
$\langle s_2,9\rangle$
$\langle a_2,6\rangle$
left-column

Finally, rule 6 will fire, giving

$\langle m_1,7\rangle$
$\langle m_2,15\rangle$
$\langle s_1,6\rangle$

of the requirements they had in mind was that the system should be able to engage in an *interactive dialogue*. In particular, they wanted a system that was able to explain its reasoning. Explanation is particularly important in systems that give their users advice about which actions to take. Before end-users accept a solution they should be able to determine whether the solution that the system proposes is reasonable, and in order to be able to do so, they need to be provided with an explanation of how the system reached its conclusion. Doctors would like to know the reason for a particular diagnosis, or for prescribing a particular course of treatment, before they would follow the advice of a medical expert system.

Davis, Buchanan, and Shortliffe (1977) claim that MYCIN is a system that is capable of explaining its own reasoning. They argue that the fact that it uses production rules as its main knowledge representation language is one of the factors that makes this possible. If a user wants to know *how* the system arrived at a certain conclusion, they can ask MYCIN for an explanation. MYCIN will print out the antecedent of the rule that it used to draw the conclusion in question. Thus, MYCIN provides an explanation by retracing the rules that it used, and MYCIN's explanation facilities thus rely to a large extent on the fact that its knowledge is represented in production rules. The restricted syntax of production rules is important here as well as it simplifies the task of writing a program that translates MYCIN rules from their internal format into natural language.

Another way in which MYCIN can explain its behavior is when the system asks the user a question. MYCIN's overall control regime is backward chaining, and when it comes across some condition it might try to establish its truth by asking the user some questions. Thus, in order to determine whether postoperative infection is a possibility, MYCIN might ask the user whether the patient has undergone surgery. When queried, the user can ask MYCIN *why* this question is asked. MYCIN will respond by printing, first, the rule whose consequent it is currently trying to prove, and, second, the preconditions of that rule whose truth it has already established. Why-questions were thus interpreted as "why is it important to establish the truth of the condition?" There are, of course, other interpretations of why-questions possible, such as "why is this rule true?" or "why do you ask this question at this specific point in time?" However, as Davis (1976), the designer of MYCIN's explanation facilities, points out, MYCIN does not have explicit representations of the pieces of knowledge necessary to answer these questions. Nevertheless, Davis, Buchanan, and Shortliffe claim that MYCIN's explanation facilities are relatively successful.

It is clear that the use of production rules is of central importance in providing MYCIN's explanation facilities. This then is another advantage claimed for production rules. However, it must be said that the work on explanation facilities in the context of MYCIN acted very much as a catalyst for research in this area. As a result, a lot of work has been done that challenges the usefulness of MYCIN's explanations. We return to the problem of explanation below.

4.6. Summary

The advantages that have been claimed for production rule systems are first the naturalness of production rules for expressing the type of heuristic knowledge, or rules of thumb, that expert problem solvers use. Second, production rule systems are very modular with the advantages that this entails in terms of maintainability of a knowledge base, and the possibility of incremental construction of a rule base. Third, the restricted syntax of production rules makes it easier to write programs that can examine their own knowledge base. Fourth, because production rule systems examine working memory very often, it becomes possible to quickly focus in on a hypothesis that looks particularly promising without being forced to so do at a premature stage. Finally, production rules have been claimed to facilitate the construction of programs that can explain their reasoning.

5. DISADVANTAGES OF PRODUCTION RULE SYSTEMS

Although production rule systems have a number of advantages, they also lead to problems. We discuss the disadvantages in this section along with suggested remedies.

5.1. The explanation problem

In section 4.5. we saw that production rules have been claimed to be of great help in the construction of systems that can explain their own behavior. However, this claim has come under attack. Clancey's (1979) system GUIDON, and his later work on NEOMYCIN (Clancey & Letsinger, 1981; Hasling, Clancey, & Rennels, 1984), showed the limitations of using production rules alone for generating explanations.

Several evaluation studies had shown that MYCIN was quite successful as a problem solver in the domain of infectious diseases. Since one of the aims underlying MYCIN was to build a program that could explain its reasoning to its users, Clancey expected it to be relatively straightforward to turn MYCIN into a tutoring program. However, the resulting program, GUIDON, fell far short of expectation. It transpired that a lot of knowledge that was necessary to generate acceptable explanations had not been explicitly represented in MYCIN, and could therefore not be used in GUIDON. Clancey (1983) specifically mentions two types of knowledge that have been omitted: The *diagnostic approach* that experts take, and their *understanding* of the rules. Both pieces of knowledge are important for a program that was intended as a tutorial program. They are also important for generating good explanations. We discuss these particular types of knowledge below.

Experts not only possess a great deal of domain knowledge, they also have knowledge about how to apply this knowledge to a particular problem. In Chapter 2, we used the term *strategic knowledge*. Acceptable explanations often refer to strategic knowledge. For example, when experts explain their reasoning, they are usually able to say why they pursued one hypothesis before they tried another one. Thus, a satisfactory explanatory program should be able to formulate the strategic decisions that were taken during this particular problem-solving session. As Clancey points out, MYCIN does not explicitly represent the strategic knowledge. It is hard-wired in its control regime, and as a result MYCIN is not able to say, for example, why one hypothesis was pursued before another. Because most other production systems also have a hard-wired control regime, they suffer from this problem as well.

A second type of knowledge that is not explicitly represented in MYCIN and that is relevant for explanation, is *support knowledge*. Support knowledge provides the underlying justification for a rule. Thus, if a rule base contained the rule "if the lights of a car are dim, then its battery is flat," then the support knowledge would explain this rule in terms of the underlying mechanism, pointing to the fact that lights need electricity to shine, and that the battery provides the electricity that is needed. Adequate explanation programs need to be able to call on this support knowledge.

As an aside, support knowledge can also be important because it can be used to determine the limitations of an individual rule. As Clancey (1983) points out, because experts know the justification of some rule, they can choose to violate it in difficult and/or nonstandard situations. MYCIN, for example, uses the rule: "if a patient is less than 8 years old, then don't prescribe tetracycline." The support knowledge behind this rule is that tetracycline leads to chelation in growing bones which causes permanent blackened teeth. Because permanent blackened teeth are socially undesirable, a doctor should not prescribed tetracycline for young children. An expert who uses this rule usually knows the underlying support knowledge, and can sometimes use this knowledge to decide to ignore the rule. Thus, if the choice is between blackened teeth, and some other more serious permanent problems (caused by some other drug, or caused because no action is taken), then an expert will prescribe tetracycline.

Clancey's work then has considerably extended our understanding of what is required for adequate explanation, and he has shown the limitations of using a simple production rule system. Many researchers are currently working on systems that can produce more sophisticated explanations. We already mentioned GUIDON and NEOMYCIN. Other examples are Swartout (1981, 1983) and Neches, Swartout, and Moore (1985). However, all of these systems either considerably extend the architecture of the basic production rule system, or follow a completely different approach. The conclusion, therefore, is that the explanation argument in favor of production rules sounds less convincing than it did some years ago.

5.2. Efficiency problems: Determining the conflict set

Another potential disadvantage of production rules follows from the way in which the invocation of rules is controlled. On every recognize-act cycle, the interpreter goes through the rule base, matching the condition part of a rule against working memory. As a result, it will create a conflict set, from which it then has to select the rule to execute. Although this process makes the problem-solving process of a production rule system in principle very flexible, it is clear that this process is computationally expensive and potentially very inefficient. There are two sources of inefficiency corresponding to the two stages in the recognize part. First, with large rule bases, determining the conflict set may be an expensive process. Second, if the conflict set is very large, then conflict resolution may become very expensive. In this section we look at problems in determining the conflict set, while in the next we look at conflict resolution.

Determining the conflict set can be a very expensive process. Each condition will have to be matched against working memory, and matching itself can be a relatively expensive procedure, especially when conditions can contain variables. Variable bindings have to be constructed and passed on to the other conjuncts in the condition. Also, if a variable can be bound in more than one way, because it matches more than one working memory element, all these bindings will have to be tried. We should also notice that knowledge bases can be very big, and many matches may have to be tried to find the conflict set.

One way of getting around this problem has been proposed and implemented by Forgy (1982) and is now used in many production rule systems. Forgy's algorithm, called the Rete match algorithm, is based on two observations. First, many rules have conditions in common. Therefore, if you can find a way of making sure that the work done in trying to match one rule against working memory is not duplicated for rules that have conditions in common, then there will be an obvious gain in efficiency. Second, working memory changes only a little on each recognize-act cycle. Thus, most of the conditions that matched on the previous recognize-act cycle will still match, while most of the conditions that did not match still will not match. In fact, one only has to consider those working memory elements that were modified, added, or deleted. By restricting attention to these, the efficiency in the recognize part of a recognize-act cycle can be improved considerably.

The Rete match algorithm works by constructing a tree-structured sorting network or index for the conditions in the various rules. When a rule base is loaded, a compiler will compile the conditions of the various rules into a network of this kind. Each node in this network is either a single-input node or a two-input node. Roughly speaking, a single-input node represents a test to see whether an object-attribute-value triple matches a working memory element. A two-input node represents a test to determine whether a variable that occurs in two conjuncts in the left-hand side of some rule has been assigned the same value in both matches. The Rete match algorithm achieves some of its efficiency because the compiler will use the same node in the network for conditions that occur in more than one left-hand side, rather than building duplicate nodes in the network. Because the matcher uses the network to do its matching, conditions that occur in more than one rule are matched only once against working memory.

Another way in which a system that uses the Rete match algorithm achieves an improvement in efficiency is by storing with each single-input node in the network a list of working memory elements that it matches. With each two-input node, the system stores two lists representing the working memory elements that matched the two conditions with the common variable. It thus stores the results of the match of the previous recognize-act cycle. On a new recognize-act cycle it therefore can restrict its attention to those working memory elements that have been deleted, changed or added. All it needs to do, is to update the lists associated with the various nodes in the network. Obviously, by having a good indexing mechanism, the algorithm can quickly find the nodes in the network that could match with the new working memory element.

As a result of using the Rete match algorithm, determining the conflict set is a very quick process. This has made it possible to write programs with large rule bases in OPS5, the first system to use the Rete match algorithm. McDermott (1982), for example, describes R1, an expert system for configuring VAX computers, which has more than 700 rules. There are two (minor) disadvantages. First, because the program has to compile the conditions of the various rules into the sorting network, loading rule bases is a relatively slow process. Second, although OPS5 does in principle allow the construction of new rules in the right-hand sides of rules, rules that are constructed during a particular session give rise to a sorting network of their own. This, of course, slightly reduces efficiency as you now have to check a number of sorting networks. Also, the new sorting network only notices working memory elements that were added after the rule has been created, and can therefore never match working memory elements that were in working memory before the rule was built. However, these disadvantages are minor compared to the increase in run-time efficiency.

Forgy's Rete match algorithm certainly solves part of the problem of the inefficiency of production rule systems. It becomes possible to determine the conflict set relatively quickly. However, the interpreter still has to engage in conflict resolution, and decide which rule in the conflict set to execute. We discuss the problem of conflict resolution next.

5.3. Efficiency problems: Conflict resolution

In large knowledge bases, the conflict set on each recognize-act cycle may be too large to consider executing all the rules in the conflict set. Davis (1980) uses the term *saturation* for situations of this kind. When a conflict set is saturated, the interpreter has to engage in conflict resolution, and select a subset of the potentially executable rules for actual execution. Clearly, conflict resolution is a process that takes time as well, and is another potential source of inefficiency.

There are various possible ways of avoiding the inefficiency entailed by conflict resolution. The first, and in a sense most obvious, solution is to try to avoid the problem by refining the conditions of rules, thus making the conflict resolution set as small as possible. A second solution is to try to develop a mechanism that enables the system to cope with the problem. A third solution is to try to avoid the problem by partitioning the system into relatively small sets of rules. The different sets of rules would then be used by separate production systems that can communicate with each other. Because each component production system is relatively small, the hope is that the saturation problem never arises. We discuss each approach in some detail below.

The first solution is to refine the conditions associated with each rule. Thus, you attempt to add further conditions to the antecedents of rules that are applicable in the same situation to differentiate them from each other. If you make the preconditions in rules more precise so that they match less often with working memory elements, then the set of applicable rules on each recognize-act cycle becomes smaller and therefore conflict resolution will take less time. Because each rule has more conditions, finding the conflict set might take longer, but this problem can be eased by using the Rete match algorithm

McDermott (1978) points to some of the problems that are associated with this solution. If you add conditions to the antecedent of rules just to make sure that they never match when another rule matches, then the different rules become dependent on each other. Conditions will be added to the antecedent of a rule solely to prevent them matching simultaneously with other rules. But this dependency of rules on each other means that modularity is lost. This, of course, has several undesirable consequences. For one, it makes incremental construction of rule bases impossible. Whenever a new rule is added, you have to go through the rule base to make sure that its antecedent cannot match simultaneously with the antecedents of too many other rules. However, because the saturation problem is more likely to arise in large rule bases, the possibility of incremental construction is essential. Refining conditions to avoid the saturation problem is, therefore, not promising.

The proposal to refine the conditions in the antecedents of rules attempts to solve the saturation problem by making sure that the conflict set never is too large. The saturation problem is therefore avoided altogether. The second proposal accepts the saturation problem and attempts to guide the system in spite of it. The idea is to prune and reorder the conflict set. If you can prune the set enough, then it may become feasible to apply all the rules. Another possibility is to reorder the conflict set in such a way that the best-looking rules are tried first. Although the latter possibility will not speed up the conflict resolution process (and is, in fact, likely to slow it down), you would hope that by judicious reordering the chances of finding a solution quickly are increased. Davis (1980) presents an approach based on these ideas. He proposes to solve the saturation problem by adding to the program so-called *meta-rules*, explicit representations of pieces of strategic knowledge. Meta-rules are then used to prune and order the conflict set.

Davis's system is an example of a system with an explicit representation of (part of) its control knowledge. In Chapter 2 we briefly discussed systems of this kind and argued that one of their problems was a potential inefficiency due to the meta-level overhead. Davis is aware of this problem, and uses the technique of *localization* to avoid it. Often strategic knowledge is applicable only in very special circumstances. Thus, consider the following meta-rule from a personal investment adviser:

IF   the age of the client is greater than 60
        there are rules that mention high risk
        there are rules that mention low risk
THEN   the former should be used after the latter

This rule is applicable only if it has been established that the client is older than 60. If you therefore associate this rule with this particular condition, and make sure that it only becomes available when the truth of this condition has been established, then there will be no overhead from this rule when the system is dealing with a client younger than 60. Thus, by localizing meta-rules, you can be sure that they produce no overhead for goals and conditions to which they are irrelevant.

The interpreter makes use of the meta-rules in the following way: Given an (object-level) goal G, the system will retrieve all the rules that are relevant to G. This gives the conflict set L. The system then first determines if there are any meta-rules associated with G. If there are, then these are executed first. As a result, L might be shortened and reordered to give the revised conflict set L'. L' is then passed back to the interpreter, which can then use its standard conflict resolution heuristics to select the next rule to execute.

In applying the meta-rules on L, the interpreter may have to engage in conflict resolution yet again. After all, it is entirely possible that there is more than one meta-rule available. Davis says that in cases like these you can add meta-meta-rules. This might suggest that there is an infinite regression. However, this danger is not very real because at every level the number of applicable rules becomes smaller, and standard conflict resolution strategies becomes once more usable. Although Davis's system, TEIRESIAS, in principle, supports any number of meta-levels, he never discovered any examples of second or higher-level meta-rules.

Davis's approach is promising, and seems to avoid some of the efficiency problems associated with systems that have explicit meta-levels. However, it does not altogether avoid them. Given the basic control loop, meta-rules will be applied even when the conflict set is very small and the interpreter would have been able to solve the conflict resolution problem without any meta-level reasoning.

Davis' solution to the saturation problem is to add an extra level of rules to the system which enable it to reason explicitly about conflict resolution. Apart from the fact that it makes it possible to give a system more intelligent conflict resolution strategies, it also has the other advantages of explicit representations of control knowledge that were mentioned in Chapter 2. In particular in relation to the explanation problem that we mentioned in section 5.1, at least some of the strategic knowledge is now in principle available for explanation purposes.

A third way of coping with the saturation problem is by partitioning the system into smaller subsystems. The hope is that the overall saturation problem can be solved because in each of the smaller systems the conflict set will always be of a manageable size. One type of system that can be seen as following this strategy are the so-called *blackboard* systems. Blackboard systems were initially developed in the context of speech understanding systems. An early example of blackboard systems is HEARSAY-II (Erman, Hayes-Roth, Lesser, & Reddy, 1980), but tools for building expert systems that rely on a blackboard architecture have also been proposed, such as AGE (Nii & Aiello, 1979) and HEARSAY-III (Erman, London, & Fickas, 1981). A particularly sophisticated system is proposed in Hayes-Roth (1984).

In a blackboard system, the rule base is divided into different *knowledge sources*, each of which can be regarded as a representation of the knowledge relevant to a particular subproblem within the larger problem that the system is trying to solve. In a speech understanding system, for example, you can have a knowledge source for recognizing individual phonemes, a syllable knowledge source for recognizing syllables, a word knowledge source for recognizing words, and so on. There are various ways in which knowledge sources can be implemented, but the most interesting from the present point of view is to use production rules, and represent each knowledge source as a set of production rules, thus partitioning the rule base. In a more sophisticated system, you can imagine giving each knowledge source its own interpreter. After all, it is entirely possible that in one partition problems are more naturally solved by backward chaining, while in another partition forward chaining is to be preferred.

Knowledge sources communicate with each other via a global blackboard. Knowledge sources can look at the blackboard to decide whether there is any new information that they could use in their own reasoning, and when they derive new conclusions, and write the information that they derive to the blackboard. The blackboard thus has a similar function to working memory in a traditional production system. Like the rule base, the blackboard is often divided into different partitions, and each knowledge source can read and write to a limited number of partitions.

The control loop in a blackboard architecture is as follows. On each cycle, each knowledge source notifies a global interpreter when there is new information on its partition of the blackboard that it can use to derive yet more information. The global interpreter then makes a control decision about which knowledge source to execute. Because there usually are a small number of knowledge sources, the saturation problem does not arise at this stage. The global interpreter then selects one of the knowledge sources for execution. Execution of a knowledge source amounts to control being passed to the interpreter associated with that knowledge source. This local interpreter can then go through the normal recognize-act cycle of production rule systems. Looking at the accessible partitions of the blackboard, and matching only those rules in the knowledge source, the interpreter will execute one or more of these rules. Again, the saturation problem is unlikely to arise at this stage as the number of rules in one knowledge source is relatively limited (compared to the number of rules in the entire knowledge base). Finally, control can return to the top-level interpreter, and the cycle can begin again.

Apart from the ability to avoid the saturation problem, there are various advantages to using blackboard systems. Erman et al. (1980), for example, mention the ability to use cooperating multiple sources of knowledge. Quite often problems in the real world are solved by teams of cooperating experts. If you use a blackboard system, then you can model this in a very natural way: Each knowledge source corresponds to one of the cooperating experts.

To recapitulate, in this section we discussed what Davis has called the saturation problem, a problem that arises in any large rule based system. Although it may be possible to determine the conflict set relatively efficiently, thanks to Forgy's Rete match algorithm, the conflict set may be so large that the actual process of selecting some rules for execution becomes another important source of inefficiency. We discussed two approaches which may provide solutions, namely meta-rules and blackboard systems.

5.4. Restricted syntax and expressibility problems

Production rule systems have a restricted syntax. Although this has the advantage of facilitating the construction of self-modifying programs, it also has the disadvantage of making certain types of knowledge very awkward, if not impossible, to express. In this section, we discuss two kinds in particular, namely structural knowledge and incomplete knowledge.

The first type of knowledge that is difficult to represent in production rules is what was called *structural knowledge* in Chapter 2, knowledge concerning the types of entities that play a role in the domain. Such knowledge is often very important in problem solving. For example, if you know that the general case does not hold, then you know that none of the special cases can be true. Thus, if you know that a patient has not undergone surgery, then you also know that they have not undergone neurosurgery. As with most production rule systems, MYCIN does not have any facilities for expressing structural knowledge directly.

As a consequence, many of the rules in MYCIN have the slightly strange feature that the condition first mentions a general case, and then a special case (Clancey, 1983). Thus, MYCIN has a number of rules of the kind illustrated here.

IF there is a disease that requires treatment,
  AND the patient suffers from meningitis,
  AND the patient suffers from viral meningitis,
  AND . . . .
THEN . . . .

IF the patient has undergone surgery
  AND the patient has undergone neurosurgery
  AND . . . .
THEN . . . .

The inability to express structural knowledge leads to these strange looking rules, with the problems that this entails for intelligibility and maintainability of large rule bases.

    Although structural knowledge is difficult to represent in production rule formalisms, it might be possible to somehow represent this knowledge implicitly, or at least bury it into the rules. However, there are also particular types of knowledge that cannot be expressed at all in production rule systems. In Chapter 3, we saw that one of the advantages of logic was the fact that you could express incomplete information. We specifically mentioned disjunctive, negative, and existential knowledge. It turns out that neither disjunctive nor negative knowledge are impossible to express in pure production systems, at least in the consequents of rules, although both of them can be expressed in the antecedents. We first look at negative knowledge.

    Negative knowledge can take two forms. First, there can be the negative knowledge that an attribute of some particular object does not have a particular value. Thus, you might know that the color of my car is not red. Second, there can be the negative knowledge that there is no object with some particular attributes and values. Thus, you might know that there is no red car. In logic, this distinction can be expressed in the following two sentences:

$(\exists x)(car(x)\ \&\ \neg color(x,red))$
$\neg(\exists x)(car(x)\ \&\ color(x,red))$

    Both types of negative knowledge can be expressed in the antecedents of production rules. OPS5, for example, allows you to write things like (car ^color ⟨⟩ red), where '^' is used to refer to the attribute of some class of objects, which must have been declared before, and '⟨⟩' is used to represent the fact that the value for the attribute should not be equal to the immediately following value. Also, again in OPS5, you can put '-' in front of a condition. As a result, the match will only succeed if all attempts of matching the condition against working memory, fail.

However, it is not possible in OPS5, or indeed in any other production rule system, to express these types of negative knowledge in the consequent of a rule. One can maybe find clever ways of representing the second type of negative knowledge (e.g., by adding an attribute "exists" and setting this value to "false," if there is no object which these values for its attributes), but these different ways would lead to many complications in the formulation of the rules, and would make expression of negative knowledge, even if possible, very awkward.

Another type of incomplete knowledge that is not expressible in pure production rule systems is disjunctive knowledge. Again, disjunctive knowledge can be encoded in the antecedent of rules. The way to do this is by simply having two rules one of which mentions one disjunct, and the other mentions the other. Thus, if we wanted to express something like

```
IF p
  AND (q OR r)
THEN s
```

you could simply have the two rules

```
IF p
  AND q
THEN s

IF p
  AND r
THEN s
```

It is left as an exercise for the reader to confirm that this indeed gives the required results.

However, as in the case of negative knowledge, you cannot express disjunctive knowledge in the consequent. For example, you might have the rule that if a person owns a Ferrari, then either he is rich, or his father is. There seems to be no way to represent this rule in a production rule format.

The conclusion that follows from the above discussion is that, although there are certain advantages associated with a restricted syntax, the restrictions also lead to certain problems. In particular, there will be pieces of knowledge that are hard to express explicitly, such as structural knowledge, or that can only be expressed in an unnatural way, or that cannot be expressed at all. Clearly, for applications in which knowledge of this kind is required, production rules cannot be used alone.

5.5. Is incremental construction of a knowledge base really possible?

Finally, even the claim that production rules allow for incremental construction of knowledge bases has recently come under attack. In section 4.2. we pointed to the claim that production rule systems are very modular which made incremental combination of rule bases possible. Jackson (1986) casts some doubt on this claim. He writes that production rules often have to be written with the conflict resolution strategy firmly in mind. If you do not do this, then the first run of a program often leads to rather unexpected results. Also, it is often difficult to predict exactly what the result will be of the conflict resolution strategy. As a consequence, adding new rules may lead to all sorts of problems.

One solution that is often adopted to get around problems like these is to add control knowledge to the antecedent of a rule. As an illustration of this, consider the example knowledge base discussed in section 3 of this chapter. The reader will have noticed that the rules contain tokens such as *borrow1*, *borrow2*, and *left-column*. The reason for adding these tokens is to make sure that the rules are executed in the right order. We want to make sure that the rule that works on the left column is executed after the two rules that deal with borrowing have fired. Apart from epistemological obscurity (we mix knowledge about how to perform operations in the domain with knowledge about the order in which the operations should be performed), it also means that the rules are no longer completely independent of each other. For example, rule 6 (the rule for dealing with left columns) is completely dependent on rule 2. Rule 2 adds the token *left-column* to the knowledge base, and rule 6 can therefore only fire if rule 2 has fired.

5.6. Summary

In this section we discussed the types of problem associated with production rules. We first used Clancey's work to throw some doubt on the claim that you can write natural explanation facilities in production rule systems. In order to be able to do so, one has to extend the basic production rule architecture.

The second problem were two possible sources of inefficiency for large rule bases. First, determining the conflict set for a large rule base might become a very time-consuming process. Second, once the conflict set was determined, and turned out to contain a lot of rules, conflict resolution might require a lot of computational power. We sketched possible solutions to each of these two problems. Forgy's Rete match algorithm provides a solution to the inefficiency arising from the need to determine the conflict set. The inefficiency inherent in conflict resolution can be solved either by the use of meta-rules, as proposed by Davis, or by the use of blackboard architectures. However, it is worth stressing once more that these problems arise only for systems with large rule bases.

A third class of problems concerns the limited expressibility of production rules. The expression of negative and disjunctive knowledge seems difficult, if not impossible, in right-hand sides of rules.

Finally, it is not clear whether one can sustain the claim that rule bases can be constructed incrementally. Without this capability, a lot of the attractive features of production rules would disappear.

6. CONCLUSIONS

Production rules have been, and still are, very popular for constructing expert systems. But they have also been used in other areas, in particular in building programs simulating human problem solving. Production rules offer modularity, with all the advantages that this entails. They also provide a natural representation of the kind of heuristic knowledge that expert problem solvers use. A third advantage is the structure of the problem-solving process. When a promising line of reasoning emerges, a production rule system will tend to follow it. On the other hand, if none of present hypotheses seems preferable, then it is not forced to focus prematurely on one hypothesis. Finally, production rules seem to facilitate the construction of systems that explain their reasoning, although the latter claim has recently been questioned.

We also reviewed some the arguments against the use of production rules. For large rule bases, there are efficiency problems. Also, because of their restricted syntax certain types knowledge are difficult to express. Finally, we expressed some doubts as to whether incremental construction of rule bases is really possible.

Davis and King (1977, p. 309) wrote

[Production rule systems] therefore appear useful when it is important to detect and deal with a large number of independent states, in a system which requires a broad scope of attention, and the capability of reacting quickly to small changes. In addition, where knowledge of the problem domain falls naturally into a sequence of independent "recognize-act" pairs, [production rule systems] offer a convenient formalism for structuring and expressing that knowledge.

It is clear that there continues to be an important role for production rules.

5
Semantic Nets

1. INTRODUCTION

In the previous two chapters, we discussed two knowledge representation languages that were similar in terms of the overall organization of knowledge. In both logic-based knowledge representation languages and in production rule systems, knowledge is organized around relatively simple independent facts or rules. For example, the unit in which information is expressed in logic is the proposition. Representing knowledge in a logic-based knowledge representation language therefore amounts to organizing it as a sets of facts where each fact refers to one or more objects in the world. Of course, logic allows more complicated propositions, but even these do not in general make reference to more than a few objects in the world, or, in the case of quantified propositions, a few types of object. Similar arguments apply to production rules. In production rule systems, knowledge is organized around propositions (in the form of working memory elements), and rules, which are closely related to, although not entirely identical with, logical implications.

It has been argued that such relatively small independent units are not the most natural way of organizing knowledge. There is an intuition, going back to Aristotle, that an important feature of human memory is the high number of connections or *associations* between the different pieces of information contained in it. A satisfactory knowledge representation language should reflect this high degree of interconnectivity.

Logic-based representations or production rules clearly do not reflect this intuition. In both, different pieces of knowledge are stored independently of each other with no interconnections between them. Of course, in the *implementation* of logic-based knowledge representation languages and production rules you often use indexing schemes which make it possible to retrieve all propositions or rules that mention a certain predicate. However, this is an implementational issue which is usually hidden from the user.

Closely related to the interconnectivity intuition is the intuition that the primitive chunks of knowledge ought to be quite large and more structured. Knowledge should be organized not around a set of simple facts that are relatively independent of each other. Rather, knowledge should be organized around entities, concepts if you like, with associated descriptions.

The knowledge representation languages discussed in this chapter and the next *semantic networks* and *frames*, respectively, are both based on the intuitions mentioned above. Because both can be regarded as reactions against the proposition oriented approach of logic and production rules, they are often discussed together as examples of so-called structured object representations (e.g., Nilsson, 1980), also known as associative nets. While it cannot be denied that semantics nets and frames have a lot in common, there is sufficient difference between the two that discussing them separately is warranted: Semantic network representations are primarily based on the interconnectivity intuition, whereas frame-based representations stress the intuition that knowledge should be organized in larger chunks. In this chapter, we therefore concentrate on semantic networks, while the subsequent one is devoted to frame-based representations. However, because of the similarity between the two, we often refer to the issues raised in connection with semantic networks in the discussion of frames in the next chapter.

The outline of the chapter is as follows. We first explain what semantic nets are, and say a few words about their history. Then we discuss a particular network theory, called conceptual dependency theory, which was proposed in the context of natural language processing. Finally, we discuss some of the criticisms that have been raised against semantic nets, and some of the proposals that have been made to avoid these problems.

2. WHAT ARE SEMANTIC NETS?

As Brachman (1977) points out, the basic idea of a semantic network representation is very simple: There are two types of primitive, nodes and links or arcs. Links are unidirectional connections between nodes. Nodes correspond to objects, or classes of objects, in the world, whereas links correspond to relationships between these objects. Nodes and links are often labeled using a mnemonic device so that the user of the network language knows their intended meaning. The important point is that there is no information stored at a node as such. All the knowledge is represented by the links between the different nodes. Thus, the information stored in a node is simply the set of links that impinge on it.

Quillian (1966, 1967, 1968) introduced semantic nets in AI. Much of Quillian's pioneering work was taken up by psychologists. Work was carried out to try to determine whether knowledge in human long-term memory was represented in terms of semantic networks. For example, Anderson and Bower (1973), Norman and Rumelhart (1975), and Anderson (1976, 1985) all present theories of this kind. Collins and Loftus (1975) review the various experiments that were done to determine the psychological validity of semantic networks. They also propose an extension of Quillian's theory that avoids some of the problems that were discovered with the particular position that he took. Here we ignore the psychological issues. The interested reader is referred to Collins and Loftus (1975), Eysenck (1984), and Rumelhart and Norman (1985). For a discussion of the history of semantic networks in psychology and AI, the reader is referred to Brachman (1979).

In the remainder of this section we discuss semantic networks in more detail. Because many of the ideas were introduced in Quillian's original work, we start with a discussion of his model. Work done in linguistics was also very influential on further developments of semantic nets, and we discuss these in some detail as well.

2.1. Representing information in semantic nets

Quillian developed a theory of the structure of human long-term memory, and wrote a computer program based on this theory which he hoped would enable the machine to perform complex memory dependent tasks. His initial aim was to build a program that could understand language. Not surprisingly, this turned out to be too difficult, and Quillian therefore wrote a less ambitious program that could compare and contrast two word concepts, and express its findings in a form of pseudo-English. For the comparison task, the program used a representation of the dictionary definitions of 50 to 60 words.

Quillian distinguished between two types of node in his memory model, namely *type* and *token* nodes. The distinction corresponds to two different ways in which words may occur in a dictionary. First, words may occur as entries and have their meaning defined in the dictionary. Second, a word may also occur in the definition of another word. In the following, the occurrence of *mammoth* is an example of the first kind, while the occurrence of *elephant* is of the second kind:

mammoth
   large kind of elephant now extinct.

In Quillian's program a *type* node corresponds to the word entry in a dictionary. For each type node, there is a link that directly points to a configuration of other nodes, called a *plane*. The plane corresponds to the definition of the meaning of the word. The nodes that occur in a plane are *token* nodes. They correspond to words used in the definition of another word in a dictionary. There is a link to the type node associated with each token node. This link is useful because it might be necessary to find the definition of the meaning of a token node. Thus, if you are trying to find the connection between the words *mammoth* and *trunk*, then you need to follow the link from the token node *elephant* in the plane associated with the type node *mammoth* to the type node *elephant*. The plane associated with the type node *elephant* may then define an elephant as a large animal with a trunk, thus allowing you to establish a connection between the words *mammoth* and *trunk*. The distinction between type and token nodes which Quillian introduced was echoed in most later semantic nets.

Apart from the special link connecting a token node with its associated type node, Quillian distinguished between five different types of link. The first type of link between a node A and a node B represents the information that B named a class of which the class named by A is a subclass. Thus, you might find a link of this type between a node naming the class *mammoth*, and a node naming the class *elephant*. A second type of link represents the fact that B modifies A. Nodes of this type are of course particularly useful in Quillian's application because the meanings of words can often be defined by modifying a superclass. Thus, an elephant can be defined as an animal with a trunk. Both the subclass-superclass link and the modification link have been used in a lot of subsequent work. A third type of link, connecting any number of nodes, represents a conjunction of the nodes, whereas a fourth type of link represents a disjunction. The final type of link, connecting A with B and C, represents the information that B, the subject, is related to C, the object, by the relation specified in A.

To make the ideas a bit more concrete, Figure 5.1 represents the meaning of the English sentence *The little girl kicks the red ball*. The representation is only loosely based on Quillian's original work. First, rather than defining the meaning of a word, the meaning of a sentence has been represented. Second, rather than using different types of link, as Quillian did, we have followed the later convention of annotating a link between nodes. The meanings of the annotations *Mod(ification)*, *Sub(ject)*, and *Obj(ect)*, are self evident. The *Inst(ance of)* link is used as a link between a token node and its type node. Thus, $g53$ and $b42$ are token nodes which have *Inst* links to the types nodes *girl* and *ball*. $g53$ and $b42$ represent the particular girl and the particular ball mentioned in the sentence above.

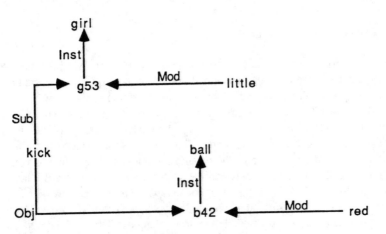

Figure 5.1. The little girl kicks the red ball.

Quillian did not have any primitive word concepts in terms of which the meanings of all other words could be defined. Thus, in a sense he allowed for circular definitions: Starting at some word W, if you followed the link to its plane, then followed the type links from the token nodes in the plane, and followed the links to the planes of these type nodes and so forth, then it was possible for you to get back to W. This is, of course, reminiscent of a dictionary, and therefore did not worry Quillian. As we will see later, others did see this as a problem and tried to define a set of primitive terms, in which the meanings of other words could be defined.

Another influence that was relevant to the development of semantic nets was work by Fillmore (1968) in transformational linguistics. Although this is not the place to go into the details of this particular approach to syntax (for introductions, see Akmajian & Heny, 1975, and Jacobson, 1978) one essential aspect of this theory is a distinction between the deep structure of a sentence, and its surface structure. The surface structure of a sentence is the form in which it appears in written or spoken language, whereas, at least to the particular school of transformational linguists to which Fillmore belonged, the deep structure of a sentence is a representation of its meaning. The surface structure can be derived from the deep structure by applying certain operations, called *transformations*. Fillmore proposed to see the deep structure of a sentence as consisting of a *modality*, to account for things like tense, aspect, mood, and so on, and a *proposition*. A proposition was seen as consisting of a verb with a number of *cases*, that had to be filled in by other constituents in a sentence. There were only a limited number of possible cases. The subject and object link mentioned in connection with Quillian's work, were just two of the possible cases, although Fillmore himself used the terms *actor* and *patient*. Other examples of cases are *benefactor* for the benefactor of a particular action (e.g., the recipient of a giving action), or *instrumental* for the instrument that was used for a particular action.

In Fillmore's proposal, each verb had a *case-frame* attached to it. The case-frame represented the cases that a verb would normally take. Thus, a verb like *hit* might have a case-frame consisting of an actor, a patient, and an instrument, reflecting the fact that someone usually hits someone with something. On the other hand, a verb like *give* would have a case-frame consisting of an actor, a patient, and a benefactor, reflecting the fact that the act of giving involves someone giving something to someone.

Fillmore's case grammar was taken up almost immediately by people working in the area of semantic nets, and links were introduced corresponding to the different cases that Fillmore distinguished. (e.g. Simmons & Bruce, 1971; Hendrix, Thompson, & Slocum, 1973). For example, you could represent a sentence such as *John hit a nail with a hammer* as shown in Figure 5.2.

In Figure 5.2, *h43*, *ha42*, and *n53* are again token nodes. The annotations *actor*, *patient*, and *instrument* correspond to three of the cases that Fillmore proposed. It is worth pointing out that the token node *h43* does not represent a particular

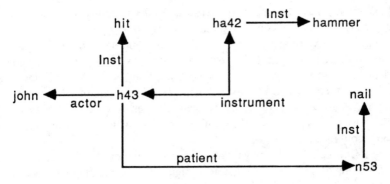

Figure 5.2. John hit a nail with a hammer.

object in the usual sense of the word. Rather, it represents an instance of the action type *hit*, that is, it represents a specific act of hitting. In some important psychologically motivated work Norman and Rumelhart and their group (see, e.g., Norman, Rumelhart, & the LNR Research group, 1975) took this idea even further, and included nodes for concepts, events, and episodes (sequences of events). They thus increased the expressiveness of semantic nets by allowing the nodes to correspond to things other than just objects, or classes of objects.

2.2. Inferencing in semantic nets

The above should give some idea about how to represent information in a semantic net. But a knowledge representation language also includes some mechanism for drawing inferences. The basic inference mechanism used in semantic networks involves following links between nodes. Two particular inference strategies have been used in particular, namely *spreading activation* and *inheritance*, although the latter can be regarded as a special case of the former. We will first briefly discuss spreading activation, and then turn to inheritance.

The notion of spreading activation, also called *intersection search*, is probably easiest explained in the context of Quillian's system. It will be remembered that Quillian was interested in a program that could compare the meanings of words. Quillian's program does not directly compare some representations of the meanings of the two words, which, for ease of reference, will be called word *A* and word *B*. Rather it tries to find a concept that is somehow relevant to both *A* and *B* by following the links starting at the types associated with each word. Each of the nodes reached in this way is tagged with a so-called *activation tag*, consisting of, among other things, the original word that led to this node being activated. Whenever a new node *N* is reached by following a link from word *A*, or from a node that could itself be reached from *A*, the program first checks whether there is already an activation tag mentioning word *B* associated with *N*.

If there is, then the program has discovered a node that can be reached from both words, and it can use this node as the basis for a comparison. If there is not, then the program checks to see if there was already an activation tag mentioning A. This may be the case because a node may be reached in more than one way from a given starting node. If there is already an activation tag mentioning A associated with N, then there is no point in creating another activation tag, and the program thus inhibits tracing out from node N more than once. If there is no activation tag at all, then a new activation tag mentioning A is attached to N, thus recording the fact that N can be reached from A.

The activation tag associated with a node not only mentions which word led to it being activated. It also mentions what Quillian calls the *immediate parent*, the node at which the semantic link leading directly to the present node originated. The effect of this is that the links become in principle bidirectional. Normally, links are unidirectional. However, in Quillian's application it is necessary to be able to follow links in the other direction as well. Noting that the node corresponding to *food* could be reached both from the nodes *plant* and *animal* is not enough to construct a sensible comparison between the two. You also have to know along which paths the program reached the node, and in order to do so, it is necessary to make the links bidirectional.

It is interesting to note that the problem of control also returns in the context of the notion of spreading activation. There are a number of ways in which you can search for a common node that can be reached from both node A and node B. You can, for example, exhaustively search all the nodes that are reachable from node A in the hope that at some stage node B will be reached. Another possibility would be to alternate between A and B. You can first activate all the nodes that are one link removed from A, then all the nodes one link removed from B, then the nodes that were reached from A, then the nodes reached from B, and so on, until a common node is reached. Quillian's program implemented this approach. Yet another possibility would be to activate only a subset of the nodes that can be reached, thus giving up exhaustive search. Of course, there are many other possibilities. However, it is worth stressing yet again that the problem of control also arises in the context of semantic nets.

Two more remarks need to be made about the notion of spreading activation. First, the notion of spreading activation has also been used to account for retrieval in human memory (Collins & Loftus, 1975). Second, Fahlman (1979) proposes a parallel computer architecture for fast implementations of intersection search. In such an architecture, each node in the semantic network would correspond to a processor, and each link between two nodes would be realized by a communication channel between the corresponding processors. Clearly, in a parallel implementation the control problem more or less disappears. On the next machine cycle, you can activate all the nodes one link removed from the presently activated nodes.

The notion of spreading activation, although influential and widely used, is not used in all associative network representations. In particular, in the formalism discussed in the next chapter, frames, spreading activation is almost never used. The notion of *inheritance*, on the other hand, has played an important role in virtually all network formalisms that have been proposed. Two types of link are especially important in the context of inheritance, namely the *Inst* link connecting a token with its type, and the *Sub* links between a class and its superclass. The idea of inheritance is simply that if a piece of information is not stored with a given node in a network, then you follow the *Inst* and *Sub* links to see if the information is stored with the superclass or the type. Thus, consider the simple network in Figure 5.3 in which yet another commonly used link is introduced, namely a *has-part* link.

If a network interpreter is asked to determine whether the sentence *Tweety has feathers* is true, then it will first look at the information stored directly with *Tweety*. It will look if there is a *has-part* link between a node which has an *Inst* link to the *feather* concept and the node representing Tweety. Given the above network, this will fail. The next step then is to follow the *Inst* link between *Tweety* and *bird* to see if there is *has-part* link between *bird* and *feathers*. Because there is, the interpreter will then be able to reply that the sentence *Tweety has feathers* is indeed true. If the interpreter was asked to determine whether the sentence *birds have lungs* was true, then, because the information is not stored directly with *bird* it would have to follow the *Sub* link and see if the information was stored with *animal*. Since it is, the sentence *birds have lungs* is true as well. Of course, these links can be combined transitively. Thus, if the interpreter is asked to determine whether the sentence *Tweety has lungs* is true, then it would have had to follow first the *Inst* link between *Tweety* and *bird*, and subsequently the *Sub* link between *bird* and *animal*.

Because both *Inst* links between tokens and their types and the *Sub* link between classes and their superclasses are used in very similar ways by the interpreter, some researchers did not draw the distinction between *Inst* and *Sub* links. They just used one link which was usually called an *ISA* link (e.g., Norman & Rumelhart, 1975). However, as we will see below, it has been

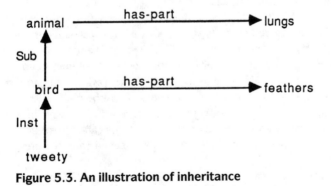

Figure 5.3. An illustration of inheritance

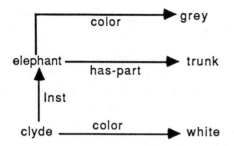

Figure 5.4. Default reasoning in associative nets.

argued that this is a mistake, and that you need to distinguish between the two.

Inheritance provides a very natural way of dealing with default reasoning. In Chapter 3 we pointed to the importance of default reasoning and claimed that it was not entirely clear how to cope with it in logic-based knowledge representation languages. In order to see how a semantic net copes with default reasoning, consider the simple network in Figure 5.4.

This network contains the following pieces of information: Clyde is an elephant; typically, elephants are grey and have trunks; Clyde is white. Given a query to determine the color of Clyde, the interpreter for the above network will first look if there is any *color* link associated with Clyde, and if there is, return the color this link is pointing to. In the above example, this strategy would return the value *white*, thus overriding the default value *grey* associated with *elephant*. Because the value for the *has-part* link is not overridden locally, that is, there is no *has-part* link explicitly associated with *Clyde*, the value for the *has-part* link, if queried, will be inherited from *elephant*. Although this treatment might seem to provide an elegant solution for the problem of default reasoning, it leads to some problematic consequences. We discuss these in the chapter on frame-based representations.

3. CONCEPTUAL DEPENDENCY THEORY

In the previous section, we mentioned the fact that Quillian did not propose any primitives in his network formalism. As a consequence, it was possible to get circular definitions: By following the links from a type node exhaustively, it was possible to get back to this node. Quillian did not see it as a problem. However, Roger Schank did, and he proposed a knowledge representation language, called *conceptual dependency theory*, that was based on a set of primitives (Schank, 1972; Schank & Rieger, 1974). The assumption underlying conceptual dependency theory is that in language understanding each utterance is translated into a conceptual structure that is language independent, and that all further processing uses the conceptual structure. In a sense, Schank's conceptual dependency structures are very similar in function to what Fodor (1975) calls the *language of thought*.

Conceptual dependency theory makes a distinction between different conceptual categories. In Schank and Rieger (1974), a distinction is drawn between the six following categories. (Schank, 1972, contains only four categories.)

PP	—	real world object
ACT	—	real world actions
PA	—	attributes of objects
AA	—	attributes of actions
T	—	times
LOC	—	locations

The categories can be related in a limited number of ways. Each of these can be regarded as specifying a different type of link. For example, one type of link connects a node of type PP and a node of type ACT and indicates that an actor acts. Another type of link connects a node of type PP and a node of type PA and represents the fact that an object has a certain attribute.

In Chapter 1, we drew a distinction between four levels at which one could discuss knowledge representation languages, one of which the epistemological level. At the epistemological distinction, one is concerned with the type of knowledge structuring primitives that are necessary for representing information, while one completely ignores the actual primitives that are necessary for representing given pieces of information. The latter is the concern of the conceptual level.

Bearing these different levels in mind, it should be clear that the distinction between the six conceptual categories in Schank's theory is at the epistemological level. However, in addition to a set of knowledge structuring primitives, Schank and his co-workers have also proposed a number of actual primitives, and Schank's conceptual dependency theory is best known for this. Not only does conceptual dependency theory propose, at the epistemological level, the *types* of knowledge structuring primitive, it also gives, at the conceptual level, a list of the actual primitives. The conceptual category that has received most attention is ACT. Schank (1973) distinguishes between 14 different types of category ACT, whereas Schank and Rieger (1974) propose 12 primitive actions.

The specific primitives that are used need not concern us here. Instead it is more important to concentrate on the implications of using a limited set of primitives, especially since this is a general issue which does not just apply to conceptual dependency theory. The arguments in favor or against using a small set of primitives at the conceptual level are independent of the underlying epistemological theory. Thus, the arguments equally apply to a logic-based knowledge representation language in which one uses a restricted set of predicates for representing knowledge.

One of the advantages of using primitives is that fewer explicit inference rules are needed. For example, consider the sentence *John bought a book*. Schank and Rieger (1974) point out that the word *buy* implicitly references two actions of transfer, one whose object is the book and another whose object is some valuable entity. Also, whenever there is a transfer (called *ATRANS* in conceptual dependency theory) then there must be an actor who does the ATRANSing, an object that is ATRANSed, a recipient, and a donor of this object. Now ATRANS is a primitive type of action that also underlies a lot of other acts, such as giving, stealing, receiving, and so on. If you did not analyze these acts in terms of an underlying primitive, then, for each of them, you would have to formulate a separate inference rule to the effect that they all involve an actor, an object, a recipient, and a donor. If you analyze them as all being a type of ATRANS, then the only rule that is necessary is one that says that ATRANS involves these four objects.

Another potential advantage of primitives is that a lot of the inferences that would otherwise have to be drawn are already implicit in the representation. Thus, if everything was stored in terms of a few primitives, then synonymous sentences would be stored in exactly the same format. Woods (1975) calls such a representation the *canonical form* of a sentence. As a consequence, rather than having to do a lot of reasoning to determine whether two sentences are paraphrases or not, you can just compare their canonical representations.

There are, however, a number of important disadvantages associated with representing everything in terms of primitives (cf. Woods, 1975; Schubert, Goebel, & Cercone, 1979; Rich, 1983). First, in many cases a lot of work needs to be done to translate a sentence into the underlying representation. Although this work may be necessary for some of the inferences, it is not necessary to do for others. For example, it is not necessary to use the underlying representation of *John hit Mary* to conclude that *Mary hit John* when we know that whenever somebody hits Mary, she will hit them back.

A second drawback is that often it is either impossible or very difficult to find the right set of primitives. An example of a domain where it seems difficult to give a set of primitives is that of kinship relationships (Lindsay, 1963). Lindsay's program uses the most obvious representation of a family as a set consisting of a father, a mother, and a set of children. The problem with this set of primitives is that there is no good representation of the meanings of such kinship terms as *uncle* or *cousin*. One may, of course, argue that Lindsay has just chosen the wrong set of primitives, but it is not clear what other set of primitives would have been better.

A third problem is that there is still a lot of inferential work that needs to be done, even if information has been stored in terms of primitives. It is trivial to determine whether two sentences are paraphrases of each other. You just check to see whether their canonical representations are identical. But quite often you also want to be able to determine whether one sentence is a logical consequence of another. It is not clear that questions of this type can be answered simply by looking at the representation. It is, in fact, more likely that you still need a full inference mechanism for problems of this type. It is, therefore, debatable whether the effort to translate sentences into their canonical representation is worthwhile.

A fourth drawback is that primitive representations are often rather complex and may require a lot of storage. It would be more efficient in terms of space to store which each concept a pointer to its decomposition in terms of a limited set of primitives, and to use this decomposition in inference, rather than replacing the concept everywhere by its decomposition. Schank and Carbonell (1979) propose to represent social and political acts in this way. The decomposition of a concept is, of course, similar to the information stored in the planes of Quillian's program.

4. THE LOGICAL FOUNDATION OF SEMANTIC NETS

In 1975, Woods published a very influential paper that criticized the then-current semantic network formalisms (Woods, 1975). Woods' work is still relevant because a lot of the points that he raises apply to at least some of the knowledge representation languages that are proposed today.

One of Woods' main points is that although the representations discussed in this chapter had been called *semantic* nets, nobody had actually made clear what the semantics of the various network representations was. Researchers gave (implicit) definitions of the types of nodes and links that were permitted, and the ways in which they could be combined. However, they usually left the semantics of the networks, what the nodes and links mean, completely unspecified. For example, consider the net shown in Figure 5.5.

Woods points out that there are at least three radically different ways of interpreting this net. First, it can be interpreted as representing the "concept" of a black telephone. Under this interpretation, the net represents a *definition* of the concept of a black telephone. Second, one can interpret this net as the representation of a specific black telephone, for example, the one on my desk. Under this interpretation the net describes a specific entity in the world, while at the same

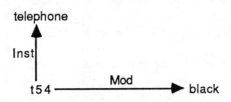

Figure 5.5. Definition of a black telephone or an assertion of its existence?

time asserting the existence of this entity. Third, the net can be interpreted as a representation of the *assertion* of some relationship between telephones and blackness. Thus, the network can be interpreted as asserting that some or all telephones are black. All readings have been used. Quillian's representations, for example, are best interpreted as definitional nets, whereas for example Schank's representations are best regarded as assertional nets.

Because this distinction between definitional and assertional interpretations of links is very important, it is worth expanding. The type of information that is represented by definitional links, let us call it *definitional information*, is analytic in the sense that it is true in virtue of the meanings of the concepts. Even if the world changed, or if the beliefs that the system has about the world changed, information stored in definitional links would remain true. On the other hand, information represented by assertional links, *assertional information*, may change as the world changes. Thus, if we interpret the links in the previous network as assertional, then the net would represent the proposition that there is a black telephone. If you destroyed all black telephones in the world, then the information represented in the net would no longer be true. However, this bout of destruction would have no influence on the concept of a black telephone, which would of course remain the same, even if it did no longer correspond to anything in the world.

The absence of a semantics is also reflected in problems with the interpretation of the *ISA* link. Brachman (1983) analyzes the various ways in which *ISA* links have been used in semantic network formalisms. Brachman catalogues a whole range of different interpretations that have been (or could have been) given to *ISA* links. Consider for example the simple network in Figure 5.6. This network can be interpreted in at least the following four ways: Y is a member of X, Y is a subset of X, Y is a kind of X, Y is a more specific description of an object (or class of objects) than X. Brachman mentions a number of factors that are relevant in determining the intended meaning of such a link. One relevant factor is the intended interpretation of the nodes. Thus, nodes can be either individual nodes, corresponding to individuals, or generic nodes, corresponding to classes of individuals. Also, nodes can be given either an intensional or an extensional interpretation. Under an intensional reading, they are interpreted as descriptions of objects; under an extensional reading, they are interpreted as standing for objects, or classes of objects, in the world. A second factor that is

Figure 5.6. A very simple ISA hierarchy.

important is whether *ISA* links are sentence-forming or concept-forming, whether they have assertional force or definitional force to use Woods' terminology. A third factor is that, although *ISA* links are normally used together with inheritance as an inference rule, there are different ways in which inheritance can be interpreted. In particular, inheritance may mean that all the properties are inherited (what might be called a universal interpretation of inheritance), or it may mean that only those properties that are not explicitly canceled are inherited (the default interpretation). Although the default interpretation is the prevalent one, it leads to serious problems when you want to define new concepts. For example, suppose that we defined the concept of a three-legged elephant as an entity that is both an elephant and has three legs. Then, if each of the properties is inherited unless canceled, then it would be possible to have a three-legged elephant for whom the property of having three legs had been canceled. We discuss this point in more detail in the next chapter.

Woods (1975) mentions other shortcomings of semantic network representations. Semantic networks are unable to represent propositions without a commitment to their truth value. The need for representations of propositions without any commitment to their truth value can be illustrated by the following pair of sentences:

Bill believes that the moon is made of green cheese.
Bill knows that the moon revolves around the earth.

The representation of the first sentence will presumably contain a representation of the sentence *the moon is made of green cheese* as a subpart, just as the second will contain a representation of *the moon revolves around the earth*. The main difference is that the latter sentence implies the truth of the embedded sentence, whereas the former does not. After all, if Bill *knows* something, then it must be true (you cannot *know* something that is false). There is, however, no such requirement for Bill believing something. Thus, in order to be able to deal with belief-sentences one should be able to represent propositions without being committed to their truth.

A related shortcoming of semantic networks is the inability to represent intensional descriptions of objects without being committed to the claim that they exist in the world. The need for such representations is illustrated by McCarthy (1979) who adapts an example due to Frege (1892). McCarthy contrasts the following pair of sentences:

Pat knows Mike's telephone number.
Pat dialed Mike's telephone number.

In the first sentence, the term *Mike's telephone number* is used *intensionally*, and refers to the concept of Mike's telephone number. In the second, the term is used *extensionally* and refers to the actual number. The difference can be brought out if we consider the following sentence:

Mike and Mary have the same telephone number.

If this is true, then it follows from the second sentence that Pat also dialed Mary's telephone number, but it does not follow that Pat also knows Mary's telephone number. The reason is, of course, that Pat might not know that Mike and Mary have the same telephone number. A further point to note is that if terms are used intensionally, then there need be no commitment that these terms correspond to object in the real world. Thus, a sentence like *Pat wants a purple wrench* does not imply that there is such a thing as a purple wrench in the world. Therefore, one needs to be able to represent objects without being committed to their existence in the world.

Woods' also highlights the problem of representing quantified sentences. It is not clear, at least for the networks discussed so far, how to represent the difference between the following two sentences:

Every man loves a woman.
A woman is loved by every man.

The difference is, of course, easy to express in logic, where the different sentences are represented as

$(\forall x)(\exists y)[man(x) \rightarrow (woman(y)\ \&\ loves(x,y))]$
$(\exists y)(\forall x)[woman(y)\ \&\ (man(x) \rightarrow loves(x,y))]$

Various authors have proposed extensions to the basic semantic network formalism in order to avoid the various problems raised by Woods. Some of the proposals are discussed in the sections below.

5. EXTENDING THE EXPRESSIVE POWER OF NETWORKS

Various proposals have been made to extend the expressive power of semantic networks in order to avoid some of the problems that Woods raises (e.g., Schubert 1975, 1976; Sowa, 1984). In this section, the discussion is restricted to two proposals. The first is a general technique that can be used for different purposes, namely partitioning the network, whereas the second approach is specifically aimed at dealing with the representation of belief sentences.

5.1. Partitioned networks

Hendrix (1975, 1979) proposes to extend the basic semantic network formalism by *partitioning*. Duda, Hart, Nilsson, and Sutherland (1978) used this technique to build PROSPECTOR, an expert system for mineral exploration. The basic idea is to partition the network by bundling together groups of nodes and arcs into what Hendrix calls a *space*. The spaces themselves can then be treated as nodes. Thus, spaces themselves can be linked by arcs to other nodes. As with any other node, a space can be embedded into a higher-level space, thus giving the possibility of a hierarchical organization of spaces.

Hendrix gives various examples of the utility of partitioned networks. One example is its use in language processing where subparts of a network that can be expressed by one syntactic unit can be grouped together. Another possible use is to represent everything that a person believes to be true, or wishes to happen, in one space. Used in this way, partitioned networks can be used to get around one of Woods' problems, namely the need to represent propositions without being committed to their truth. For example, assuming that all arcs are assertional and not definitional, a sentence such as *John believes that there is a fish with lungs* can be represented as in Figure 5.7. The *object* arc that starts at node *b42* in Figure 5.7 points to a space with the name *s1*. The information encoded within this space represents the embedded sentence *there is a fish with lungs*. Because information represented in an embedded space cannot (always) be assumed to be true within the larger space in which the embedded space occurs, one can use partitioning to represent propositions without being committed to their truth.

Another possible use of partitioning is in the representation of logical connectives and logical quantifiers, thus avoiding another problem in Woods. Adapting the proposal in Hendrix (1979) slightly, one can represent an implication as in Figure 5.8. In this figure, *i56* represents an implication, box *s0* pointed to by the *ante* link represents the antecedent of the implication, and box *s1* pointed to by the *conse* link represents the consequent of the implication. Hendrix represents disjunctions in a similar way by introducing a disjunction node.

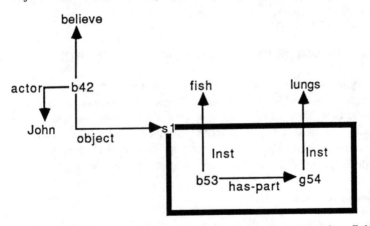

Figure 5.7. Representation of "John believes that there is a fish with lungs" in a partitioned semantic net.

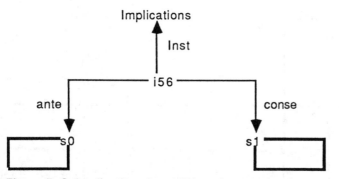

Figure 5. 8. Implications in partitioned networks.

Finally, Hendrix also uses the partitioning mechanism to represent arbitrarily quantified propositions. Again adapting Hendrix' proposal slightly, one can represent a universally quantified proposition such as *every bird has feathers* as in Figure 5.9. There are two links from the general statement *gs3*, one pointing to the quantified variable, and one to the matrix sentence of the quantified proposition. We can represent existentially quantified propositions by changing the *forall* link to an *exists* link. Scopal information can then be represented by having one space embedded in the other. Thus, in Figure 5.10 we give the representation of *every man loves a woman*, while in Figure 5.11 we represent *a woman is loved by every man*.

Fikes and Hendrix (1977) describe a set of procedures which use the network representations illustrated above to do logical deduction.

Partitioned networks have been used in a number of applications, and their utility has been demonstrated. However, they are not without their problems. A first point concerns the question whether the nodes are intensional or extensional. Some nodes, for example, those in a network partition pointed to by the object link of a belief node, seem to be intensional and are descriptions of some object. Others, for example those in the top-level partition, seem to be extensional, and stand directly for some actual object in the world. Similarly, the status of the

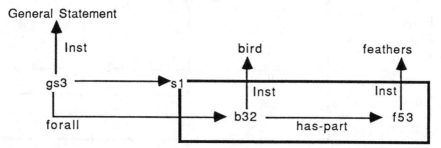

Figure 5.9. Representation of "Every bird has feathers" in partitioned nets.

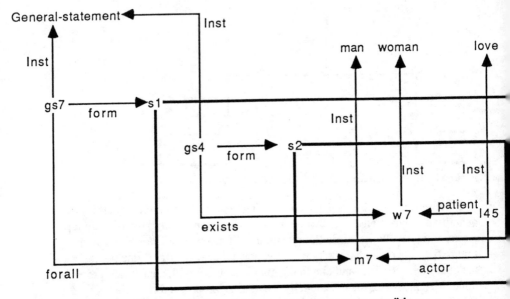

Figure 5.10. Representation of "Every man loves a woman" in a partitioned net.

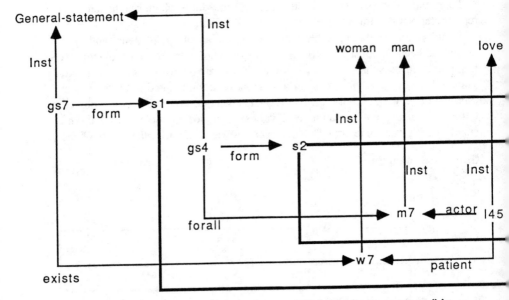

Figure 5.11. Representation of "A woman is loved by every man." in partitioned nets.

links is always not entirely clear. Some of them are clearly assertional, whereas others would seem to be definitional. In a sense, this difficulty arises from the lack of a clear semantics for the partitioned networks.

A second problem is that in the representation of arbitrarily quantified propositions, there are nodes of very different kinds in the network. There are nodes that correspond to entities in the world alongside nodes that correspond to propositions. From the point of view of epistemological clarity, this is an undesirable situation. Also, as a result of the many different nodes, partitioned networks become complicated structures, which are difficult to use. The naturalness of the simpler network languages may be obscured in partitioned semantic nets.

5.2. The SNePS networks

Another piece of work that is aimed at extending the expressiveness of semantic networks is the work on the SNePS system by Shapiro and his associates (e.g., Shapiro, 1979; Maida & Shapiro, 1982; Rapaport, 1986). SNePS is based on the assumption that every node that is represented is intensional. You need intensional representations, at least if you want to model cognitive agents that can conceive of things that do not exist in the actual world. Although many network theorists have argued that nodes should have both an extension and an intension (e.g., Schubert, Goebel, & Cercone, 1979), the designers of SNePS are not convinced that this is the case. As a result, every node in SNePS is regarded as purely intensional.

A second underlying assumption in SNePS is that each node represents a unique concept, and that each concept in the network is represented by a unique node. Thus, intensionally distinct elements are always represented by distinct representations.

Another decision in SNePS is that each concept represented in the network is represented by a node, and never by an arc. This has the consequence that (conceptual) relationships are represented by nodes as well. Arcs therefore represent nonconceptual, or structural, relationships between nodes. This means for example that SNePS does not contain any *IsA* or *Inst* links. There are a small number of structural links in SNePS which can be used by its inference engine. We mention some of them below.

To illustrate SNePS, we return to McCarthy's telephone example. In the example Mike and Mary's telephone number are the same in the world. However, they are intensionally distinct, and therefore they need to be represented by distinct nodes. Of course, one would like to be able represent the information that these concepts correspond to the same object in the world, and SNePS therefore contains a special kind of link, the so-called *equiv* link. The *equiv* link is an example of a structural link. Thus, the proposition that Mike and Mary have the same telephone number is represented in Figure 5.12. *m3* is a node that stands for the proposition in question, while *lex* is another structural link. It

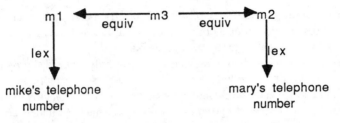

Figure 5.12. SNEPS representation of "Mike's telephone number is the same as Mary's."

points from a concept to a word in lexical memory, that is, it points from a concept to a word for verbalizing the concept.

In order to allow the inferences that one normally draws, SNePS includes a number of inference rules that rely on the existence of *equiv* links between two concepts. For example, there are certain relationships that are extensional in the sense that one can replace, say, the direct object of a verb that *lexes* this relationship by a direct object that stands for the same entity in the world. In McCarthy's telephone example, for example, one can conclude that *Pat dials Mike's telephone number* if you know that *Pat dials Mary's telephone number*. SNePS contains an inference rule which will allow one to draw this inference whenever there is an *equiv* relation between two intensions, and one intension is the object of an extensional relationship.

In order to represent the beliefs of other cognitive agents, SNePS introduces the concept of a *dominated* proposition. A dominated proposition is a proposition that is pointed to by some arc. Nondominated propositions are propositions that are not pointed to by some arc. Whereas dominated propositions represent the beliefs that the system ascribes to another cognitive agent, nondominated propositions represent information that the the system itself believes. Thus, consider the following net in Figure 5.13. Node *m1* in this net is a nondominated proposition, and represents the fact that the system believes that John believes that Mike and Pat's telephone number are identical. *m2*, on the other hand, is a dominated proposition, and is therefore not believed by the system. It represents the proposition that Mike and Pat have the same telephone number, which the system believes John believes, without believing it itself. There is obviously a similarity between SNePS' notion of a dominated proposition, and the use of spaces in partitioned networks to represent embedded beliefs.

The picture is slightly more complicated, however, because some dominated propositions may be believed by the system. Thus, John may believe (or know) something that the system also believes. In order to be able to represent this, SNePS allows one to add assertion tags to certain dominated propositions. Thus, the set of propositions believed by the system are the nondominated ones plus those that are dominated but have an assertion tag associated with them.

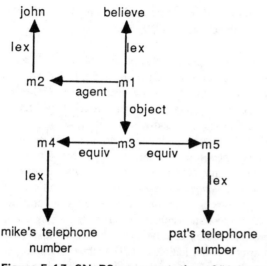

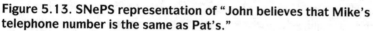

Figure 5.13. SNePS representation of "John believes that Mike's telephone number is the same as Pat's."

SNePS answers some of the problems that Woods raised. In particular, it contains intensional representations of objects. However, it has nothing to say on the subject of representing arbitrary quantified sentences, and therefore is not a complete reply to Woods' points. It is not clear how SNePS representations can be used in inference.

6. KL-ONE, SEPARATING ASSERTIONAL AND DEFINITIONAL INFORMATION

The second criticism that Woods raised against semantic network representations concerns the status of the links: Some links are used to represent analytic information, whereas others represent synthetic information. In this section we discuss KL-ONE, a network formalism that explicitly addresses this problem. KL-ONE tries to take into account the epistemological foundations of semantic networks. Although a semantic network formalism, KL-ONE is very similar to the object-oriented systems discussed in the next chapter. It is one of the intellectual precursors of KRYPTON, a hybrid system discussed in Chapter 7. The discussion of KL-ONE is based on Brachman (1979) and Brachman and Schmolze (1985). We start with a discussion of how to describe objects in KL-ONE.

The basic elements in KL-ONE are *structured conceptual objects*, or *concepts* for short. Concepts are defined as formal objects used to represent objects, attributes, and relationships of the domain being modeled. Concepts are to be seen as descriptions of objects, and so on, and hence are intensional entities. The intensional nature of the primitive objects in KL-ONE makes the language similar in this respect to SNePS.

KL-ONE distinguishes between two types of concept, *generic* and *individual* concepts. Generic concepts are descriptions of classes of individuals, whereas individual concepts are descriptions of individual objects, attributes, relationships etc. Thus, a description of cars in general is a generic concept, whereas a description of the specific car that I own is an individual concept.

The way in which KL-ONE defines descriptions is based on the observation that objects in the world have a complex relational structure, and that a description of an object must account for this internal structure. KL-ONE uses *role/filler descriptions* (*roles* for short), and *structural descriptions* to support this view. Roles represent the conceptual subpieces of an object, whereas structural descriptions account for the structuring relationships between them. Roles act as attribute descriptions, and represent a potential relationship between individuals of the type denoted by the concept and other individuals. They thus correspond to two-place relationships in logic. Structural descriptions, on the other hand, are included because quite often the roles that are associated with a concept are *inter*dependent. The (simplified) KL-ONE net in Figure 5.14 will make these concepts clearer. It represents a (partial) description of the concept of a *message*, and a definition of the concept of a *reminder* (to oneself). Arrows of the following form illustrated in Figure 5.15 are KL-ONE's representations of roles. The arc from the role to the concept (marked *v/r*) is a *value restriction* and is used to indicate a restriction on the range of individuals that can fill this role. Thus, in the above example, we have three roles associated with the concept *message*, namely a *sender* role which has to be filled by a person, a *recipient* role which also has to be filled by a person, and a *body* role which has to be filled by a text. Thus, a message is described as a thing with a sender, which must be a person, a

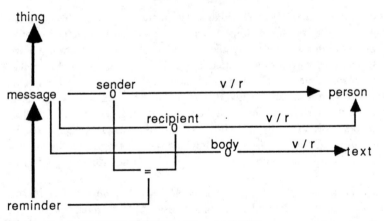

Figure 5.14. KL-ONE definition of a reminder.

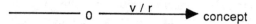

Figure 5.15. A role in KL-ONE

recipient, which must be a person as well, and a body, which must be a text. KL-ONE also allows you to associate number restrictions with a role to express *cardinality* information, information about how many entities can in principle fill a role. Thus, in the above example, one may also want to put a number restriction on the sender role saying that there is exactly 1 sender, and another on the recipient role saying that there is at least 1 recipient.

The concept *reminder* is defined as a subtype of message (the emboldened arrow is explained below), with a structural description associated with it. Structural descriptions are used to represent interdependencies between roles. In the present case the structural description indicates that a reminder is a message for which the recipient and the sender are identical.

Another way in which a subconcept can be defined is illustrated in the network in Figure 5.16. In it the concept of a *starfleet message* is defined by putting a restriction on one of the roles associated with the *message* concept. Thus, a *starfleet message* is defined as a message all of whose senders are starfleet commanders. Another way of describing lower-level concepts is by adding further number restrictions. Thus, if one defined a *message* as having exactly one sender and at least one recipient, then one could define a *private message* as a message with exactly one recipient.

The main inference mechanism is *structured inheritance*, and the emboldened arrow in the last example indicates a structured inheritance link between the *reminder* concept and the *message* concept. KL-ONE, in common with other network formalisms, uses a specialization hierarchy of concepts. Structured inheritance is the inheritance of information by a concept lower down in the

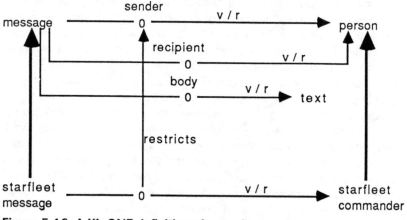

Figure 5.16. A KL-ONE definition of a starfleet message.

specialization hierarchy from some object higher up in the hierarchy. The fact that it is structured means that the information that is inherited must preserve the complex structure associated with a higher-level concept, expressed in roles and structural descriptions.

Concepts lower in a concept hierarchy always inherit all the information associated with a higher-level concept. There is, therefore, no treatment of default values in the descriptional part of KL-ONE. The only properties that are represented in this part of the system are necessary properties. Nonnecessary conditions are dealt with in the assertional part of the language. The main argument is that if one allowed default properties in the descriptional part of the language, then one would run into the problems mentioned in the previous section in connection with Brachman's analysis of the multitude of uses *ISA* links have been put to. Thus, in KL-ONE's descriptional language all the properties associated with a given concept are necessary properties, and they are therefore always inherited by concepts lower down in the concept hierarchy. Lower-level concepts however may contain more information, either by adding new roles, or by adding structural descriptions.

In addition to the descriptional part, KL-ONE also has an assertional component, although this part of KL-ONE was not as fully developed as the descriptional part. Assertions are made relative to a *context*, and they therefore do not affect the concept hierarchy. The notion of a context is similar to Hendrix' notion of a space, and can thus be used to reason about beliefs, desires, hypothetical situations, and so on.

One can assert the existence of some thing satisfying a particular concept by connecting it through a link called a *description wire* to a *nexus* within a *context*. A nexus is just a placeholder that ties together the various descriptions that apply to the same object in some context. A description wire is also taken to be within the context, indicating that the description only applies within this context. The interpretation of a description wire changes slightly depending on whether it links an individual concept to a nexus or a generic concept. In the latter case, it corresponds to an existentially quantified statement in logic. Thus, a description link from the concept *man* to a nexus in some context can be regarded as the representation of the logical statement $(\exists x)[man(x)]$. A description link between an individual concept and a nexus is an existence statement. Thus, suppose that we have an individual concept *Spock*, then a description wire from this concept to some nexus should be interpreted as asserting Spock's existence in this context.

KL-ONE has the advantage of a clear epistemological basis. It also explicitly distinguishes between a definitional or descriptional part, and an assertional part. It therefore avoids some of the problems that Woods raises against semantic networks. However, it must be said that KL-ONE does not solve all the expressibility problems. In the version reported in Brachman and Schmolze (1985) the assertional part was not fully developed, and it is not clear how one would represent arbitrary quantified sentences in KL-ONE.

7. THE SEMANTICS OF SEMANTIC NETWORKS

The last of Woods' criticisms against semantic network representations is perhaps the most damning: Although semantic networks had been called *semantic* networks, nobody had actually specified what the semantics of the language was. Given the advantages of having a clear semantics, discussed in Chapter 3 in connection with logic, this is of course a problem.

Since Woods' paper, there have been various attempt at providing a semantics for semantic networks. Given the advantages of a model-theoretic semantics of the kind defined in logic (see Chapter 3), we restrict the discussion to proposals for a semantics of this kind. It should be noted, however, that there have also been attempts at defining a procedural semantics (e.g., Levesque & Mylopoulos, 1979).

The easiest way of providing a model-theoretic semantics for semantic networks is by providing an algorithm for translating network representations into sentences of some logic (although Sowa (1984) directly defines a model-theoretic semantics for semantic networks). The idea then is that the meaning of a network representation is identical to the meaning of the logical sentence into which it is translated.

One of the problems in providing a general model-theoretic account of semantic network representations is the fact that there is no uniform notation. We therefore merely illustrate the way in which one might translate a semantic network into a proposition of first-order predicate calculus, and we will then briefly point out the limitations of this way of doing things.

Earlier we mentioned KL-ONE's distinction between two types of concept, namely generic concepts and individual concepts. Individual concepts correspond to object in the world, and can thus be translated as individual constants in logic. The expressions that most directly correspond to generic concepts are predicates. Both refer to classes of objects. We therefore assume that a node i corresponding to an individual concept translates into the logical constant i, whereas a node G corresponding to a generic concept translates into the one-place predicate G.

Given these basic translations, we can now turn to the translation of the various links. The translation of an *Inst* link between an individual concept i and and a generic concept G is:

$$i \; ^{Inst} \; G$$

translates as

$G(i)$

An *ISA* link between two generic concepts *G1* and *G2* is translated as follows:

$$G1 \xrightarrow{\text{ISA}} G2$$

translates as

$$(\forall x)[G1(x) \rightarrow G2(x)]$$

The translation of links is dependent on two factors: The nature of the originating concept (where the link starts) and the nature of the destination concept (where the link points to). If the link is between two individual concepts, then there is relatively little difficulty. Links are translated as two-place predicates. Thus, the network given below translates as

$$\text{clyde} \xrightarrow{\hspace{1cm}\text{color}\hspace{1cm}} \text{grey}$$

color(clyde, grey)

If the link is between a generic concept and an individual concept, then again the translation is relatively straightforward: The network translates as

$$\text{elephant} \xrightarrow{\hspace{1cm}\text{color}\hspace{1cm}} \text{grey}$$

$(\forall x)[\text{elephant}(x) \rightarrow \text{color}(x,\text{grey})]$

If the link is between two generic concepts, as illustrated below, then the translation is

$$\text{elephant} \xrightarrow{\hspace{1cm}\text{has-part}\hspace{1cm}} \text{trunk}$$

$(\forall x)[\text{elephant}(x) \rightarrow (\exists y)[\text{trunk}(y) \ \& \ \text{has-part}(x,y)]]$

The various links in a network, after they have been translated, can then be conjoined. Thus, the following net is translated as:

$$\text{elephant} \xrightarrow{\hspace{1cm}\text{has-part}\hspace{1cm}} \text{trunk}$$

Inst

Clyde

$(\forall x)[\text{elephant}(x) \rightarrow (\exists y)[\text{trunk}(y) \ \& \ \text{has-part}(x,y)]] \ \& \ \text{elephant}(\text{clyde})$

The reader will have noticed that given this translation, and given the inference rules for first-order predicate calculus, you can infer $(\exists y)[\text{trunk}(y) \ \&$

has-part(clyde,y)], which is of course in accordance with the inference rule of inheritance.

There are two problems with this translation. First, the translation of the links corresponding to the cases associated with a concept that represents an action, is rather unnatural. Thus, the representation of *John hit Mary with a newspaper* translates as

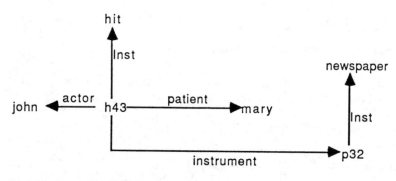

hit(h43) & actor(h43,john) & patient(h43,mary) &
instrument(h43,p32) & newspaper(p32)

A more natural translation would be seem to be

(∃x)[newspaper(x) & hit(john,mary,x)]

This is, of course, a problem with the particular translation algorithm used here. You can either accept the translations that follow from this simple algorithm, or you can complicate the translation algorithm so that it results in more natural translations, for example, as proposed by Simmons and Bruce (1971). Either way, there is no problem, in principle.

A more serious problem is independent of the particular translation algorithm that one uses. It concerns inheritance. Consider for example the network in Figure 5.4 which we repeat here. If we translate this in the normal way, then we get

(∀x)[elephant(x) → color(x,grey)] &
elephant(clyde) & color(clyde,white)

Now if we add the axiom that a given object can have only one color, then the above translation is contradictory. Clyde would have to be both white and grey. But the network is not contradictory. After all, information that is associated with higher-level objects is inherited only when there is no contradictory evidence lower down. Thus, a link emanating from a generic concept should be translated as a universally quantified proposition, but should be translated as a default rule.

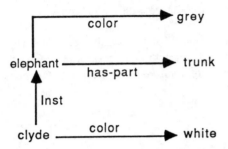

Figure 5.4. Default reasoning in associative nets.

Thus, using Reiter's default logic as introduced in Chapter 3, you could maybe give the following translation for the network below

elephant(x) | *color(x,grey)* ⊢ color(x,grey)

elephant ————— has-part —————▶trunk

Although this gets around the objection that noncontradictory networks are translated as contradictory sets of logical propositions, it is an open question whether this is an acceptable solution. As we have seen in Chapter 3, default and non-monotonic logics are themselves somewhat problematic, and the question about their semantics has not been entirely solved. We return to these problems in the next chapter when we discuss some of the proposals that have been made for a semantics for frame-based representations.

8. CONCLUSION

In this chapter, we introduced semantic network representations, a knowledge representation language that has proven quite popular. The main underlying assumption was that knowledge is organized in a highly interconnected way. Thus, in semantic nets, knowledge is represented as connections between nodes, where nodes correspond to concepts, and the links correspond to relations between these concepts. We introduced the two main inference procedures that have been used in representations of this type, namely spreading activation and inheritance. We discussed various problems associated with semantic nets, and some of the proposals to avoid these. It must be said that as a knowledge representation language semantic networks seem to have been superseded by the frame-based representations discussed in the next chapter. However, as will be clear in that chapter, many of the merits of semantic network representations, and the problems associated with them, can also be found in frame-based representations.

6
Frame-based Representation Languages

1. INTRODUCTION

In logic-based knowledge representation languages, as well as in production rules, knowledge is organized in relatively small independent chunks. Intuitively this does not appear to be the most natural way to organize knowledge. In the human mind, knowledge does not seem to be organized as a set of facts. Rather, knowledge seems to stored in larger chunks as a set of conceptual entities with associated descriptions. Moreover, there are very many connections between the various chunks of knowledge. A natural knowledge representation language should reflect these intuitions. Although both of these intuitions underlie both semantic network representations and the frame-based representations that will be discussed in this chapter, the interconnectedness intuition is more directly reflected in semantic nets, whereas the second intuition is more clearly visible in the frame-based representations.

The clearest formulation of the basic intuitions can be found in Minsky (1975). Minsky argues that in order to explain the apparent power and speed of mental activities, there ought to be more structure to the chunks of knowledge than there is in logic, and the declarative and procedural aspects of a given chunk must be more tightly connected. He then introduces the concept of a *frame* which he defines as "a data-structure for representing a stereotyped situation." Frames are retrieved whenever the system encounters a new situation. They are formed on the basis of previous experiences in similar situations and can best be seen as a structure representing expectations of the system about situations of this kind.

Another intuition that led Minsky to propose the notion of a frame was the belief that the procedural and declarative aspects of a piece of knowledge should be more tightly connected. There should be a structure that allows you to represent together both the factual knowledge and the procedural knowledge about a typical object or situation. In Chapter 2, we referred to Winograd's discussion of the distinction between procedural and declarative knowledge representation languages. The conclusion was that declarative representations have many advantages but that there are particular types of knowledge that are best represented in a procedural way. Winograd himself proposes frames as representational structures as a possible solution to this problem.

Since Minsky introduced his notion of a frame, many knowledge representation languages have been developed based on this concept. Some early examples are KRL (Bobrow & Winograd, 1977; for a critical discussion and a reply, see Lehnert & Wilks, 1979, and Bobrow & Winograd, 1979), FRL (Goldstein & Roberts, 1977), UNITS (Stefik, 1979), and many others. Frame-based representations also form the basis of many of the mixed representation languages discussed in the next chapter. Rather than discuss any one of the frame-based knowledge representation languages in particular, we concentrate on the properties that are common to them all.

The notion of frame is very similar to the notion of a *schema* that was developed in psychology by Bartlett (1932). Bartlett introduced the notion to account for the fact that often the way in which you perceive some piece of information is strongly influenced by the particular expectations that you have. In one experiment Bartlett presented British subjects with North American Indian folk stories and found that when asked to recall these stories the subjects had "made sense" out of the stories from their own cultural perspectives. Thus, certain incomprehensible details were not recalled, and certain things were included, even though they did not occur in the story, in order to make the story more coherent.

Given this description of a frame, it should not come as a surprise that the type of reasoning in frame systems is often a process of *recognition*. The designers of KRL, Bobrow and Winograd (1977), explicitly write that "Reasoning is dominated by a process of recognition in which new objects and events are compared to stored sets of prototypes, and in which specialized reasoning strategies are keyed to these prototypes."

In the remainder of this chapter the notion of a frame is discussed in more detail. Then we list some of the advantages that have been attributed to systems of this kind, and some of the problems. Finally, we discuss *object-oriented* programming, an AI programming technique that has recently become popular, and which is to a large extent based on frames.

2. WHAT ARE FRAMES?

Frames are structures that represent knowledge about a limited aspect of the world. Examples are knowledge about chairs, or knowledge about a child's birthday party. Information is stored in a frame by associating descriptions with it. Thus, frames, like the concepts in many of the semantic network representations discussed in the previous chapter are essentially intensional entities: They are *descriptions* of objects. The descriptions in a frame are called *slots*. A slot usually consists of two parts: A slot-name, which describes an attribute, and a slot-filler, which describes either a value for that attribute or a restriction on the range of possible values. We return to the notion of slot later.

As Bobrow and Winograd (1977) point out, a natural way of describing an entity is by comparison with a known entity, and further specification of the described entity with respect to a more general entity. This is reflected in the hierarchical structure of frame systems. Frames lower down the hierarchy can be seen as *specializations* of the frames higher in the hierarchy.

In most frame systems, you can distinguish between two types of frame. The first type of frame, called a *class-frame*, is a description of a class of entities in the world. An example is a *car* frame in which general knowledge about cars is stored. The second type of frame is the *instance frame*. An instance frame is an intensional description of an individual entity in the world. An example is a frame that represents knowledge about a specific car. This distinction is identical to the distinction between generic and individuals conceptual entities that was made in KL-ONE.

Just as classes of objects often consist of various subclasses, a class-frame can have several class-frames below it. Thus, the *car* frame may have a *sports car* frame below it. This relationship, which is of course the *Sub* link of the previous chapter, reflects the fact that a sports car can be described as a special type of car: a sports car can be described by further specifying the description of a car. Instance frames are similarly almost always instances of class-frames. Thus, an instance frame which corresponds to a specific car is an instance of the more general *car* frame. Of course, this relationship is similar to the *Inst* link of the previous chapter, and also reflects the intuition that a specific car can be described by further specifying the general description of a car.

It is often possible to describe a given situation from more than one perspective. Many complex objects and events cannot be described in terms of one set of primitives only, but need to be described from different points of view. Thus, to use the example of Bobrow and Winograd (1977), kissing can be seen either in pure physical terms, or in social terms. Viewed in the first way, kissing would be described in terms which are similar to acts such as eating or testing someone's temperature with your lips. Viewed as a social acts, kissing would be described in terms similar to the ones in which hugging, caressing, and so on, are described.

Descriptions from multiple perspectives are realized in most present frame systems is by allowing class-frames to have reverse *Sub* links, or *Super* links as they have been called, to more than one other frame. Similarly, instance frames can have *member-of* links, a reverse *Inst* link, to more than one class-frame. Thus, in the kissing example, the *kissing* frame would have *super* links to both the *social act* frame and the *physical act* frame.

In Minsky's original conception of frames, and in the exposition of the frame ideas by Kuijper (1975), the slots in a frame are hierarchically ordered. At the top level, there are slots that describe properties that every instantiation of the frame must have. The slots lower down describe properties that are usually, but not necessarily true. Quite often the slots lower down are filled by slot-fillers that describe an expected or default value for the property. However, particular instantiations may override this value. As an example, the *dog* frame would have a slot high up in the hierarchy that represented the property of having lungs. After all, every dog has lungs. On the other hand, the number-of-legs property would be lower down and have the default value 4. After all, it is possible for a dog to have only three legs.

In many implementations of the frame idea the hierarchical ordering of slots in frames is lost. Although there are exceptions such as UNITS (Stefik, 1979), most often all slots are treated as default slots. This leads to many difficulties, some of which will be reviewed later. There are other implementations of frames in which all the slots are treated as being necessary (so that they only describe information that must be true of every object, situation etc. to which the frame applies). Such implementations are of course unsatisfactory for applications where default reasoning is necessary.

It should be noted that frames are not just used to describe objects in the world or classes of objects. They can also be used to describe actions (either individual actions or types of action) or prototypical courses of events. One class of frames that should be mentioned separately are *scripts*. The notion of script was introduced by Schank (Schank, 1975b; Schank & Abelson, 1977). A script is a frame for a prototypical sequence of events. The best known example is the restaurant script. It is a large knowledge structure that binds together knowledge about the objects and people that you typically find in restaurants, and their functions, and knowledge about the sequence of events that typically take place in restaurants such as being seated, looking at the menu, ordering, eating, paying the bill, and leaving. Scripts have been used in SAM, a natural language understanding program which investigated how knowledge of context can be used to help in understanding stories (Cullingford, 1981).

Recently, Schank (1981) revised the theory and argued that scripts do not exist as such but are constructed from smaller entities called Memory Organization Packets (or MOPs). The main reason for changing the theory was that the various scripts often had certain parts in common, which were represented separately for each script. Thus, both the restaurant script and the visit-to-a-hairdresser script had paying the bill in common. MOPs were introduced to capture these similarities between scripts. A MOP then can best be seen as a frame which is smaller in scope that a script. Its function is to organize the experiences that an agent has had with the same type of entity, or in a similar type of situation, on different occasions, into units which represent the essential similarities between these different episodes. A MOP, as a script before it, can then be used to make predictions about new future events based on previously encountered events which are in some sense similar to the one the agent finds itself in at the moment. Scripts (now called *superscripts*) can then be constructed by combining various

MOPs into a new structure which is not itself stored permanently. Examples of MOPs are a *professional-office-visit* MOP (which can be used both in a *visit-the-dentist* and a *visit-a-solicitor* script), or a *contract* MOP. The *contract* MOP can be used in a wide variety of scripts including a *visit-a-dentist* and a *restaurant* script. In both cases there is an implicit contract involved. In both cases, you receive a service in return for which you pay some money.

3. SLOTS

The descriptions associated with a frame are called slots. A slot consists of a slot-name and a slot-filler. There are different types of slot, and in this section we discuss some of these.

The simplest type of slot is an attribute-value pair. It is used to ascribe a value to an attribute that has been defined for the particular frame it has been associated with. A slot of this kind can have different types of filler. A first type of possible slot-filler is a primitive of the programming language in which the frame representation language has been implemented. For example, if you associate a *name* slot with the *person* frame, (and the system has been implemented in a language that has strings as a data type), then the slot may be filled by a string. Thus, a slot might be of the following form:

⟨name "Mickey Mouse"⟩

A second type of possible filler is a pointer to another frame in the knowledge base. The fact that attribute-value slots can be filled by pointers to other frames reflects the interconnectedness of human knowledge which was so essential in semantic net representations. The pointer from a slot to another frame is of course very similar to the link between two nodes in a semantic network.

Two more remarks need to be made about attribute-value slots. First, for many systems it is possible to have sets as slot-fillers. Thus, if a particular car is owned by more than one person, then the *owner* slot will be filled by a set of strings, or a set of pointers to frames representing people. Second, many frame systems allow you to associate information about the status of the filler in a slot of a class-frame. In particular, many system allow you to represent explicitly that the filler was a default filler and can be overridden by subclass-frames or instance frames.

Although attribute-value slots are probably the most frequently used slot, they are not always applicable. In many cases no definite value for a slot is known. However, there is information about possible values for a slot. Most frame systems therefore allow you to associate restrictions with slots. In Chapter 3 we saw that one of the great strengths of logic was its expressive power. Logic provides a good language for representing incomplete knowledge, knowledge about incompletely known situations. The restrictions associated with slots provide frame systems with some of this ability as well, although, as we will see later, not all.

The restrictions associated with a particular slot are reminiscent of the value/restriction links used by KL-ONE. However, in many frame systems, the restrictions are more expressive and therefore more complicated than those allowed by KL-ONE. Different frame-based knowledge representation languages differ considerably in the restrictions that you can put on a slot, but the following are some typical examples.

Many frame systems allow the use of the logical connectives NOT, OR and AND in the formulation of restrictions on slots. Restrictions of this kind can be used for example to represent the information that the gender of every person is either male of female. You could put the following restriction on the *gender* slot associated with the *person* frame.

⟨gender (restrict (OR male female))⟩

A second example of restrictions is the use of functions or predicates in the underlying programming language to restrict the range of values that the slots-fillers in the slot can have. Restrictions of this kind may be used for example when you do not know the exact length of a car, although you do know that it is more than 13 feet. You can represent this as

⟨length (restrict (GREATER-THAN 13))⟩

A third possible restriction can be used when you know that every instance of a given class-frame must have as a filler for some slot an instance of another class-frame. Thus every car owner must own a car. We can represent this by having an *own* slot on the *car-owner* class-frame with the restriction that the filler of this slot for instances should be a car:

⟨own (restrict (a car))⟩

Sometimes you may have more specific information about restrictions on slot-fillers. For example, you may want to represent the information that every person has a female person as their mother. Thus, you can associate with the frame *person* a slot *mother* which must be filled by an instance of the *person* frame whose *gender* slot has been restricted to *female*. This can be represented as:

⟨mother (restrict (a person with
                (gender female))))⟩

In many systems, restrictions can be recursively applied inside the restrictions. Thus, we could restrict the *owner* slot of the *car* frame to be a person whose age is greater than 18 as follows:

⟨owner (restrict (a person with

⟨age (restrict (GREATER-THAN 18))))⟩⟩

A third type of information that can be attached to a slot is a procedure. One type of procedure that may be attached to a slot is a routine that is called whenever a value for a slot is required which has not been not explicitly stored. Quite often it is not possible to store a value because no value is available when the knowledge base is constructed. It may however be possible to compute this value when it is needed. In KRL (Bobrow & Winograd, 1977), such a procedure is called a *servant*. We can illustrate a servant by looking at a domain that was used in GUS, one application of KRL (Bobrow et al., 1977), namely booking flights in a travel agency. In an application of this kind, the knowledge base will contain a *flight* class-frame. Associated with this frame there will be such slots as *departure-date, departure-airport, destination, traveler* and *price*. You can imagine also associating a *discount* slot with the *flight* object. Suppose that the discount given depends on the age of the person acting as the filler of the *traveler* slot. Children under 12 get 50% discount, people over 65 get 25% discount. Given the age of the traveler, the following procedure will then calculate the discount available.

IF	(age of traveler) < 12
THEN	discount == 50
ELSEIF	(age of traveler) > 65
THEN	discount == 25
ELSE	discount == 0

Because the discount depends on factors that were not known when the class-frame was created, it could not be stored directly. You therefore store a servant with the discount slot of the *flight* class-frame. Whenever the value of the *discount* slot is needed for an instance of the *flight* frame, the system will first determine the age of the traveler, and then run the above procedure to determine the value of the *discount* slot for an individual flight.

Another type of procedure that can be stored with a slot is called whenever the slot in question receives a value or is updated. In KRL, such procedures are called *demons*. For example, in a program that simulates driving a car, you may associate a routine with the *gasoline* slot in the *car* frame that generates a warning whenever the value of this slot falls below a predefined value.

This way of associating procedural information with frames is called *procedural attachment*. Procedural attachment allows you to represent procedural information in what is to a large extent a declarative knowledge representation language. It is this feature that gives frames the capability of representing the procedural and declarative aspects of a given chunk of knowledge together in one structure. As we will see later in this chapter, object-oriented programming gets a lot of its power from the ability to store both declarative and procedural information.

Earlier we distinguished between class frames and instance frames. We also referred to the hierarchical organization of frame systems. This organization gives rise to special slots. A class frame generally contains a special *superclass* slot. The *superclass* slot refers to the class frame the present frame is a subset of. In systems that allow a given class to be a subclass of more than one superclass, the *superclass* slot can be filled by more than one class frame. Thus, an Alfa Romeo can be seen both as a type of car, and as a type of industrial product manufactured in Italy. In a class frame representing Alfa Romeos, the *superclass* slot would be filled by two class frame, namely the *car* frame and the *italian-product* frame. Although most class frames will have a *superclass* slot, the class frames at the top of the hierarchy are obviously exceptions.

Just as a class frame usually has a *superclass* slot, an instance frame has a special *member-of* slot. The *member-of* slot contains class frames representing sets of objects of which the present instance is a member. Again, in many systems, an instance can be a member of more than one class, and *member-of* slots can therefore often be filled by more than one class frame. One difference is that all instance frames have *member-of* slots. Thus, instance frames are only allowed if the instance has been declared to be a member of one or more classes which are represented in the knowledge base by class frames.

Another distinction that is often made is between two types of slot that can be attached to class frames. If you regard a class frame as a description of a class of entities, then there might be certain properties that are true of the entity as a class, and not of the entity as a prototype. This difference gives rise to a distinction between *own* slots and *member* slots in the frame-based knowledge representation language KEE (Fikes & Kehler, 1985). Own slots can occur in every type of frame and describe properties that are true of the entity or class of entities represented by the frame. Thus, if we have a *car* frame, then one of its own slots might be *longest*, reflecting the fact that the set of cars has one member that is the longest. We can contrast this with member slots which are slots that describe not an attribute of the class itself, but rather of all members of a class. Thus, an *engine-size* slot associated with a *car* class frame is a member slot because every car has an engine size. It is not an own slot because the set of cars obviously does not have an engine-size. As instances have no members, it follows that all slots in an instance frame are own slots.

4. REASONING WITH FRAMES

An important intuition underlying frame systems is the belief that people cope with new situations by retrieving information that was stored on the basis of previous experiences in situations that were in some sense similar to the present situation. In order to be able to model this in a frame system, the system must engage in two different styles of reasoning. The first step concerns the decision which of the many frames in the knowledge base is applicable to the current situation. The system must compare descriptions of incoming stimuli with frames in the knowledge base, and retrieve the class frame that best matches the situation. The reasoning mechanism responsible for retrieval of the best applicable frame is called the *matcher*. However, merely retrieving the relevant frame is not sufficient. A further step involves applying the frame to the current situation. The frame contains general information. However, in order to cope with the specific situation the system finds itself in, it will have to apply general information to the situation. The main inference mechanism responsible for applying general information to specific instances is *inheritance*.

Although both matching and inheritance are equally important, a lot of modern frame-based systems do not provide a matcher. (A notable exception to this rule is KRL (Bobrow & Winograd, 1977, 1979; Bobrow, Winograd, & KRL Research group, 1977) which contains a very sophisticated matcher.) Indeed in object-oriented programming, the AI programming methodology that has its roots partly in frame-based knowledge representation languages, inheritance is the only inference mechanism used. We will nevertheless first say a few words about matching before turning to inheritance.

4.1. Matching

A first step in the reasoning process, which leads to the generation of expectations then, concerns the discovery of those frames that can be applied to the situation the system currently finds itself in. Given a partial description of the situation, find the frames in the knowledge base that are consistent with this situation. Thus, the system has to *match* a description of the specific situation that it is facing with a general description of situations of this kind.

Matching is a problem that has been studied in the context of other knowledge representation languages as well. The unification algorithm discussed in Chapter 3 is in fact a matching algorithm. Similarly, in production rule systems, you need a matcher to decide whether the condition of a rule matches a working memory element.

Although frame-based systems are not unique in having matchers, matching in the context of systems of this kind is much more complicated than in other knowledge representation languages. There are several reasons for this. First, the structures to be matched are much more complicated than in other knowledge representation languages. In a unification algorithm, for example, you always match two formulas. Although formulas can have a complex internal structure, compared to frames they are rather simple.

A second reason for the greater complexity of matching in frame-based languages is the consequence of the default properties that are associated with class frames. Class frames do not only represent information that is always true of all its instances. Some instances can override the values of certain slots. The matcher therefore has to take into account the possibility of clashes between the descriptions associated with the frame and the descriptions true of the current situation. For example, although you would expect dogs to have four legs, a three-legged dog is still a dog, and the matcher must be able to recognize a three-legged dog as a dog.

A final reason for the complex character of the matcher concerns the range of possible results that may arise when matching a situation and a class frame. In a unification algorithm, or in the matcher used in production rule systems, there are two possible outcomes of the matching process. Either the formulas do not match, or else they do and a binding of the variables is returned as a result. However, in frame-based languages, the position is less clear-cut. Descriptions associated with a frame in the knowledge base need not always be true of the current situation, and perfect matches are very rare. Matches between incoming stimuli and frames are often a matter of degree. Often many frames at least partially match the incoming stimuli, and the matcher has to return the *best* match.

To illustrate matchers, we discuss a simple example. Despite its simplicity, it will give the reader some idea of the intricacy of a matcher in a frame-based system. Suppose that we have the following frames in the knowledge base, constituting a description of a situation the system is facing. Imagine for example that the system has just read the sentence *Bob, who lives in London, and who is an unpleasant chap, owns a dog called Pluto.*

⟨e1,

　　　　　　　　　　⟨member-of person⟩
　　　　　　　　　　⟨name "Bob"⟩
　　　　　　　　　　⟨lives-at "London"⟩
　　　　　　　　　　⟨owns e3⟩
　　　　　　　　　　⟨personality unpleasant⟩⟩

　　　⟨e3,

　　　　　　　　　　⟨member-of dog⟩
　　　　　　　　　　⟨name "Pluto"⟩
　　　　　　　　　　⟨is-owned-by e1⟩⟩

Suppose moreover that apart from *person* and *dog* frames, there is a *dog-owner* frame. We represent the information that each dog owner owns a dog, and that they must have a dog license. We also assume that dog owners are typically nice people.

　　　⟨dog-owner,

　　　　　　　　　　⟨superclass person⟩
　　　　　　　　　　⟨owns (restrict dog)⟩
　　　　　　　　　　⟨must-have (restrict dog-license)⟩
　　　　　　　　　　⟨personality (default pleasant)⟩⟩

It will be clear from an intuitive inspection of these frames that Bob is indeed a dog owner. Although this is a relatively simple example, any matcher will have to do some rather complex reasoning in order to reach this conclusion. First, it has to establish that Bob is at least a potential dog owner because he is a person. For example, because Pluto is a dog, the matcher can immediately rule out the possibility of Pluto being a dog owner. Establishing that Bob is a potential dog owner is relatively straightforward. It involves a match on the *member-of* slot of *e1* and the *superclass* slot of *dog-owner*. Note that if we had declared *e1* to be a member of the *american-person* frame, which in turn is a subclass of the *person* frame, then this step would have been more complicated. The matcher would have had to establish that if Bob is an American person, then Bob is also a person.

A second step which the matcher must make is to establish that the filler of the *owns* slot in frame *e1* (i.e., the thing owned by Bob) does indeed meet the restriction on the *owns* slot in the *dog-owner* frame. Thus, it has to establish that *e3* is indeed a dog. In order to do so, it will have to retrieve frame *e3* from the knowledge base and look at its *member-of* slot.

There is a clash between the fillers of the *personality* slot of *e1* and *dog-owner*. However, because the filler of the *personality* slot in the *dog-owner* frame is a default, instances are allowed to override this filler. Therefore, the clash does not cause the matcher to give up, and the system will correctly conclude that Bob is a dog owner.

4.2. Inheritance

Once the matcher has decided that Bob is an instance of the *dog-owner* frame, the system can then use this to generate expectations about him. For example, it can now derive that Bob must have a dog license. We now turn to this type of reasoning, inheritance.

We have already mentioned that frame-based knowledge representation languages, like semantic networks, have a hierarchical nature. In both languages this hierarchical organization of knowledge bases is exploited by using inheritance as an inference mechanism. Whereas in semantic nets the inference mechanism relied on the presence of *Sub* and *Inst* links, in frame-based languages it uses the *superclass* and *member-of* slots.

The basic inheritance mechanism is very similar to that used in semantic nets. When you ask for the value of a slot associated with a certain frame, then the system will first check the slots that are directly associated with that frame. If the frame contains the slot, and if the slot has a value, then this value is returned. If the frame does not contain the slot in question, then the reasoner behaves slightly differently depending on whether the frame is an instance or a class. If it is a class, then the reasoner will check the slots associated with its superclass (i.e., the frame that fills its superclass slot). If there is a value, then this is returned; if there is not, then the superclass of this class is checked, and so forth until a value has been found or until there are no more superclasses to look through. If you are interested in the slot value associated with an instance, then you check the filler of its member-of slot. If there is a value there, then this is returned; otherwise, the superclasses of this class are checked until a value is found or until there are no more classes to check.

Earlier we pointed out that that conceptual entities can often be described from different points of view. This is reflected in many frame-based knowledge representation languages by allowing class frames to have more than one filler in their *superclass* slot. Similarly, instance frames can have more than one filler of the *member-of* slot. This obviously complicates the inheritance mechanism: There are more paths that need to be explored if a value cannot be found locally. This type of reasoning is called *multiple inheritance*.

The problem in systems that allow multiple inheritance is the order in which superclasses should be searched. This is yet another manifestation of the control problem. One solution would be first to explore one path completely and to consider the other paths only when the first one fails (a kind of depth-first search). Alternatively, you can imagine first looking at the slots directly associated with the class frames in the *superclass* or *member-of* slot, and only exploring their superclasses if this search fails. This would result in a kind of breadth-first search.

Both depth-first and breadth-first search have certain advantages and disadvantages. Depth-first search is more efficient: Once a frame has been retrieved from the knowledge base, it can be used both to see if the required information is available, and if it is not, to determine directly which frame to search next. Breadth-first search is less efficient: When you have checked a class frame for the required piece of information, and failed, you cannot simply search its superclasses. This is because the frame whose slot-value you are trying to find out may have had other as yet unchecked super-classes, or other class frames which it was an instance of, and in a breadth-first approach these will have to be checked first. If none of these yield the required information, then you may have to retrieve the same frames later to determine what their superclasses are. Clearly, this is less efficient. (You could also store the superclasses in some special data-structure, but this is less space-efficient than depth-first search. Either way you lose.) On the other hand, breadth-first search has the advantage that, if there is more specific information which applies, then it will be found. In depth-first search, if the default information associated with some high-level frame is overridden by a more specific frame on another inheritance path, which is to be searched later, then the overriding value may not be found. To illustrate this point, consider the small knowledge base illustrated in Figure 6.1. Suppose that we want to determine the writing style of Bertrand Russell. Then in depth-first search, the inherited value is *boring* from the *intellectual*-frame through the *academic*- and the *philosopher*-frame. In breadth-first search however, the inher-

⟨e1
    ⟨member-of philosopher nobel-prize-winner⟩
    ⟨name "Bertrand Russell"⟩⟩
⟨philosopher
    ⟨superclass academic⟩⟩
⟨academic
    ⟨superclass intellectual⟩⟩
⟨intellectual
    ⟨superclass person⟩
    ⟨writing-style boring⟩⟩
⟨nobel-prize-winner
    ⟨superclass intellectual⟩
    ⟨writing-style excellent⟩⟩

Figure 6.1. An inheritance hierarchy.

ited value is *excellent*, because we will look at the *nobel-prize-winner*-frame before looking at any of superclasses the *philosopher*-frame.

A third alternative of searching inheritance hierarchies, and one which is used quite often, combines many of the advantages of depth- and breadth-first search. Often there are *joins* in a multiple inheritance network, superclasses that can be reached from the object in question along more than one inheritance path. For example, in the knowledge base in Figure 6.1, the *intellectual*-frame is a join because it can be reached from instance frame *e1* both through the *philosopher-academic* link, and through the *nobel-prize-winner* link. The strategy then is to search depth-first only up to joins. Thus, in the example in Figure 6.1, we would first visit the *philosopher*-frame, then the *academic*-frame, and then the *nobel-prize-winner*-frame. This control regime has some of the efficiency advantages of depth-first search, while on the other hand also making it more likely that more specific information overriding a default value is found.

One final remark needs to be made. The discussion above may suggest that inheritance is used only when you try to retrieve the slot associated with a frame. This style of reasoning is reminiscent of backward chaining or goal-directed reasoning in logic and production rules. Although many available frame-based systems operate in this way, it is not necessary to do this. You can imagine a kind of forward chaining or data-directed reasoning as well. In this case, the system would propagate slots and values downwards whenever a particular situation was recognized as an instance of a more general situation. Indeed, the generation of expectations relies on this downward propagation.

5. ADVANTAGES OF FRAME-BASED KNOWLEDGE
REPRESENTATION LANGUAGES

Several advantages have been claimed for frame-based knowledge representation languages. Many of these advantages are at the epistemological level and concern the way in which knowledge can be organized in frame-based representation languages.

Fikes and Kehler (1985) claim that frame-based knowledge representation languages capture the way in which domain experts typically think about their knowledge. The structure of the domain about which the knowledge is modeled is directly reflected in the knowledge base. Thus corresponding to a class of entities in the domain there will be a class frame in the knowledge base, and for each individual entity in the domain, there will be an instance frame. Moreover, the organization of knowledge about some entity (or class of entities) as descriptions stored with the instance frame (or class frame) is in many cases more natural than an organization of knowledge as a set of facts. Obviously, if knowledge is represented in a natural way, then this will improve the ease with which it can be grasped by a domain expert. This, in turn, will result in fewer difficulties in maintaining knowledge bases.

A second and related advantage of frame-based representation languages concerns the way in which entities are described. The most important way of describing an entity in frame-based knowledge representation languages is by specialization, that is, by comparing the entity to other things that you already know about. Again, Fikes and Kehler (1985) claim that domain experts find this way of defining things very easy to use.

The hierarchical structure of frame-based knowledge bases not only has advantages from an epistemological point of view. The inference procedure that uses the taxonomic structure, inheritance, has its own advantages. Although inheritance does not give you the full inferential power of first-order predicate logic, it is very powerful and captures a lot of the inferences that we normally draw. Moreover, it has the advantage over for example the inference procedures of logic-based knowledge representation languages in terms of efficiency. In Chapter 2 we discussed work by Levesque and Brachman (1985) concerning the tradeoff between expressive power and computational tractability. The more expressive a language was, the more computationally intractable its inference rules. Frame-based languages relinquish some of the expressive power of logic-based knowledge representation languages, but gain an increase in efficiency. For many applications, they seem to strike the right balance: On the one hand, you can express whatever you want to express, while on the other hand the inference procedure is efficient enough.

Another advantage of the hierarchical structure of frame-based knowledge bases concerns default reasoning. It was stated in the context of semantic networks that inheritance copes with default reasoning very well and very naturally.

A default value is a value that is true of an object unless there is evidence to the contrary. However, given the overall organization of the knowledge base, if there is such evidence to the contrary, it has to be stored with the object in question. Therefore, because one always checks local slots first, if there is information to the contrary, then the inference procedure will find it.

We shall pursue this point further as it provides a clear illustration of Levesque and Brachman's assertion about the tradeoff of expressibility and computational tractability. In Chapter 3 one of the arguments against a logical treatment of default reasoning followed from the semi-decidability of first-order predicate calculus (FOPC). In default logic, in order to determine whether a default rule could be applied, you had to make sure that there was no information to the contrary. However, determining whether there is information to the contrary is the part of FOPC that is undecidable. If you have not found any evidence after a limited time, you never know whether this is because there is no evidence to the contrary, or because you have not looked hard enough. As a result, default and nonmonotonic logics are not even semidecidable.

In frame-based knowledge representation languages, this problem does not arise. Given the way knowledge is organized, we know that if there is evidence to the contrary, then it must be stored in the taxonomic hierarchy between the class frame or instance frame of which we are trying to prove that it has the default property, and the class frame with which the default property is directly associated. Thus, suppose that we have the default color grey associated with the class frame *elephant*, and that we are trying to establish the color of the instance frame corresponding to the elephant Clyde. Then, in a framebased representation language, all one has to do is determine whether the default color is overridden either at the instance frame itself, or at any of the intermediate class frames. (A possible example of such an intermediate class frame might be *african-elephant*.) Determining whether this information is present at a given frame is decidable, and the undecidability problem therefore does not arise.

The situation becomes slightly more complicated for frame-based language that allow multiple inheritance. Whereas there is always a single inheritance path in the case of systems without multiple inheritance, in systems with multiple inheritance there can be a number of inheritance paths leading up from the instance or class frame for which one is trying to determine whether the default property holds. If all paths go through the class frame with which the default property is associated, then there is no problem. One simply checks all the paths. Thus the knowledge base in Figure 6.2 is not problematic. We are trying to determine whether the color grey associated with the *elephant*-frame is inherited by frame *e2*. As all the paths leading from frame *e2* go through the *elephant*-frame, there is no problem, and we can simply conclude that the color grey is not inherited.

However, in cases where the different paths do not cross in this way, there are

⟨elephant

⟨superclass animal⟩
⟨color grey⟩⟩

⟨african-elephant

⟨superclass elephant⟩⟩

⟨royal-elephant

⟨superclass elephant⟩
⟨color white⟩⟩

⟨e2

⟨member-of royal-elephant african-elephant⟩
⟨name "clyde"⟩⟩

Figure 6.2 A frame-based knowledge base.

potential problems. One can simply follow all the paths up to the top of the hierarchy. If there is no frame reachable from the frame for which we are trying to determine whether its inherits some default value, that overrides the default value, then there is no problem: The default color is inherited. If there is such a frame, and it lies between the present frame and the class frame with which the default property is associated, then we know that the default property is overridden. This is essentially the situation we had in Figure 6.2. The problem arises when there is such a frame, but it does not lie between the class frame and the present frame. Thus, if we had declared e2 to be an instance of the class frame *valuable-object* as well, and we had associated the default color *golden* with this object, then there would have been a problem. In these cases, we can draw no conclusion whatsoever. We simply have two conflicting default values, and no conclusion can be drawn. Providing that the inheritance hierarchy is finite, the whole process is of course still computable, even if we sometimes have to say that we do not know the answer.

6. PROBLEMS WITH FRAME-BASED KNOWLEDGE REPRESENTATION LANGUAGES

Although frame-based knowledge representation languages have many advantages, most of which are at the epistemological level and concern the structuring of knowledge, there are also certain problems, most of which are at the logical level and concern such things as the meaning and the expressive power of the formalism. There are three main difficulties. The first one concerns the absence of a clear semantics for frame-based representation languages. Closely related to this are problems that arises from the use of default inheritance for inference. Finally, there are problems with the expressive power of frames. We discuss each of these in turn.

6.1. The lack of a semantics

In Chapter 3 we saw that one of the arguments in favor of using a logic as a knowledge representation language, was the fact that its semantics was clear, with all the advantages that this confers. The problem with frame-based representation languages is that none of the languages that were originally proposed had a semantics defined for them.

Hayes (1979), himself a proponent of using logic as a knowledge representation language, attempts to fill this semantic gap for frames. He defines a translation algorithm from KRL into expressions of the language of first-order predicate calculus (FOPC). Rather than discuss his algorithm in detail, we will illustrate it by looking at the following two frames:

⟨e1

　　　　⟨member-of person⟩
　　　　⟨sex male⟩
　　　　⟨name "harry"⟩
　　　　⟨occupation (restrict (a profession))⟩⟩⟩

⟨person

　　　　⟨superclass animal⟩
　　　　⟨sex (OR male female)⟩
　　　　⟨mother (restrict (a person with ⟨sex female⟩))⟩⟩⟩

Hayes proposes to have a logical constant in the language for each instance frame, and a one-place predicate for each class frame. The *member-of* slot of the instance frame can then be translated as asserting that the individual corresponding to the instance frame has the property corresponding to the class frame. In a similar vein, the *superclass* slot of a class frame is translated as an assertion that everything that has the property expressed by the sub-frame also has the property associated with the superclass. Thus, assuming that *e1* is the logical constant corresponding to the instance frame, and *person* the one-place predicate corresponding to the class frame, we get the following two propositions:

person(e1)
$(\forall x)[person(x) \rightarrow animal(x)]$

The treatment of attribute-value slots is also straightforward. Slots correspond to relationships between entities. Thus, the simple-attribute slots associated with instance frame *e1* lead to the following logical propositions:

sex(e1,male)
name(e1,harry)

The treatment of restrictions on attribute value slots are treated in a similar way. A restriction of the form "(restrict (a x))" on a slot means that there must be a filler for this slot which must be an x. We can express this in logic by means of existential quantification. Thus, we can express the last slot associated with the instance frame as:

(∃x)[profession(x) & occupation(e1,x)]

Slots of class frames are treated in a similar vein. The main difference is that they make assertions not about individuals but about all individuals of this particular type. Thus, the two slots associated with the *person* frame are translated as follows:

(∀x)[person(x) → (sex(x,male) v sex(x, female)))]
(∀x)[person(x) → (∃y)[(person(y) & sex(y,female) & mother(x,y)]]

Although the above might seem to be an adequate translation of frame-based representations into the language of FOPC, there are three problems with it. They concern procedural attachment, member and own slots, and inheritance. We discuss each of them in turn. In the course of the discussion we point out some of the other problems associated with frame-based knowledge representation languages.

The first problem concerns procedural attachment. Earlier we saw that in most frame languages you can associate procedures with slots. Procedural attachment was a useful concept because it allowed frames to tie together the procedural and the declarative knowledge about an entity or class of entities. A complete translation of frame languages into logic then will also have to deal with this procedural information. One way of achieving this would be by providing a translation algorithm into logic of the programming language in which the routines can be defined. This, of course, is not straightforward although Hayes seems to prefer this solution.

An alternative way of handling procedural attachment is to give up the search for a logical translation of the entire frame language. One could maintain a logical translation of the declarative aspects and handle the procedural aspects in another way. One such method is to use the technique of semantic attachment that was used in Prolog and later also proposed by Weyrauch (1980). In Prolog the truth of the so-called *evaluable* predicates is established not by using the theorem prover but rather by executing a piece of associated code. In order to deal with procedural information in frames one could imagine using the technique of semantic attachment so that slots with associated procedures become evaluable predicates.

A second problem with Hayes' proposed translation algorithm is that it is not clear how it could be generalized to take into account the distinction between member and own slots. KRL did not draw this distinction and the problem therefore did not arise. However, many of the later frame-based representation languages do. Member slots represent information which applies to instances of a given class frame, whereas own slots apply to the frame itself. As far as member slots are concerned, Hayes' proposal is unproblematic. There are also no problems for own slots in instance frames. However, Hayes' proposal cannot be applied to own slots in class frames. Own slots in class frames represent information that is true of the class frame as an object in its own right, and under Hayes' proposal there is no constant that refers to set corresponding to the class frame.

Nado and Fikes (1987) provide a slight change to Hayes' basic translation algorithm that might seem to solve this problem. In Hayes' proposal class frames correspond to predicates and the only constants that he needs are constants corresponding to individuals in the domain. Nado and Fikes add another type of individual constant, which we will call a *class constant*. Intuitively, class constants stand for sets.

Rather than introducing one-place predicates as the translation of class frames, Nado and Fikes use class constants. Own slots in class frames can then simply be translated as asserting a relationship between the class constant corresponding to the frame, and whatever entity corresponds to the value of the slot. Member slots (or *prototype slots* as they are now called) are translated as universally quantified sentences. The way in which instance frames are translated stays largely unaltered. The only exception is the *member-of* slot. It now also gives rise to a two-place predicate. Thus, whereas the slot ⟨member-of person⟩ associated with *e1* used to be translated as *person(e1)* it is now translated as *member-of(e1,Person)* (where capitalized words are class constants).

In order to illustrate the new translation algorithm, consider the following *person* frame. The *superclass* slot is an own slot. Being a subset of the class of animals is a property of the entire set of persons and not of each individual member of the class. The second own slot *oldest*, represents the information that the oldest member of the sets of persons is Methuselah. The intended meaning of the member slots will be clear.

⟨person

                own slots   ⟨superclass animal⟩
                                ⟨oldest Methuselah⟩
              member slots

                                ⟨sex (OR male female)⟩
                                ⟨mother (restrict (a person with ⟨sex female⟩)))⟩

This frame is translated into the following set of propositions in the extended language that Nado and Fikes use.

subset(Person,Animal)
oldest(Person,methuselah)
(∀x)[member(x,Person) → (sex(x,male) v sex(x,female))]
(∀x)[member(x,Person) →
    (∃y)[member(y,Person) & sex(y,female) & mother(x,y)]]

Although Nado and Fikes' proposal gets around the problem of dealing with own slots associated with class frames, it does so at the cost of complicating the logical language into which the frame system is translated. The logical language contains two different types of constants: Normal constants and set-constants. Because of the increased (syntactic) complexity of the language, its model-theory has to become more complicated as well. Unfortunately, Nado and Fikes omit to define the model-theory. But defining the semantics is crucial: Translating one formal representation language into another formal representation language for which no semantics has been defined, might be an important result in so far as it establishes that the second language is at least as expressive as the first, but it cannot be used to provide a semantics for the first language.

The semantic difficulties with Nado and Fikes' language arise because their language contains class constants. In the standard model-theory for FOPC, constants are interpreted as referring to simple unanalyzed individuals. One cannot make use of any internal properties of these entities, unless you make them explicit in the definition of an interpretation for the language in question. Thus, calling the individuals that function as the interpretation of class constants *sets*, does not mean that the axioms of set-theory are automatically true of them. You cannot simply assume (as Nado and Fikes seem to do) that

$$(\forall X)(\forall Y)(\forall Z)[(subset(X,Y) \ \& \ subset(Y,Z)) \rightarrow subset(X,Z)]$$

In order to make Nado and Fikes' proposal acceptable from a logical point of view, you would therefore have to define constraints on the interpretations of individuals referring to sets. Although it is no doubt possible to do so, it does complicate the situation.

In both Hayes' proposal and in Nado and Fikes' class frames are treated as referring to sets of individuals. In Hayes' proposal class frames are translated as one-place predicates, and the meanings of one-place predicates in FOPC are sets of individuals. In Nado and Fikes' account, class frames are interpreted as constants that refer to sets. Although this set interpretation might be the most natural when it comes to translating frame-based representation languages into FOPC, it goes against an important intuition that underlies frame-based languages. The intuition is that general knowledge is organized around prototypes (see Rosch, 1975, for a similar proposal in a psychological theory about semantic memory, and Putnam, 1977, for a proposal to see the meaning of *natural kind* terms such as *elephant* and *lemon* as involving prototypes). Although there are various ways of defining exactly what a prototype is (see, e.g., Lehnert & Wilks, 1979), the way in which the term is most often used is as a set of descriptions which are inherited by instances only by default. Treating class frames as sets of individuals, rather than as prototypes, makes it more difficult to deal with default inheritance. Both Hayes and Nado and Fikes are aware of this problem, although they offer different solutions.

Hayes' treatment rests on the observation that a default inference contains an implicit reference to the state of the knowledge base when the default proposition was inferred. A default inference rule is applied only if the knowledge base contains no evidence to the contrary. Hayes proposes to represent these references to the knowledge base explicitly. For example, suppose that we have a *legs* slot attached to the *person* class frame with as default value 2, then under Hayes' proposal this would be represented as:

(∀x)[person(x) → ((∃y)[KB ⊢ 'legs(x,y)'] v legs(x,2))]

There are three problems with this proposal. First, we need to know the exact intuitive meaning of (KB ⊢ 'ф'). Does it mean that the proposition ф must itself be in the knowledge, or does it mean that ф must be derivable using only non-default propositions? It certainly cannot mean that ф is derivable from the entire knowledge base as we would then get into a circular argument. Second, even if the intuitive meaning becomes clear, we need to give a semantics for a logical language that allows a system to talk about itself in the language that it itself employs. Hayes is aware of this problem and gives the impression that he regards it as a rather straightforward extension of the semantics for FOPC. However, defining such a semantics is less than trivial. Third, even if we could give the right semantics for the extended language, there would be still be problems as the system would give the wrong results. Consider for example the following simple knowledge base:

⟨elephant

      ⟨superclass animal⟩
      ⟨color grey⟩⟩

⟨royal-elephant

      ⟨superclass elephant⟩
      ⟨color white⟩⟩

⟨clyde

      ⟨member-of royal-elephant⟩⟩

Intuitively, the color of Clyde should be white. However, assuming that both *color* slots are filled with default values, the translations would be:

(∀x)[elephant(x) →
  ((∃y)[KB ⊢ 'color(x,y)'] v color(x,grey)])
(∀x)[royal-elephant(x) →
  ((∃y)[KB ⊢ 'color(x,y)'] v color(x,white)])

Now, we know that both *royal-elephant(clyde)* and *elephant(clyde)* will be in the knowledge base. Given that we have not stored the color of Clyde directly in the knowledge (and we cannot derive it using nondefault propositions alone), we have two choices here. We can either use the first proposition to derive that Clyde is grey, or we can use the second proposition to conclude that Clyde is white. The problem, of course, is that in frame-based representation languages there is an order in which the system searches for default values (it always tries the most specific class frame first). In logic, this ordering is lost.

Nado and Fikes' solution to the problem of default inheritance is a generalization to frame-based representation languages of work done by Etherington (1987b). He provides a semantics for semantic networks with default inheritance by defining a translation algorithm for a specially defined semantic network formalism into Reiter's default logic (Reiter, 1980). Nado and Fikes follow Etherington. For example, suppose that we have the default value *grey* associated with the *color* slot in the *elephant* class frame, then this can be translated into

member(x, Elephant) | *(color(x,grey))* ⊢ color(x, grey)

We can read this as: "If x is an elephant, and it is consistent to assume that the color of x is grey, then x is grey." Clearly, this is the right intuitive translation of the default value. However, as we saw in Chapter 3, the question remains about the semantics for Reiter's default logic. Nado and Fikes' account is only satisfactory if Reiter's default logic can be given an adequate semantics, and that question is not (as yet) resolved.

6.2. The perils of inheritance

A point that is related to the absence of a clear semantics for frame-based knowledge representation languages concerns the problems that arise out of the use of inheritance as the only inference procedure. Brachman (1985) raises a number of issues concerning the use of inheritance.

A first question is what exactly is not being inherited when a class frame or instance frame does not inherit a slot associated with a higher class frame. You can make a distinction between the value of slot not being inherited, and the slot itself not being inherited. The case where the value of the slot is not inherited is not too difficult to represent. You simply override the value of the slot lower down. For example, if one represents Clyde as an elephant that overrides the default color of elephants, because he is white, then one can simply explicitly attach a *color* slot to Clyde, and fill it with the value *white*.

Sometimes, however, Brachman suggests, you want to be able to cancel not merely the value of the slot but the slot itself. For example, one may want to represent that Clyde is an elephant which has lost its trunk in a freak accident, and one way of doing so would be by canceling the *trunk* slot. In this case, one would want to represent explicitly the information that the slot has been canceled. Otherwise, there would be no good way of representing the difference between Clyde not having a trunk, and Tweety, the canary, not having a trunk.

It is not clear that canceling the inheritance of the *trunk* slot is actually the best way of representing the fact that Clyde has lost its trunk. As one can still talk about Clyde's trunk, even when he has lost it (e.g., "Clyde's trunk is buried near where he lost it"), one would still need a frame for representing Clyde's trunk. The object could then still be used as the slot-filler of the *trunk* slot in Clyde, although one would have to represent that it is no longer attached. Cancellation of slots seems to be necessary only if the slot represents a property of an entity, rather than a relation between entities. As the former hardly ever seems to be the case, there may be other ways of dealing with Clyde's loss of his trunk.

A second serious problem which arises when default inheritance is the only inference mechanism, is the lack of any definitional capability. It becomes impossible to define new composite concepts. Suppose that we defined a *three-legged-elephant* class frame:

⟨three-legged-elephant
   ⟨superclass elephant⟩
   ⟨legs 3⟩⟩

Then if we use default inheritance as the only inference mechanism, then any slot can be overridden, including the *legs* slot. So, one could define Clyde to be a three legged elephant with only two legs.

It might be argued that the fact that no definitions are possible is not too disastrous. Various philosophers have argued (e.g., Putnam, 1977) that for most natural kind terms definitions are impossible anyway. It is impossible to specify necessary and sufficient conditions for something to be an elephant. Indeed, this observation led Putnam to propose that the meanings of natural kind terms should be regarded as prototypes.

However, there are various reasons why this argument does not hold, and why the lack of definitional capabilities is problematic. The first reason is a purely theoretical one. Although there might be many domains for which definitions are not necessary (and perhaps impossible), there are domains, such as mathematics, where they are. If frames are to be seen as a knowledge representation language that may provide an alternative to for example logic-based knowledge representation languages, then there is a real problem as the applicability of these systems is restricted to particular types of domain. The second reason is more practical, and shows that even in nonmathematical domains it is essential that one be able to define new composite concepts. Consider for example a universally quantified sentence, such as *all elephants in London zoo are more than 10 years old*. The only way in which such a sentence can be represented in a frame-based knowledge representation language is by introducing the new composite class frame *an-elephant-in-London-zoo*. The age slot associated with this frame should then have the restriction *(greater-than 10)*. The point is that each instance of this frame has to inherit the fact that it lives in London zoo. Thus, in order to represent universally quantified sentences in a natural language understanding system one needs to be able to define new concepts.

In general the inheritance mechanism in frame-based knowledge representation languages has been default inheritance. However, not all systems take this approach. The UNITS system (Stefik, 1979) is a prime example. UNITS distinguishes between four types of inheritance roles which can be attached to slots, and Stefik mentions a fifth one which was not implemented, although adding it would pose no problems. The inheritance role attached to a slot determines how the slot is treated by the inference procedures.

The first type of role, the S role, simply means that the value of this slot is inherited by all subclasses and instances of this frame. Thus, the value of an S role is necessarily true of all instances of this frame.

The second type of role is the R role. The values of slots with R roles are restrictions on the values of the corresponding slots in frames lower down the inheritance hierarchy.

The third type of role associated with a slot is role U. Slots with this role represent information that is not inherited by any subclasses or instances of the frame. In the earlier discussion of various types of slots, we briefly mentioned the frame-based representation language KEE. KEE, which grew out of UNITS, distinguishes between own and member slots. Slots with role U correspond to own slots.

The fourth type of role in UNITS is the O role. A slot with an O role is optional. Stefik clarifies this by saying that the slot in an instance need not be filled with a value, and gives as an example the *exonomes* slot in the *bacterium* frame which has role O. According to Stefik, this represents the fact that not every bacterium has to have exonomes. Thus, from the clarification it seems that slots with role O describe attributes that not all instances of this frame need to have. In other words, it describes attributes which are not necessarily inherited by instances of the slot.

The O role can be contrasted with the M role, the role which was not implemented in UNITS. A slot with an M role represents an attribute and a value which can be overridden by frames lower down in the hierarchy. Slots with M roles therefore represent values for attributes, where the value need not be inherited, even if the attribute is. Slots with O roles on the other hand represent attributes which are not necessarily inherited. The M and O roles associated with slots thus provide an alternative way of dealing with the problem of whether values or attributes are canceled in inheritance by default.

Because UNITS distinguishes between slots with inheritance role S and slots with inheritance role M, it gives the user the ability to define new composite concepts. The definitional properties in a new composite concept are properties which are necessarily inherited by all its subclasses and instances. Therefore, they have to be represented in slots with role S. Other properties, which are merely true by default, of course, are represented by slots with role M. By having a more sophisticated inheritance procedure that takes into account the inheritance role associated with a slot, UNITS enables the user to represent both universally true sentences, and sentences which are merely true by default. It allows for the definition of new composite concepts.

6.3. Expressive limitations

Another problem for frame-based knowledge representation languages concerns the limited ability to express incomplete knowledge. We saw that this was one of the strengths of logic. Frame-based languages are able to represent certain types of incomplete information. For example, many of them allow the use of logical connectives in the formulation of restrictions on the values of slots. Thus, one can represent something like *the color of Mike's car is either red or white* by attaching the restrictions (OR red green) to the *color* slot in the instance frame corresponding to Mike's car. However, there are certain types of incomplete knowledge which are not expressible at all.

Although you can express certain disjunctions, you cannot express all arbitrary disjunctions. In fact, the only disjunctions you can express are disjunctions about the value of some property of some object. It is not clear how the following disjunctions can be expressed:

Either Mike's car is white, or it is more than 5 years old.
Either Mike's car is white, or my car is green.

A second problem concerns expressing existential knowledge. There is no problem in expressing something like *every person has a mother who is a female person*. One simply attaches a *mother* slot to the *person* class frame and adds restrictions to it. However, there are problem expressing existential knowledge when it is not in the scope of a universal quantifier. For example, in a detective story, we know that there is a murderer without knowing his or her identity. We can, of course, express this by creating an instance of the *murderer* class frame, say *e53*. The problem is that in most frame-systems, representing something as an instance frame implies that the entity corresponding to it is distinct from all other entities represented by instance frames. Thus, representing the murderer as *e53* implies that he or she is distinct from all other entities represented by some instance frame, such as the butler, the jilted lover, the penniless heir, and so on. This is not the case in logic, where an existentially quantified sentence does not commit you to saying that the entity which makes the existentially quantified sentence true is distinct from all entities that are mentioned in the set of propositions.

UNITS again provides a potential solution to this problem. It contains so-called *indefinite nodes* which behave like instance frames but correspond not to constants in a logical language, but rather to existentially quantified variables. An indefinite node has a number of slots that can be used for determining its identity. The first kind of slot is an *anchor* slot. It can be filled by an instance frame, indicating that the instance is identical to the entity represented by the indefinite node. The second type of slot is a *co-reference* slot. It can be filled by another indefinite node to represent the fact that the corresponding entities, whatever their true identity is, are equal. Of course, when the system finds a filler for the *anchor* slot, or for the *co-reference* slot, then this implies that the information contained in the indefinite node applies to the filler of the *anchor* or *coreference* slot as well.

7. OBJECT-ORIENTED PROGRAMMING

Frame-based knowledge representation languages are closely related to a new style of AI programming, so-called *object-oriented* programming. In this section, we briefly introduce this style of programming. Stefik and Bobrow (1986) is a more detailed introduction to object-oriented programming. They also discuss the difference between the various object-oriented languages.

The basic building blocks in an object-oriented system are objects. Objects are modules which, in the most natural applications of this style of programming, correspond directly to the types of object found in the domain of the application program. Thus, if you were using an object-oriented program to simulate a factory, then the various objects would correspond to the various machines that are performing particular tasks.

Each object has two types of information associated with it. First, there are attributes and values for those attributes. Thus, in our factory example, each machine object might have the attribute *manufacturer* with as possible value *philips*. This type of information corresponds to the information stored in attribute-value slots in frames.

The second type of information associated with an object is called a *method*. A method is basically a small program that can be used to perform certain calculations. Thus, in our factory example, we might have an output-method that calculates how many units the machine can manufacture each hour. Because this depends on such variable things as operating temperature, flow of input material, and so on, this is not a fixed value, and therefore cannot be stored directly but has to be computed whenever it is needed.

As in frames, there is a distinction between two types of objects, instances and classes. (As we will see later, the situation is more complicated, but for the moment this will do.) Instances correspond to specific entities in the world, such as machine *wvh42*. Classes, on the other hand, correspond to types of object, such as all machines of a particular type. The overall organization is hierarchical. Instances are always an instance of a particular class, and one class may be a subset of another. Object-oriented systems then use inheritance as one of their main reasoning mechanisms.

Objects communicate with each other by sending *messages*. The idea of using messages is due to Hewitt (1973, 1977). In order to explain what messages do, we will contrast this notion with the flow of control in standard programming languages. In normal procedural languages, you start off a computation by invoking a procedure with certain arguments. In an object-oriented system, you send a message to an object, which in the majority of cases will be an instance. A message consists of two conceptually distinct elements, namely a method and a list of arguments. Sending a message to an object results in the method being executed with the list of arguments as input. The system uses the hierarchical organization of a program to determine which method to invoke. Each object has certain methods associated with it. If the method mentioned in the message is stored directly with the receiving object, then there is no problem. If it is not, the system will look in either the object of which the present object is an instance, or the object of which the present object is a subclass. This will be done recursively, until either a method has been found, or until no more objects can be tried, in which case the system generates an error. Something similar happens when an object is asked for the value of a given attribute. If the value is not stored locally, then the system will go up the hierarchy looking for values higher up.

It is important to realize that even in those cases where a method is found higher up the hierarchy, it is always executed in the context of the object the message was sent to. What this means is that if a method makes reference to the value of some attribute, then the value that will be used is the one associated with the object that the message was sent to, and not the value of the attribute associated with the object where the message was found. Thus, suppose that we have a method *return-manufacturer* associated with an object *machine*, which just returns the value for the *manufacturer* attribute. Suppose moreover that we have the (default) value *philips* for this slot associated with the *machine* object. Suppose finally that we have a special subclass of *machine* called *press*, which has the value *siemens* in its *manufacturer* slot. Sending the message *return-manufacturer* to the object *press* will result in the method associated with the object *machine* being executed in the context of the object *press*. and will return *siemens* as its result.

Executing the methods associated with an object often results in another message being sent to some other object. Thus, in our factory example, in order to determine the maximum output of a machine *wvh42* one might send it the message *give-maximum-output*. As the maximum output of a machine will depend on the input that it receives, executing this method will result in *wvh42* sending requests to the machines that feed it to determine what its maximum input is.

Earlier we said that there are two kinds of objects in object-oriented programming languages, namely classes and instances. Strictly speaking this is not true. There is another kind of object, called a *meta-class*. Although messages are not usually sent to classes, it is sometimes useful. For example, one may want to send a message *new* to the *machine* class telling it to create a new instance of itself. Meta-classes are then used to determine how a particular class should deal with such a message. A class is in effect an instance of a meta-class. Just as an instance may use a method defined in its class to determine how to deal with a message, a class will look in its meta-class, which is usually stored in a *meta-class* slot, to see how to cope with an incoming message. Thus, when we send the message *new* to the *machine* class, it will use the definition of this method in the meta-class in its *meta-class* slot. Many object-oriented systems contain one or more predefined meta-classes, but users often have the freedom to add new meta-classes to the system. Thus, they can to a certain extent determine how a class frame deals with for example a *new* message.

To illustrate the power and usefulness of meta-classes, consider the following example. Suppose that there is a meta-class which defines the *new* method as follows: if a class *class* receives the message ⟨*new name*⟩, simply create a new instance frame called *name* and fill its *member-of* slot with *class*. Thus, if we were to send the *machine* class the message ⟨*new nr63*⟩ the following object would be added to the knowledge base:

⟨nr63 ⟨member-of machine⟩⟩

Now it might be the case that whenever an instance of the *machine* class is created, the user would like to be queried about the value of certain slots that every machine has. One can achieve this by making a new meta-class called for example *machine-meta-class* and putting a pointer to this meta-class in the *meta-class* slot of *machine*. The method *new* associated with *machine-meta-class* would then ensure that every time the message *new* was sent to the *machine* class, the user would be queried about the value of the *manufacturer* slot of the new instance.

Object-oriented programming languages are becoming more popular. Many of the AI tool kits discussed in the next chapter are implemented in an object-oriented style. Part of the appeal of languages of this kind is that they have all the advantages of frames in terms of naturalness of expression, and so on. There is a close correspondence between the program and that part of the world that the program models. This, in turn, leads to very modular programs. There can be little doubt that programming languages of this kind will become increasingly important.

8. CONCLUSION

In this chapter we discussed frame-based knowledge representation languages. The advantages of languages of this kind are primarily at the epistemological level: The organization of knowledge around entities, and the use of inheritance as the main inference procedure, seem to be very natural. Inheritance provides a natural way of dealing with default reasoning. There is also the implementational advantage that inheritance is easy to implement by means of fast special purpose routines.

The advantages are considerable and have led to a very widespread use of frame-based knowledge representation languages. In addition, many people are using object-oriented programming languages. Nevertheless, there are some problems that arise in the context of frame-based languages. Interestingly enough, they are mostly at the logical level. The first problem is the absence of a clear model-theoretic semantics, at least if one allows default inheritance. A second problem lies in expressing incomplete knowledge. However, it is not clear for how many applications the types of incomplete knowledge that cannot be expressed in frame-based knowledge representation languages are important. Since frame-based languages are widely used, the implication is that people can get by without using the types of incomplete knowledge that cannot be expressed.

7
Mixed Representation Formalisms

1. INTRODUCTION

In the previous chapters, we discussed various knowledge representation languages. The reader will have noticed that each of them has certain advantages and certain problems. Quite often the representational problems which can be solved naturally in one knowledge representation language are difficult for another, and vice versa. Thus, to take an example, default reasoning is a problem for logic-based knowledge representation languages while semantic nets and frame-based representations provide a very natural way of dealing with this type of reasoning. On the other hand, semantic nets and frames have problems when it comes to defining new concepts, a problem that can be handled quite naturally in logic.

Given these observations it seems attractive to attempt to combine the various representational formalisms in a new mixed knowledge representation language. There are various large mixed representation systems on the market which embody most of the knowledge representation languages and AI programming techniques that have proved useful. ART, KEE, and KnowledgeCraft are prime examples.

There are many advantages to systems that combine more than one knowledge representation language (cf. Vilain, 1985). First, the resulting system may be computationally more efficient. Often it is possible to force a particular piece of knowledge into a given knowledge representation language, but the cost of doing this is a loss in the speed with which inferences can be drawn. Thus, you could represent an object hierarchy as a set of logical axioms, but the inferences take longer to draw in such a representation than they would if you had used a frame-based representation language with inheritance.

A second, closely related, advantage is naturalness of expression. Although it is often possible to represent a piece of knowledge in a given representation language, and although it can often be done without any great loss in computational efficiency, you may prefer to express it in another language for reasons to do with clarity of expression. In Chapter 4 we mentioned Clancey's point about the difficulties of expressing structural knowledge in production rules. Although it is in principle possible to represent structural knowledge in a production rule language, even if only implicitly, it is not very natural, especially when you compare it to representing knowledge of this type in a frame-based language.

A third advantage of hybrid representation languages is the fact that they may extend the expressive capabilities of any one representation language. For example, we saw that it was very difficult to represent arbitrary disjunctions in frame-based representation languages, whereas they can be expressed in logic. Combining a frame-based representation language with a logic-based representation language would therefore increase the expressive power of the frame-based language.

A final point in favor of hybrid representation languages lies at the heart of KRYPTON (Brachman, Fikes, & Levesque, 1983; Brachman, Gilbert, & Levesque, 1985). Recall that Woods criticizes associative network representations because it is not clear whether the links have assertional or definitional import. KL-ONE, one of the semantic network formalisms discussed in Chapter 5, is an explicit attempt at separating assertional information from definitional information. KRYPTON is an extension of this idea and uses different knowledge representation languages for representing these different types of information. Hybrid knowledge representation languages thus enable you to represent different types of knowledge in different languages. The result is a representation that is clearer from an epistemological point of view.

There are a number of different hybrid representation languages in existence. Rich's (1982, 1985) system *Cake*, for example, uses both a special purpose representation for representing information about programs and programming, and predicate calculus. The same information is represented in both languages and the basic idea is to use each of these to do the reasoning most natural to it.

Cake differs in an important aspect from the so-called *essential* hybrid representation languages. Whereas Cake represents all information in both its languages, essential hybrid representation languages use different representation languages for representing different types of knowledge. The aforementioned system KRYPTON is one example and will be discussed in more detail below. KL-TWO (Vilain, 1985), another program derived from KL-ONE, is another example. KL-TWO uses two different representation languages for dealing with propositional and quantificational reasoning respectively. Thus, McAllester's Reasoning Maintenance System (McAllester, 1980) is used for propositional reasoning (see Chapter 3), whereas NIKL, a new implementation of KL-ONE (Kaczmarek, Bates, & Robins, 1986), is used for quantificational reasoning.

For reasons of space, we cannot discuss all the various mixed representation languages in great detail. Rather, the discussion in this chapter focuses on two rather different kinds of approach. First, we discuss the approach that underlies many of the AI tool kits, that have become available over the past few years, such as ART, KEE, and KnowledgeCraft. Second, we discuss KRYPTON.

2. AI TOOL KITS

One of the most important developments over the past few years has been the design of AI tool kits. ART, KEE, and KnowledgeCraft are probably the best known. (Since these systems are proprietary commercial products there are no widely accessible standard references for systems of this kind, apart from the documentation that you receive when you buy a licence.) The philosophy behind these systems seems to be to make available in one system a wide variery of knowledge representation languages and inference techniques. As a result, these systems provide a large number of different knowledge representation languages and AI programming techniques, and the different representation languages are integrated in a more or less coherent way.

The AI tool kits usually make available all the different knowledge representation languages discussed in the previous chapters. The systems contain an object-oriented programming language, and thus provide a frame-based representation language. Also, there usually is a rule-based representation language together with a variety of global and local control regimes. Thus, sets of production rules can be interpreted in a backward or a forward chaining fashion, and there are a variety of ways of performing conflict resolution. In addition, most AI tool kits also contain a logic-based representation language (usually some form of Prolog). Many systems also include some form of reason maintenance. Finally, because the majority of these systems have been implemented in Lisp, you can also use procedural representations (i.e., Lisp programs).

Within systems of this kind, the various representation languages are more or less integrated. For example, rather than using object-attribute-triples (or attribute-value pairs) in the conditions of production rules, you can access the value of a slot in a frame in order to determine whether the preconditions of some rule hold. Conversely, you can often associate sets of production rules as a method with a slot in an object. Thus, rather than using a piece of arbitrary Lisp code as the method definition associated with an object, you can use a set of production rules. Whenever the object then receives a message, rather than executing a small Lisp program, it will use a rule-interpreter on the production rules to find the answer. Because of the large range of different global and local control regimes, this obviously extends the range of possibilities. This particular combination of objects and rules was pioneered by Jan Aikins in a program called CENTAUR (Aikins, 1983).

Although most AI tool kits are at the deepest level large Lisp programs, usually the only representation language directly implemented in Lisp is the object-oriented or frame-based language. All the other representation languages are themselves implemented in the frame-based language. Thus, a production rule, for example, is internally represented as a frame. A possible representation would be to see a production rule as a frame with an *antecedent* slot and a *consequent* slot. Different global control regimes are also represented as objects.

The difference between a forward chaining and a backward chaining rule interpreter can then be implemented by associating different *select* and *execute* methods with them. Forward chainers have a *select* method that looks at the *antecedent* slot of a frame representing a rule, whereas backward chainers have a *select* method that looks at the *consequent* slot.

Because most things are represented as an object in AI tool kits, the user can change most aspects of such systems. Objects are accessible to users and can be modified by them. The user therefore has access to the implementational details of the various representation languages. The system discussed in the next section, KRYPTON, is based on an opposing view namely that the implementational details should be hidden from the user. KRYPTON's designers refer to this view as the *functional* view of knowledge representation languages. We discuss it in detail below.

One advantage of the nonfunctional view of knowledge representation, as it is realized in the AI tool kits, in the freedom that it gives the user. Almost everything can be changed. If you do not like a particular feature of the system, you can change it by altering the frame corresponding to that feature. For example, if you do not like the way in which a particular rule interpreter works, then you can change the corresponding object.

AI tool kits also provide a very good development environment. A development environment is a set of software tools that make construction and maintenance of a program easier. An example of a very simple development tool is an editor. Program construction is made much easier when you have an editor so that you can look at your program and change it whenever you discover an error, or to use programmer's jargon, a bug. Life without an editor would be very hard indeed. For example, without an editor, you could only fix a bug in a procedure by retyping the whole definition of the procedure. Since bugs can often be fixed by making small local changes, an editor, which allows you to make such local changes without having to retype the whole definition, will obviously make development of the program much easier. The AI tool kits contain a whole range of different software tools and these greatly facilitate program construction. In addition to sophisticated editors, such systems often have very good debugging facilities such as steppers and tracing packages. Also, there are often very sophisticated statistical packages which allow you to determine in which part the program spends most time when it is trying to solve some problem. This obviously allows you to determine which parts of the program need to be made more efficient. Given the fact that most aspects of an AI mixed programming environment can be changed by a user, and given the complexity of these systems, a good development environment is essential.

While the enormous array of different representation languages made available is an obvious advantage in terms of flexibility, it also leads to certain problems. A given piece of knowledge can often be expressed in many different ways. Thus you could represent *if x is a bird, then x is an animal* either as an implication in a logical language, or as a production rule, or by representing the *bird* frame as a subtype of the *animal* frame. The problem is that the designers of systems of this kind often give no guidelines about when to use which representation language. As a result, programmers tend to develop idiosyncratic ways of representing particular pieces of information. Thus one programmer might represent as much knowledge as possible in production rules, while another programmer might prefer objects. This is likely to lead to difficulties in maintaining knowledge bases, or extending them. If everybody has their own style, then changing a knowledge base created by somebody else is very difficult. The problem is made worse by the fact that the AI tool kits are often used for developing large application programs which are constructed by more than one programmer.

Although the above discussion has been rather brief, it should have given the reader some idea about the advantages and disadvantages of AI tool kits. The main advantage is in terms of flexibility and power: You can choose the most appropriate representation language for the particular piece of knowledge that you want to represent, and if you do not like the way in which a particular feature has been implemented, then you can change it. The other side of this coin is the fact that too much flexibility can lead to *ad hoc* styles of representing knowledge, with all the disadvantages that this entails in terms of maintainability and extensibility of knowledge bases. In the next section, we discuss a mixed representation language that attempts to give a more principled way of combining different representation languages.

3. KRYPTON

KRYPTON is a mixed representation system which grew out of KL-ONE, a semantic network formalism discussed in Chapter 5. It is based on two assumptions. The first underlying assumption is the functional view of knowledge representation. The second one is that one must distinguish between assertional and definitional information.

The functional view of knowledge representation (Levesque, 1984) is best regarded as a proposal to see knowledge bases as abstract data types. The notion of abstract data type is derived from computer science. (For a thorough and highly readable introduction to these ideas, see Abelson & Sussman, 1985. The example discussed here is derived from their discussion of this issue.) Sometimes, you want to write computer programs that use more complicated data structures than the ones that are provided by the programming language itself. For example, the computer programming language might only support integers, and the desired program may need to reason with fractions. One way of achieving this would be by constructing a compound data structure consisting of a pair of integers, with the first integer functioning as the numerator and the second the denominator. The idea of abstract data types, then, is to specify how the compound data object is used separately from the details of how it is constructed from the more primitive data objects. The programs that use the new compound data objects can then reason with the "abstract" specifications without having to worry about how the compound data structure is actually implemented.

In order to be able to use the abstract data structure in a computer program to do some actual computation, you will, of course, have to define specific functions that implement the abstract data structure in real data structures. Two slightly different types of functions are necessary: a *constructor*, which constructs an instance of an abstract data structure, and *selector(s)*, which allow you to select parts of the abstract data structure. For example, in our fraction example, we need to have the following constructor

(make-fraction ⟨n⟩ ⟨d⟩)
   which takes the integers ⟨n⟩ and ⟨d⟩ and returns a fraction with ⟨n⟩ as numerator and ⟨d⟩ as denominator.

In addition, you need two selectors, each of which takes as its argument a compound data structure representing a fraction. This fraction, of course, must have been constructed using the constructor *make-fraction*.

(numerator ⟨x⟩)
   which returns the numerator of the fraction ⟨x⟩
(denominator ⟨x⟩)
   which returns the denominator of the fraction ⟨x⟩

Once the constructor and selectors have been defined, you can then use them in defining operations on instances of these abstract data structures. For example, suppose we wanted to define a function for adding fractions, then you would define this in the following way:

```
(defun add-fractions (x y)
   (make-fraction
      (+ (* (numerator x) (denominator y))
         (* (numerator y) (denominator y)))
      (* (denominator x) (denominator y))))
```

The important thing to note about this definition is that it relies on the availability of selectors and constructors, and that you do not need to be aware at all of the way in which the abstract data structures are, in fact, realized. Thus, you abstract away from specific implementations of fractions. One obvious advantage is, of course, that you can then change the actual implementation to whatever you want (for example for efficiency reasons), without having to worry about having to change the rest of your programs.

Levesque (1984) proposes to regard knowledge bases as abstract data types in this way. You can then specify abstract operations that you need to be able to perform on knowledge bases. There are two obvious ones, namely TELL and ASK. TELL is an operation that takes a knowledge base and an assertion and returns a new knowledge base, to which this assertion has been added. There are, of course, various additional requirements that you might want to put on this operation. For example, if the assertion that is to be added was derivable from the knowledge base beforehand, then TELL might return the same knowledge base as before. After all, the information to be added is not really new.

The second operation on a knowledge base is ASK. It takes a knowledge base and a query, and can return three possible answers: Yes, if the query follows from the knowledge base; no, if the negation of the query follows from the knowledge base; unknown, if neither the query itself nor its negation follows from the knowledge base. The situation becomes more complicated if you are also allowed to ask wh-questions, such as "what is the capital of California?" as opposed to simple yes-no questions "is there a capital of California?" The bulk of Levesque's paper is then devoted to designing a language that is rich enough to be used both as a language in which to query a knowledge base, and in which to assert propositions into a knowledge base.

The functional view of knowledge bases goes against the spirit of at least some of the object-centered representation languages, and some of the AI tool kits discussed above. These systems often make the implementational details accessible to the user, and the user can then change the representation language at will. Often the meaning of the representation language is specified only in terms of the data structures that are used to implement it. Thus, inheritance is often defined in implementational terms: "A ISA B" means that all the information stored with B is also accessible to A, unless there is contradictory information stored with A. The important point is that the term *stored* concerns implementation. Representation languages of this type then answer the question "What structures should the system maintain for the user?" KRYPTON, on the other hand, because it is based on the functional view of knowledge representation, focuses on the question "What exactly should the system *do* for the user" (Brachman, Fikes, & Levesque, 1983).

The second assumption underlying KRYPTON is the need to distinguish between assertional and definitional information. Woods criticizes both semantic network representations and frame-based representation languages on the grounds that it is often not clear whether the links or slots are intended to represent assertional information or definitional information. KL-ONE made an explicit distinction between these types of information. However, the assertional part of KL-ONE was not particularly well-developed. KRYPTON takes the idea of separating definitional and assertional information one step further, and contains two completely separate components, the TBox (Terminological Box) and the ABox (Assertion Box). The TBox is used for representing definitional and terminological information, while the ABox is used for assertional information.

The TBox is used for representing terminological information. The TELL operation appropriate to this component allows the user to construct taxonomies of structured terms, whereas the ASK operation can be used to answer questions about analytical relationships among these terms. The language used in the TBox is reminiscent of KL-ONE. Thus, the basic entities in this component are concept expressions, corresponding to the concepts in KL-ONE, and role expressions, corresponding to slots in pure frame-based language, and to roles in KL-ONE. In general, concepts and roles are formed by combining or restricting other concepts or roles.

The language of the TBox in KRYPTON gives the user a number of primitives for defining new concepts and roles. An example is *ConGeneric,* which takes any number of concepts, and returns a concept that is the conjunction. Thus, you might define a bachelor as an unmarried male, and the way in which this would be represented in KRYPTON's TBox would be as (*ConGeneric man unmarried*), assuming that *man* and *unmarried* are already available, either as defined or as primitive concepts. Another primitive is *VRGeneric,* which takes as arguments a concept, a role, and a concept. It corresponds to the notion of a value restriction on a role in KL-ONE. Thus, we can define the concept of a person with a Greek father as (*VRGeneric person father greek*). You an combine the different primitives in KRYPTON's TBox. Thus, a person with an unmarried mother could be defined as (*VRGeneric person mother (ConGeneric woman unmarried)*). KRYPTON gives a number of other primitives, but it is beyond the scope of this chapter to discuss each of these.

If we regard the TBox as an abstract data type, then we can define one constructor function and two selectors functions. The constructor function TELL simply adds a definition of some to the TBox. Thus:

TELL: bachelor (ConGeneric male unmarried)

would add the definition of a bachelor as an unmarried male to the TBox. The two selector functions are called ASK_1 and ASK_2. ASK_1 takes as input two symbols and returns *yes* if the first symbol is subsumed by the second, *no* if it is not, and *unknown* if this cannot be determined. Thus, after the above TELL operation

ASK_1: bachelor male

will return *yes* as the concept of bachelor is subsumed under the concept male. The second selector, ASK_2, also takes as input two symbols. It returns *yes* if the concepts corresponding to the symbols are disjoint, *no* if they are not, and *unknown* if this cannot be determined. Two concepts are disjoint if the set of individuals to which the first concept applies has no elements in common with the set of individuals to which the second applies. Thus, if we asked

ASK$_2$: male female

then this would return with *yes.*

The language of KRYPTON's ABox is a form of the language for first-order predicate calculus (FOPC). The reason for this choice is the fact that an assertional component needs to be able to represent incomplete knowledge, that is, knowledge about incompletely known situations, and we saw in Chapter 3 that FOPC is good at this. There is one difference between FOPC and the language used in KRYPTON's ABox. Normally, in logic you are free to choose whatever predicates and terms you want as the primitive, domain-dependent expressions. However, KRYPTON contains a component for specifying primitive predicates, namely the TBox. Therefore, rather than treating the predicates in the logic as primitive, KRYPTON allows the user to define them further in the TBox.

The main advantage of this scheme over standard FOPC is the fact that you can separate the definitions of the predicates from propositions that correspond to truths about the domain. In standard FOPC, there is no way of distinguishing between definitional information and assertional information because both are expressed in the same language. Thus, to use an old philosophical example, although both *man is a featherless biped* and *man is a rational animal* are true, the first is taken to be a historical accident, and therefore is assertional information, while the second can be seen as a "definition" of the concept *man,* and therefore is definitional information. We represent these sentences in logic as:

$(\forall x)[man(x) \leftrightarrow (featherless(x) \ \& \ biped(x))]$
$(\forall x)[man(x) \leftrightarrow (rational(x) \ \& \ animal(x))]$

There is no way of distinguishing between these two different types of sentences. In KRYPTON, on the other hand, it is possible to distinguish between these two different types of information: The first sentence is represented in the ABox as a logical sentence, while the second is represented in the TBox.

Brachman, Gilbert, and Levesque (1985) define a model-theoretic semantics for KRYPTON. The semantics for the language of the TBox is defined as follows. There are primitive concepts in the TBox. Their meaning is simply defined as a set of individuals. This is, of course, similar to the way in which the meaning of one-place predicates are defined in logic. Similarly, we interpret roles as two-place predicates, that is, as sets of pairs of individuals. The meanings of the defined concepts in the TBox are then defined in terms of the meanings of the primitive concepts. For example, if *C* is defined as (*ConGeneric C' C"*), then the meaning of *C* is the intersection of the meaning of *C'* and *C"*. Thus, the meaning of (*ConGeneric male unmarried*) are those individuals who are both in the extension of *male,* and in the extension of *unmarried.* The meaning of (*VRGeneric C R C'*), as all those *x* in the set denoted by *C,* such that $\langle x,y \rangle$ is in the set denoted by *R* only when *y* is in the set denoted by *C'*. Thus, the meaning of (*VRGeneric person father greek*) is the set of all x in the set denoted by *person* such that $\langle x,y \rangle$ is in the set denoted by *father* only when y is in the set denoted by *greek*.

The semantics for the language used in the ABox is relatively straightforward. The ABox uses *FOPC* and the semantics of *FOPC* is well known. The only complication arises from the fact that the meanings of the one-place predicates should be compatible with the meanings of the concepts in the TBox. But this can easily be achieved by insisting that the meanings of the one-place predicates, that is, the set of individuals assigned to a one-place predicate, is identical to the meaning assigned to the corresponding concept in the TBox. Thus, if the language in the ABox contains the one-place predicate *bachelor*, which is defined in the TBox, then we make sure that the set denoted by *bachelor* is identical to the set denoted by this concept in the TBox. After this, the semantics of the ABox can be defined in the normal way as in Chapter 3.

The architecture of KRYPTON means that the theorem prover that is used for the ABox cannot be a standard theorem prover. It has to be able to take into account the definitional information stored in the TBox. There are two ways in which this can be achieved. The first, and in a sense, the most straightforward way would be to translate the definitions in the TBox into sentences in the ABox. Brachman, Gilbert, and Levesque (1985) reject this approach for two reasons: First, if you did this, then the distinction between definitions and propositions that are contingently true would disappear. You would no longer be able to distinguish between *man is a featherless biped* and *man is a rational animal*. Second, translating definitions to sentences in the ABox will invariably slow the theorem prover down. Thus, there are efficiency reasons for rejecting this approach as well.

A second possible solution is to implement a special-purpose theorem prover that can take into account definitions in the TBox. KRYPTON uses a theorem prover developed by Stickel (1983). Stickel extended a particular type of theorem prover (called a *connection graph* developed by Kowalski, 1975) into a theorem prover that could take into account a set of definitions.

In Chapter 3 we discussed resolution refutation theorem provers. The only inference rule in systems of this kind is resolution: If one clause contains a sentence ϕ, whereas another contains a sentence $\neg\psi$, and ϕ and ψ unify with unification σ then you can derive a new clause by applying σ to the other literals in the two clauses and collecting the resulting literals into the new clause. The basic idea is to find contradictory sentences and unification is the mechanism used for determining whether two sentences are contradictory. KRYPTON extends the basic resolution step in two ways. First, it extends the unification algorithm. Second, it does not have to rely on unification as the sole mechanism for determining whether two sentences are contradictory.

KRYPTON slightly extends the unification algorithm to take into account the definitions in the TBox. Normally, two sentences unify only if their predicates are identical. But because the TBox further defines predicates, KRYPTON does not need to restrict the unification algorithm in this way. Suppose, for example, that *man* is defined as a subconcept of *animal*. Then we know that $man(x)$ and $\neg animal(x)$ are contradictory, and the unification algorithm can be changed to reflect this. Thus KRYPTON's unification algorithm will also unify sentences when the predicate in one is a subtype of the predicate in the other. Obviously, KRYPTON's theorem prover can use the ASK_1 operation defined for the TBox to this end.

Apart from generalizing the unification algorithm KRYPTON makes use of the knowledge represented in the TBox in two further ways. The first extension corresponds to the ASK_2 operation that we defined for the TBox. ASK_2 returned *yes* if two concepts were disjoint. Suppose for example that the TBox replies *yes* to the query

ASK_2: male female

Then the sentences $male(x)$ and $female(x)$ are contradictory as well and they can be resolved against each other. KRYPTON thus extends the basic resolution step and will resolve sentences against each other if the information in the TBox allows one to conclude that the concepts corresponding to the predicates in the sentences are disjoint.

Another way in which KRYPTON makes use of the knowledge in the TBox is by using what can be called *conditional resolution*. You can complicate resolution by introducing the notion of a *residue*. A residue can be regarded as a statement that two sentences can be resolved against each other, provided that the residue is known to be false. For example, suppose that we defined *bachelor* as the conjunction of *male* and *unmarried*. Then, $male(a)$ could be resolved against $\neg bachelor(a)$ provided that we knew $\neg unmarried(a)$ to be false. The reason is that if $\neg bachelor(a)$, then either $\neg male(a)$ or $\neg unmarried(a)$. If we then know that $\neg unmarried(a)$ is false, then $\neg male(a)$ must be true, and this of course resolves against $male(a)$. Thus conditional resolution is another mechanism that the theorem prover in KRYPTON's ABox uses to utilize the knowledge in the TBox.

There are many more things that could be said about the way in which KRYPTON has been implemented. KRYPTON, for example, embodies certain techniques for doing some of the inferencing when the system is built, rather than when the system is consulted. The intuitive motivation behind this is that you want maximal speed out of a system when it is built, even at cost of some slow-down at the time at which the system is built (Elfrink & Reichgelt, 1988, 1989, present a purely logic-based system also based on this intuition). However, the above discussion should have given the reader a flavor of KRYPTON.

One of the problems with KRYPTON, as with KL-ONE, is the fact that it cannot deal with default reasoning. The TBox is exclusively used for definitions, and therefore cannot be used for representing default propositions, while the language in the ABox is the language of FOPC and in Chapter 3 we argued that default reasoning cannot be dealt with in straightforward FOPC.

Given the basic distinction between the ABox and the TBox, the only way in which KRYPTON could be extended to deal with default reasoning would be by extending the language used in the ABox. After all, defaults seem to be more to do with things that are contingently true about the world, rather than with the definition of concepts. Thus, the best way to enable KRYPTON to deal with default reasoning would be to replace the language used in the ABox by a language for some default or nonmonotonic logic. This would obviously also entail certain changes to the inference machinery that is used in the ABox. Clearly, the viability of this move would depend on the availability of a satisfactory default or nonmonotonic logic, a topic which we discussed at great length in Chapter 3.

Summarizing then, KRYPTON is a hybrid representation language that has the advantage of being much more principled than the AI tool kits discussed in the previous section. It also avoids some of the problems that Woods raised in connection with semantic network representations and frame-based systems. In particular, it has a clear distinction between definitional and assertional information.

8
Parallel Distributed Processing

1. INTRODUCTION

In Chapter 1 we discussed the knowledge representation hypothesis. Virtually all the work that has been done in AI to date is based on this hypothesis, and assumes that any artificial intelligent process will contain separate structural components which external observers take to be the representation of the knowledge that the system has, and which play a causal role in the behavior that the system displays. As a consequence, a clear separation is assumed between the knowledge that the system has, and the way in which the system uses this knowledge to solve certain problems. Recently, however, a new approach has come to the fore that challenges these assumptions. The new approach is known as *connectionism*, or *parallel distributed processing* (PDP). There are subtle differences between connectionism and the PDP approach but for the purposes of our present discussion we simply ignore them and use the terms interchangeably.

We start with a very brief introduction of the basic ideas behind the connectionist approach. This should give the reader some feel for what models of this kind amount to. It will also set the scene for the subsequent discussion of the motivation behind the PDP approach. We then discuss PDP models in more detail. Finally, we critically review connectionism. It must be said that, although its roots go back a long way, the PDP approach is a relatively new development that has not yet been fully explored. As a result, both the discussion of the details of the approach, and the critical review is not claimed to be definitive.

2. WHAT IS THE PDP APPROACH?

Unlike most approaches in AI, where one is primarily interested in the software, the programs that implement the knowledge representation language, the PDP approach starts of with a specification of the hardware, the machine on which the programs should run. A PDP machine, or a network, consists of a large number of *nodes* or *units*, each of which is connected to a large number of other nodes.

Each connection between two nodes has a *connection strength* associated with it. Each node is a very simple processing unit, which, if we simplify slightly, can do three things. First, it can store a single value, called its *activation value*. Second, it can pass its activation value to the nodes to which it is connected. Thirdly, it can calculate a new activation value on the basis of its old activation value and the activation values that are passed into it by nodes that are connected to it. How strongly the activation values of the nodes feeding into a node influence the new activation value depends on the connection strength of the connection between them. One of the attractive features of connectionist models is that they are able to learn new information automatically. Learning in a connectionist model amounts to simply changing the connections strength on the connections between the different units. As we shall see in section 5, this very simple account of learning turns out to be surprisingly powerful.

We expand this very brief description of PDP models in sections 4, where we discuss various different PDP models in more detail, and section 5, in which we discuss the different methods in which connectionist network can be trained. First, however, we discuss the motivation behind connectionism in some detail. The discussion is to a large extent based on McClelland, Rumelhart, and Hinton (1986).

3. WHY ADOPT THE PDP APPROACH?

One important motivation for the PDP approach is neurological. Human intelligence is "implemented" in the human brain. It might therefore be possible to create artificial intelligence by building a machine that mimics the human brain. The PDP approach can be seen as an attempt at constructing a computer that is structurally similar to the human brain, and determining whether this machine can be used in such a way that interesting phenomena emerge.

The human brain consists of a large number of nerve cells, or *neurons*, with very many connections between them. A neuron communicates with another by sending messages in the form of electrical pulses down its *axon*. When the message reaches the end of the axon, chemical substances are released into the synapse, the connection between the sending neuron and the receiving neuron. These chemical substances are called *neurotransmitters*, and they change the state of the receiving neuron. Depending on what other inputs this neuron receives, the state of this neuron may change enough for it to send a message down its own axon. Neuro-transmitters may be excitatory, making it more likely that the receiving neuron will send a message down its axon, or inhibitory, making it less likely. Neurons receive inputs from an enormous number of other neurons. It has been estimated that a single neuron receives inputs from between 1,000 and 100,000 other neurons. Conversely, a neuron does not send its output to a single other neuron. In fact, a neuron sends its output to between 1,000 and 100,000 other neurons. Clearly, this is a very simple account of what happens in the brain, but for our present purpose it will do. For more details, the reader is referred to Carlson (1986).

The parallels between connectionist models and the brain will be obvious. Units or nodes in a PDP model can be compared to neurons, while the process of sending an activation value down a connection to another unit corresponds to a neuron sending a message down its axon. However, the similarities between connectionist network and the brain are liberally drawn, and there are a large number of differences between the processes in a connectionist network and the processes that take place in the brain. Some of these differences will be mentioned below. For more details, see Crick and Asanuma (1986).

A second related motivation concerns the speed with which each component in the brain works. Compared to components in modern digital computers, neurons are slow processors and it takes a relatively long time for a message to travel down an axon. The PDP researchers conclude from this that, given the speed of mental processes, it is not possible for the brain to compute solutions to problems in a serial fashion, that is, by considering one possible solution after the other, until a solution is found. Rather, they argue, the brain works in parallel and considers different solutions to a problem simultaneously. Thus, when faced with the problem of completing a partially specified pattern, the brain will consider all possible completions at the same time and decide which completion matches the partial pattern best. A serial computer would have to consider each possible completion in turn until it finds one that matches the partial pattern. One aspect of the PDP approach then is to search for highly parallel algorithms. We will see how parallelism can be realized in connectionist models when we discuss some of these models in more detail.

But apart from these neurological motivations, there are also psychological reasons for adopting the PDP approach. Various PDP researchers started life as psychologists trying to explain human cognitive behavior in terms of schemata, entities that, at least as far as the underlying intuitions are concerned, are identical to frames. One of the motivations for using schemata in this context is that they seem both general and flexible enough to explain how we use old knowledge to deal with novel situations. Schemata store knowledge that applies to a class of objects or events, and are therefore general. On the other hand, they do not completely specify every detail of the type of object or situation that they stand for. Clearly, this flexibility is required because a novel situation may not completely match the information stored in a schema, and the system may have to adapt its schema to accommodate the situation it finds itself in. However, it was found that the difficulties in implementing the schema idea in such a way that most of the intuitions were preserved were too great. In order to implement a schema, you have to specify precisely which properties the implemented schema has, and this specification entails that the schema looses most of the flexibility that made it such a useful notion in the first place (see, e.g., Rumelhart, Smolensky, McClelland, & Hinton, 1986). One reason for adopting the PDP approach is a reaction to the fact that structured representations do not have the flexibility and the generality necessary to explain human cognitive behavior.

Another psychologically inspired motivation has to do with the fact that human memory is content addressable. We can access the same piece of information in memory using many different cues. Thus, we can get at the same information from the following diverse cues:

A picture of Richard Burton
The name "Richard Burton"
The description "The most famous of Elizabeth Taylor's husbands"
The description
    "The actor who played the older husband in the film version of
    Who is afraid of Virginia Woolfe" and so on

The content addressability of human memory was also the main motivation behind the development of matchers in frame-based knowledge representation languages. As we shall see, PDP models also support content addressability.

Another attractive feature of PDP models is the fact that they tend to degrade more gracefully. The best way to describe this feature is by contrasting it with the behavior of for example logic-based knowledge representation languages. If you want to retrieve a specific pattern in such a language, then the pattern has to match the information in the knowledge base exactly. If there is no exact match, then the information will not be retrieved. Human memory does not seem to have this all-or-none quality. When presented with a given input, you will probably be able to retrieve the requested information even if the input does not quite match the information that you have stored. Thus, if you were presented with the description:

The American actor who played the older husband in the film
version of *Who is afraid of Virginia Woolfe*

then you will still be able to retrieve the relevant information even if you know that Richard Burton came in fact from Wales. Clearly, PDP models again have the feature of graceful degradation in common with frame-based knowledge representation languages that retrieve the frame which matches the input best.

Another attraction of the PDP models is that systems of this kind are capable of learning. Learning is obviously of prime importance to an intelligent entity. It allows it to use previous experiences in novel situations, thus increasing the chance that it will cope successfully with the situation that it finds itself in. Although learning has received ample attention within the nonconnectionist tradition in AI (see Michalski, Carbonell, & Mitchell, 1984, for an overview), and although its importance has long been recognized, it has not occupied the central position in research into knowledge representation formalisms. It is, however, central to the PDP approach, and given the importance of learning for intelligence, this is another obvious attraction of this approach.

Clearly then there are many motivations and arguments for the PDP approach. In the next two sections we discuss a few PDP models in more detail in the hope that some of the abstract arguments become more concrete.

4. PDP MODELS

As said before, the PDP approach starts with a specification of a machine. The various models within the PDP approach differ in the precise details of the hardware. Although some of these machine specifications have indeed given rise to actual pieces of hardware, for example, the connection machine (Hillis, 1985), most of these specifications are simulated, but this is a reflection on the current state of computer technology. Deciding which of the different specifications is best is still very much a research topic.

A PDP model consists of a large number of units, or nodes. Each node is a very simple processor. The only information that it can store is an activation value. One of the differences between the various PDP models concerns the range of possible activation values that they allow the units to take on. Most models use one of the following three possibilities: First, the activation value is either 0 or 1; second, the activation value can be any real number between −1 and 1; third, the activation value is any real number between 0 and 1. It should be stressed that the units, are very simple objects which can only store activation values. They therefore correspond to what Hinton (1981) calls *microfeatures*, very simple primitive features in terms of which the world could be described.

In PDP networks, there are a large number of connections between the units. In general, connections are unidirectional. Each connection has a connection strength associated with it, where the strength can be any number, positive or negative. Units communicate with each other along the connections. The connections can be interpreted as *microinferences* between the microfeatures as represented by the different units. A positive connection means that whenever one microfeature is present the presence of another microfeature can be "microinferred"; a negative connection licenses a microinference about the absence of the other microfeature.

There are many different possible patterns of connectivity. In the rest of this chapter, the discussion is restricted to two different patterns of connectivity. A first example is a pattern of connectivity in which each unit is connected to all other units. Figure 8.1 provides an example of such a network. The second example is a pattern of connectivity in which the units are organized in layers, with each unit connected only to the units at the next layer up, as illustrated in Figure 8.2.

In order to see how units communicate with each other, recall that each node

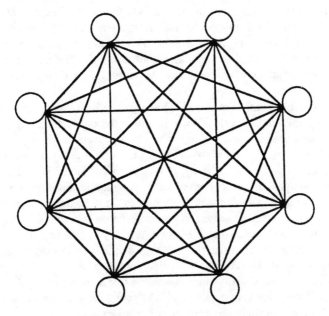

Figure 8.1. Total connectivity.

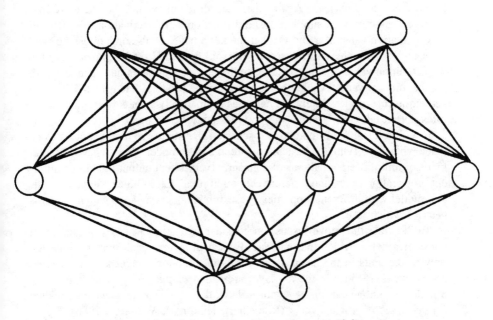

Figure 8.2. A layered pattern of connectivity.

in a network has a certain activation value. On the basis of the activation value, you can determine the *output* of the unit. In many models the output of a unit is simply its activation value, but there are more sophisticated models where the output of the unit is calculated by a threshold function of the activation value. In models of this kind, a unit will only have an output if its activation value exceeds a particular value.

A unit will in general be connected to a large number of other units, and it will be able to communicate with other units along the connections between them. The *input* of a unit i to some other unit j can be calculated by multiplying the output of unit i by the connection strength between i and j. If this number is negative, then i is said to *inhibit j*; if it is positive, then i is said to *excite j*.

Processing in a PDP model is a process of calculating new activation values of units based on the inputs that they receive from the units that they are connected to. This process is called *propagation*. Propagation is a two-stage process. In order to determine the new value of some unit j, you first have to combine the inputs that j receives from the various units that it is connected to into what is called the *net input* of j. The rule by which the inputs are combined is known as the *propagation rule*. Usually, the propagation rule amounts to simply adding the various excitatory inputs to the unit and subtracting the inhibitory inputs to arrive at the net input, but there are more complex propagation rules.

The second stage of the propagation process involves changing the activation values of the units on the basis of their net input. The rule used in this process is called the *activation rule*. Again, there are different possibilities here. A first possibility is to have a simple threshold function as the activation rule: Set the new activation value of a unit i to 1 if the net input exceeds some threshold, and set it to -1 or 0 otherwise. A second possibility is to also take into account the old activation value of a unit, and make the new activation value dependent both on the old activation value and the net input. Models that use this kind of activation rule are less likely to change as dramatically as nets whose activation rules do not take into account the previous activation value.

It will be clear from the above discussion that there are many choices to be made when specifying the basic hardware in a PDP model. We can have different kinds of unit, different patterns of connectivity, different output functions, different propagation rules, and different activation rules. Each choice obviously leads to a model with different properties. Research is underway as to which model is best for which task.

To illustrate the above discussion consider two different types of net. First, consider a net in which the units are divided in layers. Each unit is connected only to the units in the layer above. Units in the bottom layer are called *input* nodes, whereas those in the top layer are called *output* nodes. The units in the middle are known as *hidden* units. Networks of this kind have been called *layered feedforward* networks (Rumelhart, Hinton, & Williams, 1986). Figure 8.3 is an illustration of a layered feedforward network with 4 layers.

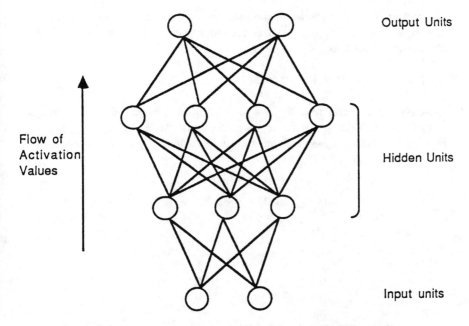

Output Units

Flow of
Activation
Values

Hidden Units

Input units

Figure 8.3. A feedforward net with 2 layers of hidden units.

We consider a layered feedforward net in which all units have as their activation value either 0 or 1. The output of a unit is simply its activation value. We use the following simple propagation rule: Determine the net input of a unit i by summing for each connection between a unit j and i, the product of the output of j and the strength of the connection. We use a threshold function as the activation rule: If the net input to a unit i is above some threshold, then set the activation value of i to 1; if the net input is below the threshold, then set its activation value to 0.

To illustrate the propagation and activation rules, consider Figure 8.4 which depicts a hidden or ouput unit i with the connections feeding into it. The input to node i is calculated by summing the products of the connection strengths and the

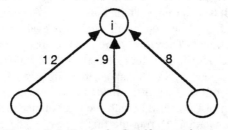

Figure 8.4. Part of a feedforward net.

activation values of the nodes feeding into the connections. Thus, if we assume that all the units feeding into i have an activation value 1, then the input to i in the above configuration is

$$(12 * 1) + (-9 * 1) + (8 * 1) = 11$$

If we assume that the threshold above which i changes its activation value to 1 is 5, then it is clear that given this input the activation value of i will indeed be set to 1. The following table gives the activation value of i given the inputs to the units feeding into it:

Inputs	Value into i	Activation
1 1 1	11	1
1 1 0	3	0
1 0 1	20	0
1 0 0	12	1
0 1 1	-1	0
0 1 0	-9	0
0 0 1	8	1
0 0 0	0	0

One of the motivations behind the PDP approach was the desire to have algorithms that were as parallel as possible. In order to see that propagation can be done in parallel, consider a simple layered feedforward net, in which there is only one layer of hidden units. Thus, we have a layer of input units all connected up to units in the layer of hidden units. In their turn, the units in the layer of hidden units are all connected to units in the output layer. Suppose that to start off with the activation values of all the units in the net is 0. We then feed an input into the net by setting the activation values of the input units. Then the activation values of the hidden units can all be calculated in parallel. Given the pattern of connectivity in this net, the activation value of a node in a layer of hidden units depends only on the activation values of the input units. So, once all activation values of the input units have been determined, the activation values of the hidden units can all be determined at the same time. Whatever changes we make to the activation value of one hidden unit will be irrelevant to the activation value of any other hidden unit. Therefore, there is no temporal ordering between the times at which the activation values of the different hidden units need to be calculated, and we may as well compute them in parallel. Clearly, a similar argument holds from the level of the hidden units to the level of output units.

In a layered feedforward network with one layer of hidden units, we need only two cycles of computation. During the first cycle we calculate new activation values for the hidden units. We also calculate the activation values of the output units during this cycle of the computation, but because the activation values of the hidden units were all 0 when we started this cycle of computation, the activation values of the output nodes will not change. On the second cycle we might again try to calculate the activation values of the hidden units but as the activation values of the input units will not have changed, they will remain the same. However, because the activation values of the hidden units were changed in the previous cycle of computation, the inputs to the output nodes will have changed, and therefore their activation values will now have to change. Thus, on the second cycle of computation, we will determine the activation values of the output nodes. We could go through a third cycle of computation but this clearly would not change any activation values. A network that is in a state where further cycles of computation would not significantly change the activation values of any of its units is said to have *settled into a stable state.*

Obviously, for feedforward networks with more layers of hidden units, we need more cycles of computation before the network settles into a stable state. However, it is easy to see that the network will always settle into a stable state, and that only relatively few cycles of computation are necessary to reach a stable state. However, for systems with more complex patterns of connectivity the situation is not as straightforward. Two problems arise. First, networks may never settle into a stable state. Second, even if they do settle, then this may take a very long time. The next example will illustrate this.

Consider a model in which every node is connected to every other node, such as for example the very simple network in Figure 8.5. We assume that the activation value of a unit in this network is a real number between -1 and 1. The connections in this network are unorthodox in that they are bi-directional. Thus, just as unit i is connected to unit j with connection strength 2, so unit j is connected to unit i with the same connection strength, and so on.

The activation rule that we use in this example is more complicated. However, it has been used in a lot of serious PDP models and it is therefore worthwhile to discuss it in some detail. In order to determine the activation a_i of a unit i, first determine the input into i, $input_i$, simply by summing all the inputs feeding into i. If $input_i$ is positive, then we increase a_i by an amount which depends on the distance between the previous activation level and the highest possible activation level of 1. If $input_i$ is negative, then we decrease a_i by an amount which depends on the distance between the previous activation level and the lowest possible activation level of -1. In addition, there are two global parameters, which set the rates of excitation and decay respectively. The rate of decay D tends to pull a_i back to the resting state 0, whereas the rate of excitation E determines at what rate an activation value should change. A large value for E will give network that changes rapidly, a small value results in a more static network. The propagation rule that is used then is

if $input_i > 0$, then $\Delta a_i = (E * input_i * (1 - a_i)) - Da_i$
if $input_i < 0$, then $\Delta a_i = (E * input_i * (1 + a_i)) - Da_i$

where Δa_i is the amount of change in a_i.

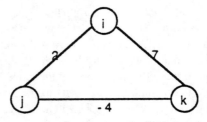

Figure 8.5. A very simple network.

In the remainder of this section we assume that E = .15 and D = .15.

The expression above calculates the amount of change in a_i. Obviously, in order to calculate the activation value of a_i on the next cycle of computation, we will have to add the amount of change to the old value if it is positive, or subtract it if it is negative.

In order to see how the above activation rule works, assume that initially the activation values of i, j and k, a_i, a_j, and a_k, have been set to .5, .3, and $-.4$ respectively. On the first cycle of computation, the input into i is (.3 * 2) + ($-.4$ * 7) = -2.2. The input is negative, and therefore should pull the activation value of i to its lowest possible value of -1. Applying the formula for calculating the amount of change given above, the amount of change for i given this input should be $-.58$. We then subtract this from the previous activation value of i to give the new activation value of $-.08$. The following is a table of the activation values of the units after a number of cycles of computation. The reader can see that the network settles into a stable state after about 10 cycles of computation.

	a_i	a_j	a_k
1	0.50	0.30	−0.40
2	−0.08	0.52	0.14
3	0.25	0.27	−0.34
4	−0.14	0.43	−0.16
5	−0.16	0.39	−0.48
6	−0.47	0.47	−0.62
7	−0.67	0.52	−0.83
8	−0.81	0.58	−0.88
9	−0.84	0.61	−0.90
10	−0.84	0.63	−0.89
11	−0.84	0.63	−0.90
12	−0.84	0.64	−0.90
13	−0.84	0.64	−0.90

By changing the initial activation values of i, j, and k, we may create a different stable state. For example, if we started the network off with the initial values .5, .3, and .6 respectively, it will settle into a stable state with the activation values .83, −.66, and .89 respectively. Thus, by starting off the network in different start states, we can achieve different stable states. This illustrates how even a very simple network can be used to represent different pieces of information. Clearly, a more complicated network will have many more stable states that can be reached, and it thus becomes possible to represent many more different pieces of information.

As said before, there are two problems that may arise in networks of this kind. First, sometimes a network will take very long time to settle into a stable state. For example, even our simple network with just 3 nodes requires 10 cycles of computation before it settles. A more complicated network may take much longer.

A second problem is that a network of this kind may never settle into a (completely) stable state. It may, for example, oscillate between one state and another. The latter happens in the above network, if we change the connection between i and j to 7, and start off the network with activation values of −.4 for both j and k. The network will oscillate between a state in which i has the activation value 1, while j and k have activation value −1, and a state in which i has activation value −1, while j and k both have activation value 1. Hopfield (1982) has shown that in certain cases you can avoid some of these problems if you adopt a different regime for updating activation values: Rather than updating the activation values of all units at the same time, you update the units *asynchronously*. Each unit has a fixed probability that it will update its activation value on a particular cycle of computation. It turns out that this way of updating units can keep networks out of oscillations. The disadvantage is, of course, that you lose the possibility of updating all units in parallel.

5. LEARNING IN PDP MODELS

In the previous section we saw the importance of the connection strengths in determining whether a network will settle at all, and if so, in which stable state. This obviously leads to the problem how to decide values for connection strengths. The way this problem is solved in PDP models is by letting the network itself decide. A network can be trained and learn to make the appropriate response. Learning in a PDP model is, in fact, a very simple process and merely involves changing the strengths on the connections between the different nodes, according to some rule called the *learning* rule. Each PDP model contains in addition to the elements specified in the previous section, a specification of some learning rule. As we will see later on, this simple model of learning turns out to be very powerful.

5.1. Paradigms of learning

Four slightly different types of learning have been studied in the context of PDP models. Rumelhart and Zipser (1985) call these different types of learning different *paradigms of learning*. Before discussing some of the different learning rules that have been proposed, we first briefly describe the different paradigms of learning.

The first paradigm of learning is called *associative* learning. It involves learning associations between certain patterns of activation. Usually, but not necessarily, the input patterns are presented at the input nodes in a layered feedforward net. During the training phase, the output patterns of activation are presented at the output node of the network, and the network is allowed to change the strengths of the connections between the nodes. Training is stopped when the network has learned the association, that is, when for each input and output pattern, if the input pattern is presented at the input nodes, then the output pattern will appear at the output nodes. Thus, when the network has been trained, it will be able to retrieve the output pattern when it is presented with the input pattern. It turns out that quite often a network that has been trained in this way will also be able to retrieve the output pattern even if only part of the input pattern, or a distorted version of it, is given as input. These networks therefore show graceful degradation. Even a partial or distorted input pattern will lead to retrieval of the correct output pattern.

The second type of learning is in fact a special case of associative learning, namely *auto associative* learning. In auto associative learning, the input and the output pattern are always identical. Thus, when presented with an input pattern, a trained network will display the same pattern at its output nodes. Networks of this kind have been used for example in pattern-completion tasks. In such tasks, the network is presented with a partial pattern, or a distorted pattern, and retrieves the stored pattern that most closely matches the partial or distorted pattern. An example of auto associative learning can be found in Kohonen, Oja, and Lehtiö (1981) who trained a network on pictures of human faces. If the network was then presented with a partially obscured, or a distorted, version of a picture that it had seen before, it was able to retrieve the original picture. One might argue that memory in these systems is content addressable. By presenting partial information about a particular item, all the information about this item is retrieved.

The third paradigm of learning is *classification* learning. Again, it is a special case of pattern association. The network is trained to make associations between input patterns and output patterns. However, the output patterns are not unrelated patterns as in associative learning, or identical to the input patterns, as in auto associative learning. Rather, there is a fixed set of patterns which can be thought of as representing different categories. Thus, the goal of classification learning is not to learn arbitrary associations between patterns, or to enable a network to complete partially presented patterns or correct distorted ones; rather, the goal is to train the network to classify input stimuli into classes.

The final paradigm of learning is *regularity discovery*. The idea here is to train the network on a large set of instances of a particular concept, and let it *discover* salient properties of the input patterns which allow the network to classify inputs for itself. Thus, rather than training the net to classify input patterns into pre-defined categories, the network is supposed to discover interesting categories into which the input patterns can be classified for itself. Regularity discovery differs from the previous three learning paradigms in that during the training phase no output is presented at the output nodes. The network is allowed to determine for itself which output it should produce.

5.2. Learning rules

Given these different types of learning, it is perhaps not surprising that a large number of different learning rules have been proposed. However, virtually all learning rules are variants of the *Hebbian* rule. Hebb, one of the first to study PDP-like models, proposed a learning rule in 1949, the simplest formulation of which is:

> If, during the training phase, two units A and B are simultaneously excited, then increase the connection strength between them.

Although all learning rules are variants of the Hebbian rule, there is a great deal of variety in the specific details. We restrict the discussion to three specific learning rules: The *delta rule* proposed by McClelland and Rumelhart (1985), the *generalized delta rule* due to Rumelhart, Hinton, and Williams (1986), and a learning rule called *conjunctive forcing*, proposed by Kohonen, Oja, and Lehtiö (1981).

5.3. The delta rule

In order to understand the delta rule as proposed by McClelland and Rumelhart (1985), it is necessary to say a bit about the particular networks they used. McClelland and Rumelhart assume that the network of connected units can be divided into set of units called *modules*. The units within a module are all connected to each other. Each unit in a module also receives input from units in other modules and sends output to units in some other modules. Figure 8.6 is a very simple example of a system with this kind of architecture.

Restricting ourselves to a single module, we can make a distinction between two types of input to a unit. A unit receives *external* input from units in other modules, and *internal* input from units within the same module. The total input to a unit is then simply the sum of the external and the internal input. The weights of the intermodule links are assumed to be fixed. Therefore, learning can only take place by changing the weights on the connections between the units in the same module.

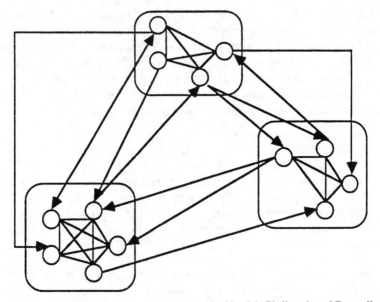

Figure 8.6. An example of the models studed by McClelland and Rumelhart.

Activation values of units are assumed to be between -1 and 1. The activation rule is a slight variant of the second activation rule discussed in section 4. In order to determine the activation of a unit i, we first determine the net input into i, simply by summing the external and the internal input. If the net input into i is positive, then we increase the activation value by an amount which depends on the distance between the previous activation value of i and 1; if the input into i is negative, then we decrease the activation value by an amount which depends in the distance between the previous activation value and -1.

To illustrate the delta rule, suppose that we are training a single module to achieve pattern completion. So, whenever a partial pattern is specified at some of the units in the module, the activation levels of the other units of the module will settle into a state which is identical to the states they were in when the network was trained on the complete pattern. Hence, during the training phase the external inputs to the various units in a module are in a sense the correct ones. Taking a very simple example, suppose that we want to train a module consisting of the 4 units a, b, c, and d on the pattern $+--+$ (where $+$ corresponds to 1 and $-$ to -1), then during the training phase we make sure that the external input to a is $+$, to b is $-$, to c is $-$, and to d is $+$. What we would like to achieve is that after training the internal inputs to the units are identical to the external inputs. If we then present the network with a partially specified pattern, then the internal inputs to the units with no external input will become identical or at least be very close to the external input during the training phase, and as a result the training pattern will be recreated.

Training in networks of this kind consists of two stages. The first stage involves calculating for each unit i, the difference δ_i of the external input and the internal input. The second stage is of the actual adjustment of weights. If there is no difference between the internal and the external input to a unit i, then we do not need to make any changes to the connections into i at this cycle of the learning phase. If δ_i is negative, then the internal units are activating i too much, and the strengths on the connections between the other units in the module and i need to be decreased, whereas, when δ_i is positive, the internal units are not activating i enough and the strengths need to be increased. The weights between unit j and unit i are thus adjusted according to the formula:

$$\Delta w_{ij} = \eta \delta_i a_j$$

where Δw_{ij} represents the *change* in weight on the connection between unit j and i, η is a global strength parameter which regulates the size of the adjustment, and a_j is the activation value of j. If η is large, then the adjustment will always be relatively large, whereas when η is small, the adjustment is smaller. It is a matter of trial and error to find appropriate values for η is.

McClelland and Rumelhart (1985) show that networks trained with the delta rule are able to extract prototypes from sets of patterns, provided that the set of patterns are, in fact, random distortions of the same prototype. Thus, if we trained the network on a set of patterns each of which may represent an individual dog, then after a while the network will complete partial dog patterns in accordance with the prototype, and will more strongly respond to the prototype pattern, even though it has never been explicitly trained on the prototype itself. The network can do this for several prototypes at the same time. For example, the network may contain both dog and cat prototypes. Finally, it turns out to be possible for the network to represent knowledge both of the prototype, and of specific instances of the prototype at the same time. Thus, the network may represent both the dog prototype, and various individual dogs that it has been trained on. This model thus seems to provide a good implementation of at least part of the concept of a schema, something which was problematic for the more traditional approaches in AI.

There are, however, problems with networks of this kind. First, the reader will remember that the PDP approach was partly neurologically inspired; it was hoped that by building a machine that was structurally similar to the human brain, one might to construct a machine that achieves humanlike intelligence. However, the delta rule is not acceptable from a neurological point of view. In order for learning to take place, a unit (or neuron) has to be able to calculate the difference between two inputs. While neurons can compute the sum of two inputs, they are not able to calculate the difference. The main problem is that neurons cannot distinguish between two different inputs. This does not matter for addition as addition is commutative ($a + b = b + a$), but it is important for subtraction as subtraction is not commutative. Therefore, the delta rule cannot be the learning rule used in the brain.

A second problem concerns the range of patterns that can be learned. In order for the model to be able to learn a set of patterns perfectly, the patterns have to obey the *linear predictability constraint*: Over the entire set of patterns, the external input to each unit must be predictable from a linear combination of the activation of every other unit. Without going into the mathematical details (see Jordan, 1986, for a clear introduction), linear predictability roughly means that the value of one unit in a pattern can be found by multiplying the value of the other units by some number (which may be different for the different units) and adding the results. Thus, a pattern like 1001 obeys the linear predictability constraint as the value of each of the four units can be found by multiplying the values of other units by some number and adding the results. For example, the value of the third unit can be found by multiplying each of the other values by 0 and adding the results. Similarly, the value of the first unit can be obtained by multiplying the fourth by 1 and the two others by any number. However, a pattern like 1000 does not obey the linear predictability constraint because the value of the first unit is not predictable from a linear combination of the others: No matter what value we multiply 0 by, the result will always be 0. If the set of patterns thus contains a pattern like this, then it does not obey the linear predictability constraint and cannot be learned by means of the delta rule. Another problem is that if the set of patterns contains patterns that differ in only one position, such as +--+ and +---, then perfect learning is impossible.

There are two ways to avoid this problem. The first is to adopt a more subtle representation of the patterns that one would like the network to learn. Rather than treat each dimension of the stimulus separately, you can use what is called *context-sensitive* or *conjunctive* encoding. The basic idea is to let the representation of each dimension be dependent on the representation of other dimensions of the stimulus. One way of achieving this is by using more units than would seem strictly necessary. Thus, whereas it might seem that a pattern consisting of four elements might be represented in a network of only four units, if the set of patterns does not obey the linear predictability constraint, then one might be able to represent this set of patterns in a network with a larger set of units. For example, if we used five units, and we represented the pattern 0001 by 00011 and 1000 by 10001, then the new set of patterns would obey the linear predictability constraint. In fact, it turns out (rather surprisingly perhaps) that *coarse* coding gives the best results: If you let each unit be activated by many different features in the stimulus, and you let each feature of the stimulus activate a large number of units, then you can represent a large number of patterns with relatively few units (Hinton, McClelland, & Rumelhart, 1986).

A second solution is to use more complex networks. The networks for which the delta rule is appropriate have no hidden units. Rumelhart, Hinton, and Williams (1986) study a generalization of the delta rule, called the *generalized delta rule* which can be used for networks with hidden units. We discuss the generalized delta rule in a later section. However, first we discuss an application of the delta rule to a problem of realistic complexity.

5.3.1. Learning past tenses of English verbs

An interesting application of the delta rule is a model of how children learn past tenses of English verbs. This model was proposed by Rumelhart and McClelland (1986). It has become the focus of a lot of attention, and it is worthwhile to discuss it in some detail. We first review what psychologists have discovered about the way in which children learn past tenses of English verbs.

Children learning past tense formation go through three distinct stages. During stage 1, they can produce the past tenses of only a small number of verbs. Most of these verbs are high-frequency and are irregular. Examples are *came*, *got*, *went*, *took*, *gave*, and so on. The crucial point is that children apparently use the correct past tense of these verbs. During stage 2, children seem to acquire implicit knowledge of a linguistic rule. There are three phenomena that point to this. First, children start to use the past tenses of many more verbs. These past tenses are regular, for example, *wiped*, *pulled*, *kicked*. Second, children will generate past tenses for invented words. Thus, if you can persuade a child that *rick* describes some action, then they will generate the form *ricked* when the action described by *rick* is seen to have taken place in the past. Third, children now overgeneralize and use the past tense rule even to irregular verbs. Thus, whereas during stage 1 they could produce the past tense of *come* as *came*, they will now generate forms like *comed* and *camed*, adding the past tense morpheme *-ed* to the root of the verb and the irregular past tense respectively. Stage 3, finally, is the adult stage in which the child realizes that some verbs have regular past tenses, whereas other are exceptions to the general past tense rule.

The way in which children learn past tense formation has always been considered to be a prime illustration of the fact that children, when they acquire their native language, seem to acquire and follow rules. Their behavior in stage 2 strongly suggests this. Therefore, it seems most appropriate to assume that linguistic knowledge is stored in the mind in the form of rules (although admittedly are not directly accessible to the child as they cannot consciously report them). However, Rumelhart and McClelland claim that this behavior can also be achieved by training a PDP model according to the delta rule, and that it is therefore unnecessary to invoke rules in order to explain it.

Rumelhart and McClelland used a relatively simply network for their simulation. The core of the network, the *pattern associator*, is a simple two-layered system consisting of a layer of input nodes and a layer of output nodes. The input

Encoding network   Pattern associator   Decoding network

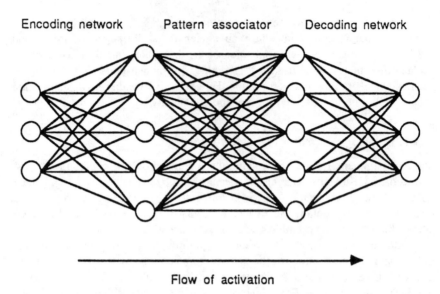

Flow of activation

Figure 8.7. The network used for learning past tense formation.

nodes are hooked up to a fixed encoding network which encodes the inputs (which are the stems of verbs), and the output nodes provide input to a fixed decoding network which decodes the output. Figure 8.7 illustrates this kind of network. The picture is simplified in that it contains far fewer units than the model that Rumelhart and McClelland actually used.

The reason for using encoding and decoding networks is that the model uses a special representation of phonological information called *Wickelfeatures*. This representation makes it easier to represent the different root forms of English and their past tenses. It also makes it easier for generalizations to emerge. However, the encoding and decoding networks are fixed and all the learning takes place in the pattern associator according to the delta rule.

Wickelfeatures are based on the idea of Wickelphones. Wickelphones are a useful representational technique in the context of PDP models as they allow one to represent a word, which is an ordered string of phonemes, as an unordered set. A Wickelphone is a triple consisting of a phoneme as well as the preceding and the following phoneme in some word. Using # for word boundaries (and assuming a very simple and naive notation of phonemes), one can represent a word like *hit* as the set {#hi, hit, it#} and something like *stand* as {#st, sta, tan, and, nd#}. It will be clear that given a representation of a word as an (unordered) set of Wickelphones, one can in general reconstruct the word. Hence, give the set {lt#, #wi, ilt, wil} it is relatively straightforward to reconstruct the word *wilt*. The main problem with Wickelphones is that there are too many of them, and Rumelhart and McClelland therefore devise the more parsimonious representation of Wickelfeatures. However, since their specific representation is not crucial to the present discussion, we will not discuss any further details.

During the training phase the system is presented with the stem of the verb at its input nodes (e.g., *come*) and the past tense of this verb (*came*) at its output nodes. The encoding and decoding network then transform these into sets of Wickelfeatures. During training, the decoding network case works in the reverse order from the way in which it normally works. Normally, it takes a representation of Wickelfeatures and will transform it into an English word. However, during the training phase, it takes the representation of an English word and transforms it into a set of Wickelfeatures.

Once the input and output are encoded, learning can take place. The output nodes of the pattern associator receive input both from the decoding network and from the input nodes of the pattern associator. By treating the input from the decoding network as input from an external module, and treating the input from the pattern associator as internal input, the model can apply the delta rule. Thus, it can find the difference between internal and external input by subtracting for each output node in the pattern associator the input fed into it from the decoding network and the input that it receives from the input nodes in the pattern associator. This difference can then be used to change the weights on the connections in the pattern associator.

The network was trained in three stages. During the first stage, it was trained on the stems and past tenses of 10 high-frequency verbs 8 of which had irregular pasts. One each pair the network went through 10 cycles of presentation. This was enough to teach the model the past tenses of these verbs, and after 10 trials the model seemed to behave in exactly the same way as a child in stage 1.

During the second stage of the trial, 410 medium-frequency verbs were added to the initial 10 verbs and the network was trained 190 times on each of the 420 pairs. The responses of the network early on in this training phase were similar to children in stage 2 of their development, that is, the network would incorrectly overgeneralize and made the pasts of irregular verbs regular (producing *comed*) or use double-marked past forms (yielding *camed*), and was able to form regular pasts of verbs it had never seen before. Towards the end of the 190 training trials, the network was behaving like an adult, and would produce the correct past tenses of the different verbs.

Rumelhart and McClelland claim that their model captures the basic three stages that a child goes through during its acquisition of past tenses of the English verbs, and that it can respond appropriately both to novel verbs that it has never encountered before as well as to regular and irregular verbs that it has come across. They claim to have provided a reasonable account of the acquisition of past without using any rules (Rumelhart & McClelland, 1986).

We return to the Rumelhart and McClelland model and their claims in a later section when we discuss the various criticisms of connectionist approaches. For the moment, let us simply observe that they seem to have produce a model that appears to go through the same stages as a child when it learns past tenses of English verbs.

5.4. The generalized delta rule

One of the limitations of the delta rule is that it is only applicable to networks with no hidden units. Networks of this kind were studied by Rosenblatt (1962) who called them *perceptrons*. Rosenblatt believed that perceptrons were powerful enough to form the basis of AI. Minsky and Papert (1969) analyzed perceptrons in detail and discovered that there were certain functions that could not be computed by perceptrons, unless one was prepared to accept an absurdly large number of units. For example, they showed that perceptrons could not calculate parity, that is, perceptrons cannot be used to determine whether a given input pattern contains an odd or an even number of units with an activation value of 1. Another restriction that we have already come across is the linear predictability contraint. Modern-day PDP researchers have therefore turned to networks with multiple layers of units, and generalizations of the delta rule have therefore been necessary.

Rumelhart, Hinton, and Williams (1986) propose a generalization of the delta rule, which they call the *generalized delta rule*. The generalized delta rule makes it possible to train multilayered networks. They studied in particular feedforward networks. The idea is to present the network with patterns at the input and output nodes during the training phase, and more or less let it determine itself what features in the inputs the hidden units should correspond to. This of course contrasts with attempts at avoiding the problem posed by the linear predictability constraint by complicating the representation of the inputs.

Training a network again involves two distinct phases. We represent an input pattern at the input nodes and an output pattern at the output nodes. The output pattern at the output nodes can be called the *desired output* or the *target pattern*. During the first phase, we let the network calculate the output pattern for the given input pattern given the strengths on the connections that it has at the moment. The actual output is then compared to the desired output, and the network calculates for each unit an error signal. Calculation of the error signal is a recursive process, and starts with calculating the error signals for the output units. Simplifying a little, the error signal for the output units is the difference between the target output and the actual output. Thus, the error signal δ_{pj} for some output unit j, given the input pattern p is given by:

$$\delta_{pj} = t_{pj} - o_{pj}$$
where o_{pj} is the actual output at node j
and t_{pj} is the desired output.

Calculating the error signal for the hidden units is a bit more difficult as there is no specific target value for them. After all, part of the motivation behind the generalized delta rule is to let the network decide for itself what the hidden units correspond to. The error signal for a hidden unit is the sum of the error signal of the units it is connected to multiplied by the weight of the connection. Thus, the error signal δ_{pj} for some hidden unit j given the input pattern p is given by

$$\delta_{pj} = \sum_{k} \delta_{pk} w_{kj}$$

where w_{kj} is the weight of the connection between unit j and unit k.

The way in which the error signal for hidden units (and incidentally input units) is calculated thus involves a backward pass which is analogous to the initial forward pass through the network. This backward pass is called *backward propagation*, as the error signals on the output units are propagated backward through the network.

Having calculated the error signals for all the units in a network, one can engage in learning which, as in the case of the delta rule, simply involves changing the weights on the connections. In fact, one can use exactly the same equations. If the actual output and the desired output do not differ, then no learning needs to take place. Otherwise, we calculate the weight changes for each connection according to the rule

$$\Delta w_{ij} = \eta \delta_{pi} a_{pj}$$

where Δw_{ij} is the rate of change in the connection beween units j and i
a_{pj} is the activation value of unit j given input pattern p
δ_{pi} is the error signal for unit i given input signal p
η is a global strength parameter.

The generalized delta rule is simply a generalization of the delta rule that allows it to cope with networks with hidden units. The generalization comes about because of the idea of backward propagation which allows you to calculate the error signals of the hidden units. Apart from this, the basic mechanisms are very similar to the delta rule.

An interesting aspect of networks that use the generalized delta rules as their learning rule is the fact that under certain circumstances some of the hidden units would seem to correspond quite closely to "higher-level" features of the input. This happens, in particular, in a network with an hour-glass appearance with a relatively small number of hidden units compared to the number of input and output units.

One problem with this approach is the question of which feature each hidden unit corresponds to. An interesting attempt at answering this question can be found in Rosenberg (1987). Rosenberg used standard statistical techniques, such as hierarchical clustering and cluster analysis, in an effort to reveal the structure of the internal representations of NETtalk. NETtalk is a connectionist speech synthesis system which can translate a written word into (a phonetic description of) an acoustic speech signal. NETtalk was trained on pairs of written words and phonetic descriptions of these words in a two-layered feedforward network by means of the generalized delta rule. NETtalk contains 80 hidden units, and Rosenberg tried to discover what features the hidden units corresponded to. He was able to divide the hidden units into separate clusters, each of which responded to a particular feature. For example, there was a major division between units that respond to consonants, and those that respond to vowels. Rosenberg was able partly to explain the structure of the hidden units in his net, although he could not say for each individual hidden unit what feature it exactly corresponded to. While he made some progress in revealing the structure of the internal representation of a network, he did not succeed in completely determining its structure. We return to this problem in section 6.1.

We have already said that the generalized delta rule is a simple generalization of the delta rule. In fact, if we apply the generalized delta rule to networks with no hidden units, then it behaves exactly like the delta rule. However, because it is a straightforward generalization, it inherits the problem that it cannot be neurologically real. Another neurological problem with backward propagation is the fact that in the brain a signal can travel in only one direction on the link between two neurons. Thus, if there is an axon between neuron 1 and neuron 2, then the signal can only travel along this axon from neuron 1 to neuron 2 and not the other way around. There may, of course, be other pathways from neuron 2 to neuron 1. However, for the generalized delta rule to work, one would have to assume that for any pair of neurons, if neuron 1 has an axon connecting it to neuron 2, then there must be an alternative pathway from neuron 2 to neuron 1. The brain does not seem to obey this constraint.

5.5. Conjunctive forcing

A final learning rule that we discuss can be found in Kohonen, Oja, and Lehtiö (1981). It is called *conjunctive forcing* (not to be confused with conjunctive encoding mentioned in the discussion of the delta rule). It has the advantage over both the delta and the generalized delta rule of being neurologically plausible. Kohonen *et al.* propose a *laminar network model*, which is similar to the modular structure used by McClelland and Rumelhart as discussed in the context of the delta rule: There are a large number of subsystems with a high degree of interaction within the subsystems, and weaker interactions between the various subsystems. In the Kohonen et al. networks, each subsystem consists of a single layer of units. It receives input from one or more other subsystems, and sends output to one or more subsystems. However, in addition, some or all of the output is also fed back into the subsystem itself. Thus each unit in a subsystem receives input from units in other subsystems as well as from all or some of the other units in the subsystem (possibly including itself), and sends output to units in other subsystems as well as all the units in its own subsystem. Figure 8.8 is an illustration of a subsystem of this kind.

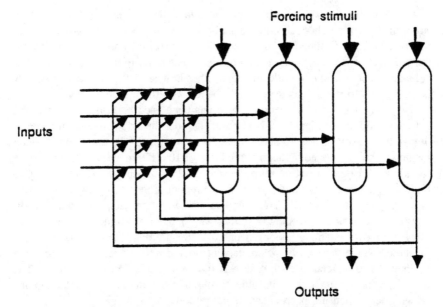

Figure 8.8. A subsystem in the network studied by Kohonen and his associates. Note that units are represented as lozenges and not as circles.

As in the earlier network, the input lines from some unit j into some unit i have a strength associated with them. Kohonen et al. use the term *synaptic conductivity*, and write m_{ji}. Clearly, the synaptic connection m_{ji} is the same as the connection strength w_{ij} (although, to confuse matters, w_{ij} denotes the strength of the connection between j and i, whereas m_{ij} denotes the synaptic connection between i and j.) In order to make the terminology consistent we use the term connection strength and use the notation w_{ij}.

In order for learning to take place in systems of this kind, one needs a *forcing stimulus*, which is simply a representation of the response one would like the network to learn whenever it is presented with the input stimulus. Each output unit then receives its own forcing stimulus, which is identical to the activation value that the unit should take on in the required output. However, in contrast to the earlier two learning rules, the output units are not clamped to ensure that their activation value is identical to the required output. Rather, the forcing stimulus merely acts as an additional input to the output units. The output of a unit is determined by adding the forcing stimulus to the inputs of the various other inputs, the latter multiplied by the connection strengths. So, the output of some unit j, r_j, is calculated as follows:

$$r_j = \sum_i (w_{ji} s_i) + f_i$$

where f_j is the forcing stimulus into j.

Learning takes place by changing the connection strengths. A connection strength w_{ij} will be changed however only when both f_i and s_j are positive. The rate of change is obtained by multiplying f_i, s_j, and some constant λ, indicating the *plasticity* of the connection. The role of λ is similar to the constant η in the delta and generalized delta rule and determines how large the changes will be. A large λ leads to rapid change; a smaller λ leads to more gradual change.

The conjunctive forcing learning rule has been used both in associative and auto-associative learning. After being trained under the associative learning paradigm, the network is able to classify patterns. Kohonen, Oja, and Lehtiö trained the network on digitized pictures of the faces of 10 different people. They choose faces only for demonstration purposes and not because they were attempting to build a psychologically valid model of face recognition. Each person's face was photographed from five different angles. The input in each case was the digitalized picture. The forcing stimulus was a pattern unique to that person, representing for example his or her name. After training, the network was then presented with a picture of a person taken from a different angle. The output that the network produced in each case was the pattern unique to that person. The network thus turned out to be able to classify the picture, even though the viewing angle had not been encountered before.

Kohonen, Oja, and Lehtiö also trained their network using the auto-associative learning paradigm. Because the output of an output unit j is fed back into the network, the activation value of j will affect the behavior of all the other output units. Each part of forcing stimulus is therefore conditioned with all the other parts of the forcing stimulus, and as a result it becomes possible to use any part of the forcing stimulus as a key to retrieve the whole forcing stimulus. In auto associative learning, the input and required output are identical. In conjunctive forcing, this means that in the learning phase the input and the forcing stimulus are identical. Since we can use any part of the forcing stimulus as a key to the entire forcing stimulus, we can use any part of the pattern to retrieve the entire pattern. Clearly, this is exactly what we want when we are interested in pattern completion. Kohonen, Oja, and Lehtiö illustrate the power of their implementation by training (in the auto-associative learning paradigm) the network on a set of digitalized human faces and showing that even if the network is presented with a partially obscured face, or with a severely distorted picture of a face, the network will still be able to recognize the face in the sense that it retrieves the matching face from the original set from which the input has been derived. It thus seems as if the network is able to achieve pattern completion and pattern enhancement. A word of caution: Even if the network is presented with a partially obscured new face, or a distorted picture of a new face, it will still retrieve one of the original faces, namely the one that most resembles the input.

6. CRITICISMS OF THE PDP APPROACH

In the previous sections of this chapter, we explained the basic ideas behind PDP models, and presented some of the arguments that have been put forward in favor of them. In this section, we will look at some of the criticisms that have been leveled against the PDP approach.

Pinker and Prince (1988) distinguish between three views that one can take of the relationship between the PDP approach and the "traditional" symbol-processing approach. The first is to see PDP models as a level between symbol processing and neural hardware. PDP models would simply be implementations of the basic operations that are necessary in symbol processing. For example, PDP models could implement matching, a basic operation that is necessary in many different knowledge representation languages. PDP implementations might force revisions in traditional models, for example, because certain operations used in traditional languages might be neurologically implausible, or because certain complex chains of operations can be done in one step in the brain. But the distinction between hardware and symbol-processing would remain. Pinker and Price dub this view of PDP models *implementational connectionism*.

A second possibility is that PDP models will completely replace symbol-processing models. It would be impossible to find any relationships between the operations of a PDP model and the operations necessary in symbol-processing models. The explanation of cognitive behavior would be solely in physical terms, and there would be no need for symbol-processing models in order to explain human cognitive behavior. At best, symbol-processing models have some heuristic value. Pinker and Prince call this *eliminative connectionism*. The Rumelhart and McClelland model of language acquisition would seem to be an example of this strand of PDP modeling.

The third possible view lies between implementational and eliminative connectionism. Rather than merely implementing symbol-processing models or rather than eliminating models of this kind, one can imagine that symbol-processing models will need to be radically revised because of connectionist models. It might well be the case that the primitive information processing operations that emerge from a PDP model are very different from the primitive operations that one would postulate on the basis of a study of cognitive behavior independent of neural implementation. This may lead to radically different symbol-processing theories. Thus, rather than taking a traditional symbol-processing theory and trying to implement it, one starts off with building a set of PDP models. One derives a set of primitive operations from these, and uses these in constructing new symbol-processing theories. Pinker and Prince call this view of connectionism *revisionist-symbol-processing connectionism*.

Most of the PDP work to date can be classified either as implementational connectionism or as eliminative connectionism. Although revisionist-symbol-processing connectionism is perhaps the most interesting possibility, the PDP approach is too new to have come up with a reliable set of primitive information-processing operations that the brain is good at. It would, therefore, seem premature to start rebuilding one's symbol-processing theories on the basis of the PDP work that has been done so far. There have been relatively few attacks on implementational connectionism. Many cognitive scientists seem to accept the value of PDP models as implementations of traditional symbol-processing theories. However, the eliminative view has received a lot of criticism. In the remainder of this section, we discuss some of these criticisms in some detail.

6.1. Are PDP models adequate theories?

A first criticism concerns the value of PDP models, at least those proposed in eliminative connectionism, as psychological theories. One would expect a theory to provide explanations of its subject matter and to make predictions. It is not clear that PDP models do either of these. To what extent is building a machine that simulates some aspect of human cognitive behavior an explanation of this aspect of human cognitive behavior, if we cannot really understand what is going on inside the machine? All we know is that certain PDP models simulate certain aspects the processes in the human brain. All this seems to tell us is that human cognitive behavior can be implemented in mechanisms that mimic the human brain. But this is hardly surprising as each of us constitutes an existence proof of this claim. An exception to this criticism is of course the work by Rosenberg who tries to determine more precisely what the hidden units in a particular connectionist model represent, and in this way hopes to get more insight in the type of processing that the machine is engaged in.

Eliminative connectionists may retort that this criticism misses the point and that a proper theory of the human cognitive system is in terms of neurology. Although there have been proponents of this reductionist position throughout the history of science (not necessarily just from psychology to neurology, but also from, e.g., economics to physics), the most powerful argument against this position is that there are particular generalizations that can only be formulated at higher levels of description. The fact that children all go through similar stages during their cognitive development is a generalization that can only be formulated at the level of psychology. It is hardly likely that this general fact can be described in terms of identical changes in the connections between identical neurons in all children. Fodor (1975) contains a very convincing rejection of the strong reductionist position. He comes to the conclusion that a more acceptable form of reductionism is one where theories at higher levels take into account restrictions that arise out of theories of the underlying levels. So, sociological theories should take into account restrictions that follow from psychological theories, and should not postulate processes which are considered to be impossible by psychologists. Similarly, psychological theories should take into account limitations that arise out of our theories about the processes that take place in the brain. Clearly, if this is the correct position to take, then eliminative connectionism, which is a form of strong reductionism, will have to be given up in favor of revisionist-symbol-processing connectionism, which would seem to be closer to the weaker form of reductionism.

6.2. PDP representations lack the necessary structure

Fodor and Pylyshyn (1988) argue that the basic bone of contention between what Pinker and Prince call eliminative connectionism and "traditional" cognitive science does not concern the role of representations in the explanation of cognitive behavior. Both agree that there are states of mind which function to encode states of the world. The main issue on which PDP theoreticians and more traditional cognitive scientists disagree concerns the primitive relations that hold between the basic content-bearing entities in the representations. According to the connectionist, for whom the basic content bearing entities are the nodes in a network, the only relation between the nodes is *causal connectedness*. One node can only influence another node in virtue of the fact that the first node is connected to the second node with a certain strength. Classical cognitive scientists, on the other hand, can also make use of a range of structural relations, of which *constituency* is one. Thus, a classical cognitive scientist may describe a given symbol as part of a larger representation, and may make use of this structural relationship in explaining a given cognitive phenomenon. Such talk of constituency makes no (direct) sense to the connectionist.

This basic disagreement comes to the fore in two essential ways. First, classical cognitive scientists take mental representations to have a *combinatorial syntax and semantics*. The assumption claim comprises three subclaims: First, it is assumed that there is a distinction between structurally atomic and structurally molecular representations. Second, structurally molecular representations have syntactic constituents that are either themselves structurally molecular or structurally atomic. Finally, the semantic content of a molecular representation is a function of the semantic contents of its constituent parts and the way in which they have been combined to form the molecular representation. The reader will have been reminded of the discussion of logic in Chapter 3. Logic probably provides the best illustration of these three claims: We distinguished between primitive expressions (as specified in the vocabulary of a logical language) and nonprimitive expressions, and gave a number of syntactic rules for combining expressions into larger, nonprimitive expressions. We also said that logical languages obeyed the principle of compositionality: The meaning of a large expression could be constructed from the meanings of its constituent expressions, and the way in which these expressions were combined syntactically to yield the larger expression. Clearly, all the other knowledge representation languages that we discussed obeyed these principles as well.

The second basic claim underlying the classical conception of representation is that processes are assumed to be sensitive to the *structure* of the representations. The operations that take place in the mind take into account the syntactic structure of the mental representations, and can be described with reference to the structure of the input representation. A corollary of this position is that structural properties can be defined at any level of abstraction, and one can therefore make use of variables in a description of mental operations. For example, in a model of inference one may claim that the mind uses the following rule: from (P & Q), infer P, where P and Q are variables. Thus, the above rule holds no matter what value P and Q have, and the inference rule can be applied independently of whether we are talking about the weather, football results, or mathematics. If one does not believe that mental representations are structured, then one cannot use such variables: A variable is basically a place holder for part of a structure, and if there is no structure, then one cannot use such place holders. If every representation is a primitive representation, then variables are of no use, since a variable could only stand for the entire class of representations.

The PDP representations proposed by eliminative connectionists in general do not obey these two principles. First, PDP representations have no internal structure. A PDP representation of a sentence like *the boy loves the girl* is holistic in the sense that there is no constituent part which can be regarded as the representation of the clause *the boy*. Information is represented in the state of activation of the entire network, and it is in general not the case that one can point to a part of the network and say that this is the representation of a particular part of the information represented by this particular state of activation. Second, because PDP representations have no internal structure, it is obviously not possible for processes to be structure sensitive. In fact, the distinction between process and representation that underlies much of "classic" cognitive science is not drawn at all in PDP models. A network that has gone through its training phase both represents and processes information.

A consequence of this lack of structure in PDP representations is that PDP models in general do not allow variables. Norman (1986) argues that variables are necessary to account for conscious, deliberate thought, planning, and problem solving. As PDP representations lack this ability, Norman comes to the (tentative) conclusion that PDP models are perhaps fundamentally limited to dealing with those parts of cognition that are closer to perception or to motor output.

The lack of structure in connectionist representations also underlies Fodor and Pylyshyn's arguments. Having argued that the main difference between classical and connectionist models concerns the question as to whether mental representations are structured or not, Fodor and Pylyshyn then give a number of arguments which they see as conclusive evidence that mental representations must indeed be structured, and that PDP models therefore are not adequate.

The Fodor and Pylyshyn argument that we will concentrate on is *systemat-*

icity. Fodor and Pylyshyn claim that our linguistic capacities are systematic in the sense that the ability to produce and understand some sentences is *intrinsically* connected to the ability to produce or understand certain other sentences. For example, if you understand the sentence *the boy loves the girl*, then you also understand the sentence *the girl loves the boy*. Linguists have concluded from the systematicity of our linguistic capabilities that sentences must have a syntactic and semantic structure.

Fodor and Pylyshyn argue that thought is systematic as well. They point out that just as it is impossible to be able to understand the sentence *the boy loves the girl* without also being able understand the sentence *the girl loves the boy*, it is impossible to be able to think the thought *the boy loves the girl* without also being able to think the thought *the girl loves the boy*. Clearly, if one infers that language has a constituent structure from the systematicity of our linguistic abilities, then one would have to infer that our mental representations have a constituent structure from the systematicity of our cognitive abilities.

The systematicity of thought is hard to account for in the connectionist approach. In a PDP model every representation is in fact atomic. Representing a piece of information in a network amounts to the network settling in a stable state of activation, and there is no clear one-to-one correspondence between certain parts of this state of activation and particular parts of the information that is represented. Thus, if a given state of activation represents *the boy loves the girl*, there is no part of this state of activation which represents *the boy*. As a result, the state of activation in which the network is interpreted as representing *the boy loves the girl* need have nothing in common with the state of activation in which the network represents *the girl loves the boy*. Therefore, there is no intrinsic reason why a network that can be in a state corresponding to *the boy loves the girl* should also be able to settle in a state that corresponds to *the girl loves the boy*.

Closely related to the systematicity argument is the *compositionality* argument. Fodor and Pylyshyn point out that the systematic connections between sentences in a language are not arbitrary. It is not the case that being able to understand the sentence *the boy loves the girl* means that you also have to able to understand the sentence *the cat is on the mat*. Rather it seems to be the case that systematically related sentences are also semantically related. This is not entirely accounted for just in terms of systematicity: You also need to assume that the contributions made by each word to the entire sentence is more or less identical from one sentence to the other. *the girl* must mean roughly the same in both *the boy loves the girl* and *the girl loves the boy*, that is, you need something like the principle of compositionality. Again, PDP models do not account for this.

Thus, to summarize Fodor and Pylyshyn's argument: The systematicity of thought, and its compositionality, indicate that mental representations are structured. PDP models cannot represent any such structure and therefore inadequate as accounts of mental phenomena.

6.3. Rumelhart and McClelland's past tense model revisited

In an earlier section we discussed the PDP model of the acquisition of past tense proposed by Rumelhart and McClelland (1986). The Rumelhart and McClelland model has achieved the status of a paradigmatic example of what PDP models are capable of, partly because language has always been thought of as "a prototypical example of how fundamental properties of a cognitive domain can be explained within the symbolic paradigm" (Pinker & Prince 1988). Pinker and Prince present a very detailed analysis of this model, and come to the conclusion that the claims that Rumelhart and McClelland make for their model do not stand up. In this section, we discuss Pinker and Prince's criticism in some detail, because it raises a number of issues which go beyond the issue of whether the Rumelhart and McClelland model is correct.

Pinker and Prince start off with a critical analysis of the general linguistic assumptions underlying Rumelhart and McClelland's model, and the use of Wickelfeatures in particular. The reader will remember that the input and output to the pattern associator in which learning took place were sets of Wickelfeatures. One of the reasons for using Wickelfeatures was that it enabled Rumelhart and McClelland to represent strings as unordered sets of entities.

There are a number of arguments against Wickelfeatures. The first argument against Wickelfeatures is that they do not allow you to represent certain classes of words unambiguously. Pinker and Prince give the example of the Australian language Oykangand which contains for the string *algal* (meaning "straight") and *algalgal* (meaning "ramrod straight"). Since words are represented as *sets* of Wickelfeatures, multiple occurrences of the same Wickelfeature are reduced to one. As a result, both *algal* and *algalgal* are represented by the set {#al, alg, lga, gal, al#}. The fact that the Wickelfeatures *alg*, *lga* and *gal* occur twice in *algalgal* is irrelevant as the whole string is represented as a set. Wickelfeature representations are therefore potentially ambiguous.

One might simply argue that this means that words should not be represented as *sets* of Wickelfeatures, but rather as *bags*, collections of items in which order is irrelevant but in which multiple occurrences of some item cannot be reduced. However, this is not possible given the basic architecture of the Rumelhart and McClelland model. For each Wickelfeature, there is exactly one input node and exactly one output node in the pattern associator part of the network. Therefore, in order to be able to represent words like *algalgal*, one would have to duplicate the number of input and output nodes corresponding to each Wickelfeature. However, new problems then arise: How many duplications of each Wickelfeature do we need, and can we still write the coding and decoding networks that form an integral part of the Rumelhart and McClelland network?

A second argument against Wickelfeatures is that an adequate notation should exclude the impossible, an argument regularly used by linguists. Here, Wickelfeature representations do not fare particularly well either. For example, Pinker and Prince point out that no language in the world seems to have the transformation of relating a string to its mirror image reversal (e.g., *pit* to *tip*, *garb* to *brag*, etc.). However, it is as easy to learn this transformation in a pattern associator as it is to learn auto association.

Rumelhart and McClelland might argue that the requirement that the representation excludes the impossible places too heavy a burden on the representation. Why should a representation be asked to carry this burden? You could just argue that impossible transformations are never learned because they do not occur in any language, and therefore never occur in any training set.

However, this rejoinder is dubious: If certain phenomena never occur in any natural language, then a theory that explains this on the basis of (assumptions about) the structure of the cognitive mechanisms responsible for language use is preferable to one which has to put the burden on the input that the language learner receives. After all, explaining the fact that a given natural language does not exhibit these phenomena on the basis of the language as spoken to the child begs the question why the language did not contain these particular rules in the first place.

Pinker and Prince also attack Rumelhart and McClelland's model because of its lack of a separate level of morphology or lexical items. Morphology is the study of the internal structure of words. In the Rumelhart and McClelland model past tenses are formed because of a direct and uniform mapping from a phonetic representation of the input into a phonetic representation of the output. The problem with this is that certain (morphological) regularities that can be seen in past tense formation are also at work in other morphological processes in English. For example, Pinker and Prince point out that regular past tenses are formed by putting either [id], [t] or [d] after the stem of the word depending on whether the final segment was a [t] or [d] itself (as in *pat* and *pad*), voiceless (as in *work*) or voiced (as in *flog*). However, a similar regularity can also be found when it comes to forming the (regular) plural of a noun in English, or forming the third person singular of a regular (verb), or putting the possessive marker after an English noun phrase. In each case, the distribution of [iz], [s] and [z] depends on identical factors. Thus, if the final segment in a singular noun is [s] or [z] (as in *loss* or *hose*), the plural is formed by adding [iz]; if the final segment is voiceless (as in *cork*), [s] is added; if the final segment is voiced (as in *dog*), [z] is added. Rumelhart and McClelland would have to postulate a different network for each of these processes in English, and it would be impossible for the brain to make use of this morphological regularity in English. Similarly, there are certain regularities and processes that can only be formulated if there is a separate level notion of a lexical item. The lack of a separate morphological level echoes Norman's criticism of the lack of variables in PDP models.

Apart from these essentially linguistic arguments, Pinker and Prince also examine the achievements of the theory as a model of how children acquire past tenses, and they find it wanting in this respect too. Pinker and Prince first look at the performance of the final system. The model does not always give one response, but rather produces several candidates with an associated strength. Rumelhart and McClelland interpret this strength as the likelihood with which a particular response will be generated. Thus, the higher the strength, the more likely an adult is to produce this form. In order to rule out responses that are entirely due to noise, they decide that only those responses with a strength more than 0.2 count as generated responses.

With this in mind, we can now look at the responses that were generated by the model after it had been trained on the entire training set. Of the final 72 stems on which the final system was tested, 6 (*jump, pump, soak, warm, trail,* and *glare*) showed no response that was above the threshold, and hence can be interpreted as not yielding any response. For 18 other stems, the model gave more than one response. Of these, 4 gave very strange candidates. For example, the system proposed *membled* as the past tense of *mail*. Three others past tenses were not systematic. For example, the past tense of *brown* was given as *brawned*. Finally, 7 others contained the past tense morpheme twice, for example, *type* gave as result *typeded*. The 4 other stems gave wrong but potentially sensible results: For example, *shape* yielded *shipt*, *sip* gave *sept*, and *slip* yielded *slept*, possibly due to interference with the past tenses *kept* and *slept*. Thus, of the 18 verbs for which there was more than one response, (at least) 14 gave results that were not expected. On a test set of 72 verbs, this is a considerable number, and one is therefore tempted to agree with Pinker and Prince's conclusion: "What we have here is not a model of the mature system."

Pinker and Prince also have a close look at the developmental evidence, and suggest that the Rumelhart and McClelland model fails here too. Rumelhart and McClelland claim, for example, that their model neatly accounts for the three stages that the child goes through. However, as Pinker and Prince rightly point out, the system only goes from stage 1 to stage 2, and from stage 2 to stage 3, due to changes in the environment, that is, due to the fact that Rumelhart and McClelland train the network on another training set. Thus, in order for them to be able to claim that their model is correct, they will have to show that the linguistic input to a child changes radically around or just before the child goes from one stage to the next.

Rumelhart and McClelland have one argument in favor of this position, namely that the verbs on which the network is trained initially have the highest frequency in English and are therefore most likely to be encountered by the child. This observation seems reasonable, but according to Pinker and Prince is unfortunately false. Grammars of early speech show that the number of regular verbs used by young children, is surprisingly consistent at around 50 percent. Furthermore, Slobin (1971) found that the percentage of regular verbs in the speech of the parents of young children was similar at 43 percent. There therefore seems to be no reason to believe that there is a marked shift in the number of regular verbs that the child is exposed to when it goes from stage 1 to stage 2. The explanation put forward by Rumelhart and McClelland would therefore seem to be false.

Another argument against the Rumelhart and McClelland model concerns the way in which the pattern associator is trained. During training, Rumelhart and McClelland present the past tense at the output nodes and the stem of the verb at the input nodes. Viewed as a psychological claim, this means that the child somehow is aware of a special relationship between past and present tenses of some verbs. But there is evidence that it is not. Instead the child simply seems to memorize past tenses in much the same way as it memorizes present tenses without being aware of a relationship between the two. For example, Brown (1973) reports that a child in stage 1 used *fell-down* about 10 times without ever using *fall* or *falling*. This suggests that *fell-down* was memorized; there is no evidence that the child knows the stem *fall*.

There also seems to be evidence that children in stage 2 treat irregular past tenses as stems themselves. For example, children use forms such as *wenting*, *ating* and *thoughting*, or use irregular past tenses as infinitives, as in *Can you broke those?*. It is interesting to point out that errors of this kind arise around the time at which children seem to overgeneralize and produce double-marked past tenses, such as *camed* or *ated*. The reader will recall that the Rumelhart and McClelland model also produced these double-marked past tenses at the end of stage 2, and Rumelhart and McClelland saw this as another piece of evidence in favor of their model. However, forms like *camed* and *ated* were generated as past tenses of *come* and *eat*. However, given the occurrence of forms such *ating*, one might argue that this is actually a wrong prediction, and that such double-marked pasts should really be treated as past tenses of *came* and *ate*, which the child mistakenly interpreted as stems.

Given this evaluation of the Rumelhart and McClelland model, what are the consequences for connectionist models in general? Is it just that the Rumelhart and McClelland model is an unsuccessful attempt at modeling a certain pattern of behavior within an otherwise promising paradigm, or are some of the problems with this model more general and arise out of the PDP approach? Pinker and Prince believe that the shortcomings of the Rumelhart and McClelland model are symptomatic of more general problems with the PDP approach.

A first general point that Pinker and Prince raise concerns the representation of individuals in PDP networks, whether these individuals be real individuals in the world, or verbs or past tenses of verbs. Individuals are represented by certain patterns of activation over the units in a given network. Moreover, each unit in the network corresponds to a certain property of the individual. Thus, the units have semantic content, and represent the microfeatures of an item.

Pinker and Prince have no objection to this kind of featural decomposition. In fact, they rightly point out that featural decomposition has been used in linguistics for a long time. Many phonological rules are formulated in terms of the features of the items to which the rule can be applied, and more recently it has been proposed to see grammatical categories, such as N, or NP, simply as sets of grammatical features (see, e.g., Gazdar, Klein, Pullum, & Sag, 1985). Interestingly enough, there have also been attempts at featural analysis in semantics (e.g., Katz & Fodor, 1963), but the consensus seems to be that these theories have failed. There are a variety of reasons for this, one of them being that the meanings of many natural kind words such as *gold, horse, lemon*, and so on, could not be analyzed in terms of a set of general purpose primitives, unless one was prepared to have such "high-level" semantic primitives as *goldness, horseness, lemonness*, and so on. Featural analysis, then, has been a successful tool in various branches of linguistics, and PDP models inherit some of the advantages of this approach. However, according to Pinker and Prince, PDP models run into difficulties because they see an individual as nothing but a set of features, and information such as ordering of the features, constituency structure, and so on, is lost. In this respect, PDP models are different from previous attempts to explain linguistic phenomena with the help of a set of features, and, according to Pinker and Prince, this lack of structure is one of the reasons for their most dramatic shortcomings.

Pinker and Prince refer to Norman's criticisms of PDP models to support this claim. Earlier, we mentioned that Norman attacked PDP models because of their lack of variables. Norman's second criticism concerns what he calls the *type-token* problem: The ability to handle different instances (tokens) of the same concept (type) at the same time. Norman gives the example of representing the sentences *John eats a sandwich* and *Helene eats a sandwich* simultaneously. When we hear these sentences, we assume that there are two different sandwiches and we therefore need two different tokens of the same type sandwich. But tokens or individuals are simply sets of features, and PDP models do not seem to allow one to represent the fact that a given bunch of features corresponds to a single individual. Conversely, it is impossible to distinguish between two individuals if they have exactly the same features. Pinker and Prince point out that this problem also arises in the context of the Rumelhart and McClelland past tense model. After all, there are certain verbs in English that have the same stem, but which have different past tenses. For example, *wring* and *ring* are pronounced identically and therefore are analyzed as the same set of Wickelfeatures, but whereas the first has the past tense *wrung*, the second has the past tense *rang*. It is impossible for any PDP model that analyses a word simply as a set of features of whatever kind to represent this distinction.

A second general point concerns the PDP learning mechanisms. Learning in PDP models is a form of the old psychological theory of associationism and therefore runs into all the problems that associationism did. For example, as Pinker and Prince point out, in a PDP model any statistical correlation between input items can be learned. While one might argue that such a powerful learning mechanism is an advantage, there are situations where this power becomes a liability. There are certain transformations that never occur in any natural language. One attractive explanation for this observation is that the human learning mechanism is constrained, and simply cannot learn certain rules. But PDP models do not seem to be constrained in this sense and therefore may be too powerful.

Another problem with the PDP learning mechanisms is mentioned by Holyoak (1987). PDP learning mechanisms require a very large number of trials. To illustrate Holyoak's point, one may cite Rumelhart and McClelland's model which needed 190 trials on each of the 420 verbs, that is, almost 80,000 learning trials, to reach a stage 3 model. But, Holyoak points out, there are plenty of examples of one-trial learning, especially in cases where the new hypothesis is consistent with prior knowledge. It is not clear how one-trial learning can be explained in a PDP model.

Furthermore, in circumstances where one-trial learning takes place, people often ignore any statistical correlations that might exist between the different input items. People often rely almost exclusively on the knowledge that they discovered to be useful on previous similar situations, even if this means that the problem cannot be successfully solved. As an illustration of this, one can refer to an experiment by Levine (1971). Levine set university students the following simple problem. Presented with two cards, the subjects had to pick one of them. The experimenter would then tell them whether the alternative they had chosen was correct. In the first stage of the experiment, the correct solution was based on the position of the correct card relative to the other. Subjects had no problem in discovering this. Then he changed the correct solution to one which involved picking a card based on what was written on it, rather than on its relative position. He found that around 80% of his subjects could *not* solve the second problem within 100 trials, thus demonstrating convincingly the influence of prior knowledge on problem solving. PDP learning mechanisms seems to be unable to take into account this kind of top-down information about a specific domain.

6.4. Conclusion

In this section, we reviewed various criticisms of PDP models. One point which can be found in a number of these critical reviews is the lack of structure in PDP representations and the importance of such structure in a number of areas of cognitive science. Whereas Fodor and Pylyshyn's arguments are rather abstract, Pinker and Prince come to similar conclusions by looking at a particular PDP model in a lot of detail. Also, Norman's review, although in general much more favorable than the Fodor and Pylyshyn and the Pinker and Prince paper, seems to point to the lack of a clear structure in PDP representations.

A second point that has not been highlighted quite as much is the difficulties in deciding on an appropriate representation of input and output information. For example, Rumelhart and McClelland's encoding of words as sets of Wickelfeatures, although certainly not unproblematic, would seem to be a major factor in the (limited) success of the model. A lot of the more successful applications of the PDP methodology seem to rely on clever representations of input and output information.

A third point concerns the learning mechanisms. The main problem is that

PDP learning is restricted to extracting statistical correlations from the set of input items. It is not clear how to restrict the learning mechanisms to explain the fact that certain rules never occur in any natural language, and therefore would seem to point to certain inherent limitations in the human language acquisition system. Also, there seems to be no place for prior information to guide the learning processes.

A final point that is worth reiterating is the question about the status of connectionist models as psychological theories. One may wonder whether models that merely simulate human cognitive behavior without giving a clear insight in how the model achieves this constitute adequate psychological theories.

7. GENERAL CONCLUSION

In this chapter, we have reviewed connectionism, a radically different approach to cognitive science. We have given some of the reasons why the connectionists have turned away from the traditional symbol-processing traditional in cognitive science, and we have described the mechanisms that have postulated in stead. We also discussed a number of critical reviews.

It is too early to judge whether the PDP approach will succeed or not. There are certainly severe difficulties some of which have been discussed, and it is not clear that it will be possible to overcome all of these. On the other hand, it seems likely that the PDP approach may have the lasting effect of making people aware of the need to take seriously the findings of neurologists about the workings of the brain. PDP models are to a large extent neurologically inspired, even if the present models are not always neurologically correct. Another lasting effect of the PDP approach may follow from the emphasis that it places on the problem of learning. Although learning has been studied within the symbol-processing paradigm, it has not occupied the position that it perhaps merits. It is certainly central in connectionist thinking, and we may see a greater interest in learning in more traditional cognitive science as a result of this.

9
Conclusion

1. INTRODUCTION

In the previous chapters we reviewed the various knowledge representation languages that have been proposed in Artificial Intelligence. We also reviewed some of the arguments that have been presented in their favor, and problems. We also discussed a recent approach, connectionism, which can be distinguished from the other theories discussed in this book in that it no longer adheres to the knowledge representation hypothesis, and no longer assumes that any artificially intelligent system must contain a separate component which is the knowledge that the system has. In this chapter we discuss some open problems and research issues in knowledge representation.

2. ANALOGICAL REPRESENTATIONS

Most of the representations that have been discussed in this book are examples of what Sloman (1971, 1975) calls *Fregean* representations. Sloman contrasts Fregean representations with *analogical* representations, which he defines as follows:

> If R is an analogical representation of T, then (a) there must be parts of R representing parts of T . . ., and (b) it must be possible to specify some sort of correspondence, possibly context-dependent, between properties or relations of parts of R and properties or relations of parts of T. (Sloman, 1975)

Clear examples of analogical representations are things like maps, and diagrams. The following is another example of an analogical representation of the situation in which block A is on top of block B:

a
b

This is an analogical representation because parts of this representation represent entities in the situation (thus, *a* in the representation corresponds to block A), and

221

certain relations between entities in the representation correspond to relations between parts of the situation (thus, *a* being above *b* in the picture corresponds to block A being on top of block B). Contrast this for, example, which the following representation in logic, a prototypical Fregean representation language:

on(a, b)

Analogical representations should not be confused with reasoning by analogy, which seems to underlie a lot of creative thinking. (For a psychological study of the importance of reasoning by analogy for problem solving, the reader is referred to Gick & Holyoak, 1980.) Reasoning by analogy concerns using knowledge about an old problem in order to discover solutions to new problems. For example, certain problems in particle physics could be solved once it was realized that an atom is in certain respects similar to a solar system. The use of analogies in problem solving involves finding mappings between features of a new problem and features of an old problem. The hope then is that these mappings can be used to "translate" the solution to the old problem into a possible solution for the new problem. Whether the problems themselves are represented in an analogical or a nonanalogical knowledge representation language is a completely separate question.

Many psychologists have proposed that the mental representation that humans use are analogical. For example, in order to explain the psychological findings concerning the representation and processing of visual mental images Kosslyn (1981) proposes analogical representations although they may be generated from nonanalogical representations in long-term memory. (Pylyshyn, 1981, attacks Kosslyn's position and argues that Fregean representations can explain these phenomena just as well.) Johnson-Laird (1983) proposes analogical representations both for reasoning and for language understanding. However, there have been relatively few attempts to build computer programs that use analogical representations. Counterexamples include Gelernter's Geometry Machine which used diagrams of the kind used by, for example, Euclid to solve problems in geometry (Gelernter, 1963) and Funt's WHISPER, a program that used analogical representations to predict the collapse of a structure consisting of a number of blocks (Funt, 1980). Kosslyn's model of imagery processing was also implemented as a computer simulation.

There are various advantages to analogical representations. First, problem solving with analogical representations is often much simpler, at least for humans. Thus, finding a route between two places on a map of the railway network of some country is much easier than finding a route in a knowledge base which contains a separate logical proposition for each pair of cities directly linked by a railway line, and the proposition that if *a* is connected to *b*, and *b* is connected to *c*, then *a* and *c* are connected as well.

A related reason is the fact that an analogical representation makes certain features of the situation self-evident (Funt, 1987). For example, by looking at a picture you can see directly whether two objects are close to each other. The problem of course is that vision is still a very difficult area. No complete artificial vision system exists yet. Thus, it might seem that in order to make use of the fact that certain features are self-evident in an analogical representation, one would have to build a full vision system.

Funt solved this problem in WHISPER by including what he called the *retina* and the *retinal supervisor*. The retina consisted of a large number of parallel processors, each of which could look at a small part of the *diagram*, the internal picture that the system had of whatever structure of blocks it was dealing with. Each processor in the retina, also called a *bubble*, could either be "marked" or "unmarked." A bubble was marked if there was a line in the portion of the diagram that the bubble looked at. A lot of the intelligence of WHISPER resided in the retinal supervisor, which would take as input relatively high level questions such as "Do shapes A and B touch?" and "Is shape C symmetrical about a given axis?" and generate as output algorithms which could then be sent to the bubbles in the retina. Thus, the retinal supervisor was responsible for translating high level requests into low-level algorithms that could be executed by the bubbles. One might therefore argue that WHISPER did indeed include a vision system.

Another argument that Funt sees for analogical representations is the fact that one can use commonsense knowledge without having to completely formalize it. To give a very simple example, if you use diagrams in geometric reasoning, then you can see that two identical right-angled isosceles triangles, when joined together along their hypotenuses, form a square. If you used a nonanalogical representation, then clearly you would have to either include this observation as an axiom, or ensure that it could be deduced from the other axioms that the system has available. But often axiomatizing this sort of knowledge is very difficult (for example, try to formalize the behavior of fluids). Clearly, a system that can use this type of knowledge without having to axiomatize it, would be a great advantage.

While analogical representations have a number of advantages, there are also certain problems that remain, and that suggest that they are not the complete answer to the problem of knowledge representation. First, as Funt himself observes, analogical representations are often not general. Thus, although one can see in an analogical representation that two identical right-angled isosceles triangles, when joined together along their hypotenuses, form a square, you can only make this observation about the two specific triangles in the diagram. You cannot make the generalization that this is true for any two identical right-isosceles triangles. A second problem is the problem that many analogical representations are to a large extent conventional, and you need to know these conventions in order to be able to use the representation. Consider for example road maps, and the knowledge that one needs to have in order to be able to read them.

A final problem is that in order to be able to use analogical representations you need a lot of difficult and complicated support machinery. For example, we have already seen that WHISPER contained a simple, but more or less fully fledged, vision system.

3. SINGLE OR MULTIPLE KNOWLEDGE REPRESENTATION LANGUAGES

There are many different knowledge representation languages around, each of which seems to be good at representing a different type of knowledge. For example, we saw that logic-based knowledge representation languages were good at expressing what we called incomplete knowledge, such as existentially quantified knowledge, or disjunctions. Other knowledge representation languages had problems with this. For example, we saw that it was difficult to represent arbitrary disjunctions in frame-based languages. However, logic-based languages had their problems with default knowledge, whereas other knowledge representation languages, most notably frames and semantic networks, were good at this. Also, as we saw in the previous section, for certain problems it might be preferable to use analogical representations.

One may regret this abundance of knowledge representation languages. However, Sloman (1985) argues strongly in favor of the position that we need to explore the uses of many different formalisms for different purposes. He argues that one of the hallmarks of an intelligent system is that it can choose between different formalisms, and that on occasions, it can create new formalisms when the situation it finds itself in demands that this be done. One is tempted to argue that the mental models that Johnson-Laird postulates to account for human performance in syllogistic reasoning (see, e.g., Johnson-Laird, 1983) are an example of such a special purpose representation.

There are a few open problems that anybody faces who advocates the use of multiple knowledge representation languages. First, the question arises when to use which knowledge representation language. In order to provide knowledge based programs that are maintainable long after the person who originally implemented the system has gone, it is necessary to avoid some of the possibly *ad hoc* style of knowledge representation that may result if everybody uses their own knowledge representation language.

As we saw in Chapter 7, KRYPTON tried to solve this problem by enforcing a rigid distinction between definitional and assertional information, and using one knowledge representation language (frames) for definitional knowledge, and another (logic) for assertional knowledge. As we have seen, KRYPTON is not without its problems. For example, it is not clear how KRYPTON could be extended to deal with default reasoning. However, for the purposes of the present discussion, the main problem with KRYPTON is that the number of knowledge representation languages is still limited to only 2, and if we are to believe Sloman's arguments, any *a priori* limitation is undesirable at this stage.

Another attempt to solve the problem of when to use which knowledge representation formalism, is the work of Chandrasekaran and his associates (for an overview of this work, see Chandrasekaran, 1987), and Wielinga and Breuker (see, for example, Breuker, 1987). Chandrasekaran's work is based on the assumption that complex knowledge based reasoning tasks of the kind typically undertaken by expert systems can be decomposed into a set of *generic tasks*. In an expert system the overall goal that one is trying to achieve can often be decomposed in a set of subgoals. A generic task is problem solving strategy that is appropriate for solving one of the subgoals. Each generic task has associated with it certain types of knowledge and a family of control regimes. Chandrasekaran then sets out to provide a set of guidelines which allow one to determine which generic task one would like the application to perform, and to choose appropriate knowledge representation languages and control regimes. Wielinga and Breuker's KADS methodology is very similar although more directly aimed at the problem of knowledge elicitation: How to get the knowledge out of an expert whose specialized problem solving abilities should form the basis of an expert system. They come up with the notion of an *interpretation model*, which in spirit looks very similar to Chandrasekaran's notion of a generic task. Breuker (1987) contains a fairly large list of interpretation models. Chandrasekaran's and Breuker and Wielinga's work point in a promising direction. Both try to formulate guidelines which might prove useful in choosing an appropriate knowledge representation language for a given application.

To illustrate, consider Clancey's (1984) discussion of heuristic classification. Many expert systems have the task of classifying some object as being a member of a limited number of classes. Thus, a patient may be classified as suffering from one of a number of possible diseases, or a potential investor may be given advice to invest in one of a number of companies that the system knows about. Clancey observes that many classification expert systems go through three conceptually different stages. First, they try to *abstract* from the data that they have obtained about the object to be classified. Thus, in the investment example, one may conclude from the finding that the investor is interested in a quick profit that they are interested in high-risk investment. The second stage in heuristic classification is to *heuristically match* the abstracted data to a class of solutions. Clancey claims that in many expert systems this match is based on an incomplete model of the world, and that is mainly here that the rules of thumb that expert have built up over the years are of prime importance. In our investment example, we may have the rule which heuristically matches the information that an investor is interested in high-risk investment with the advice that they should invest in a small but fast growing company. The final stage in heuristic classification is the need to *refine* the solution abstraction into a proper solution. Thus, if we have discovered that our investor is interested in small and fast-growing companies, the system has to make its advice more specific and suggest a particular company.

Clancey's work on heuristic classification can be regarded as an attempt at decomposing a large and complex task into a set of generic tasks. It seems likely that each generic task needs a different knowledge representation language and a different control regime. For example, the knowledge that is used during the refinement phase is very hierarchical in structure, and one is therefore inclined to use a frame-based language. On the other hand, the knowledge used during the heuristic match phase seems more suited for a production rule language. However, more work is necessary to match generic tasks to the different knowledge representation languages and control regimes.

A second problem with the view that we need many knowledge representation formalisms is in a sense similar to one of the problems which was raised against procedural representations. Sloman argues that in order to choose the right representation it is not enough just to look at the domain. The way in which the knowledge will be used is important as well. Chandrasekaran makes a similar point when he argues that knowledge representation and use cannot be separated. Clearly, the consequence of this position would seem to be that every time domain knowledge needs to be used to perform a different task, it will be necessary to reimplement the knowledge. Thus, as with procedural representations, every time a knowledge base is to be re-used, a new knowledge base will need to be constructed. Clearly, this is undesirable.

There are two ways around this problem. First, one can simply deny Chandrasekaran's claim that knowledge representation and use cannot be separated. The work on explicit representations of control knowledge which was discussed in a number of places throughout this book would then provide a solution. Using the same knowledge base to do perform another task then simply amounts to changing the control knowledge base. The disadvantage is, of course, that the resulting system is inefficient, but there is research underway that tries to avoid this problem.

A second possible way out of this problem is to store the knowledge in some application-independent format, and then translate it into a more appropriate knowledge format for every application. For example, the knowledge could be stored as a set of propositions in logic and translated into semantic networks for a specific application. Wielinga and Breuker's interpretation models, or Chandrasekaran's generic task formalisms, could be used as target representations for particular tasks.

Although this approach might go some way towards fulfilling Sloman's wish for multiple representations without falling into the proceduralist's problem, there are three open problems with it. First, it clearly does not explain at all how intelligent beings develop new representations. Second, it still requires an answer to the question of when to use which knowledge representation language. Third, the application-independent language in which the knowledge is to be stored, must be expressive enough to enable one to represent many different types of knowledge. However, the design of this language is clearly difficult. For example, we have seen that each of the languages discussed in this book seems to have certain expressive limitations. Concluding, the idea that knowledge should be stored in an application-independent format, and compiled into a application-specific language, seems a promising direction for research.

4. CONNECTIONISM

Most of the work discussed in this book has been based on the knowledge representation hypothesis. According to this hypothesis, every intelligent process must contain a separate component that can be interpreted as representing the knowledge that the system has about the world. As we have seen in Chapter 8, this view has come under attack from the PDP or connectionist approach.

It should be stressed again that the argument between the connectionists and those who believe in the knowledge representation hypothesis is not about the value of representations. Both believe that representations are necessary to explain human cognitive behavior. In this respect, both disagree with, for example, the behaviorists according to whom all animal and human behavior could be explained simply in terms of stimulus-response pairs.

The main disagreement between the connectionists and those who subscribe to the knowledge representation hypothesis concerns two points. First, the latter believe that there should be a separate component which can best be described as the knowledge base. This component can be distinguished from other components which enable the system to use this knowledge in order to solve certain problems. The connectionists do not make such a clear distinction between representing knowledge and processing it. A PDP model both represents and processes knowledge.

A second point of disagreement concerns the nature of the representations. The traditional symbol-processing approach assumes that representations are very much like a language. In particular, they believe that representations are structured and that they obey sort form of compositionality. The connectionists, on the other hand, argue that representations are distributed and that they do not exhibit any structure. Thus, for the connectionist there is no reason why the representation of the sentence *John hit Mary* and *Mary hit John* should have anything in common. Note that it can at least be argued that the hypothesis that representations are structured is in principle independent of the knowledge representation hypothesis. One can well imagine systems that have a separate component for representing knowledge, without insisting that the formalism used for knowledge representation is structured and obeys the principle of compositionality. In practice, however, these two assumptions have nearly always gone hand in hand.

In Chapter 8 we distinguished between three views of connectionism. First, one could see PDP models merely as *implementations* of traditional symbol processing theories. Second, one could see PDP models as *alternatives* to symbol processing theories. Third, one could see PDP models as proposing a number of primitive operations, which are easy for the brain to compute.

The last view of PDP models is perhaps the most interesting. The first view, implementational connectionism, shows that traditional symbol processing theories can run on machines that are in important aspects like the human brain. Clearly, to the extent that PDP models do indeed mimic the human brain, this is an interesting result. However, for symbol processing theories, this is hardly a surprising result. After all, given the assumption that our mental representations must somehow be implemented in the brain, you would expect that whatever knowledge representation language you think most closely resembles our language of thought, can be implemented on a brainlike machine. Of course implementational connectionism can still be useful. For one thing, if the PDP model does indeed simulate the brain in sufficient detail, then it will enable one to do certain experimental studies which, for obvious ethical reasons, could not be performed on functioning human brains.

The second view of connectionism is the strongest and most contentious. Under this view, the traditional knowledge representation hypothesis approach and the PDP approach are radically opposed to each other, and are competing theories that are aimed at explaining exactly the same phenomena. This view of connectionism is a form of strong reductionism. The claim is that psychological phenomena can be explained in neurological terms. In Chapter 8, we saw some reasons why this form of connectionism might be too strong. While it is no doubt true that psychology should be informed by whatever neuroscientists discover about the workings of the brain, it seems doubtful that all psychological phenomena can be explained in purely neurological terms.

The final view of connectionism holds that PDP models can be seen as showing that certain operations are easy to perform in brainlike machines. Traditional theories will then have to be revised and take these operations as basic building blocks. Thus, some of the PDP work has shown that a task like pattern completion is fairly easy for a connectionist network. Under this view of the PDP approach, new symbol processing theories should take this into account, and rather than using matching of two patterns as a primitive operation they should use pattern completion as a primitive operation. While this form of connectionism seems promising, the problem is that not enough PDP models have been built to give one a good idea about which operations are easy to perform for machines of this kind, and under what conditions. Thus, before one can revise one's symbol processing theories, more work would need to be done in order to develop some feel for these issues.

One last remark needs to be made about the PDP approach. Independently of the arguments about the psychological plausibility, both connectionist models and symbol processing models can still be useful from a purely technological point of view. Thus, even if it turns out that the strongest form of connectionism is correct, and that all psychological phenomena can indeed be explained in neurological terms, symbol processing theories might still be valuable from a technological point of view, for example, because they make representation of information easier for human knowledge engineers. Alternatively, PDP models may have to be rejected as psychological theories, while still being useful from a technological point of view.

5. CONCLUSION

The field of knowledge representation has been a major area of research in the relatively short history of AI. The many different representational formalism that have been discussed in this book bear witness to this fact. Nevertheless, there are still many open problems. Further research is necessary to clarify these points. While this book has been written principally from an AI perspective, cognitive psychologists have an important role to play. Despite the success of AI in certain areas, humans are still the most advanced intelligent systems that we know of, and a better understanding of human intelligence and knowledge representation will provide important insights that can be used to build artificial intelligent systems.

References

Abadi, M., & Manna, Z. (1986). Modal theorem proving. *8th International Conference on Automated Deduction*, pp. 172–89.

Abelson, H., & Sussman, G. (with Julie Sussman). (1985). *Structure and interpretation of computer programs*. Cambridge, MA: MIT Press.

Adams, J. (1976). Probabilistic reasoning and certainty factors. *Mathematical Biosciences, 32*, 177–86. (Edited version appears in Buchanan and Shortliffe (Eds.) (1984), chapter 12.)

Aikins, J. (1983). Prototypical knowledge for expert systems. *Artificial Intelligence, 20*, 163–210.

Aitkenhead, A., & Slack, J. (Eds.). (1985). *Issues in cognitive modeling*. Hillsdale, NJ: Lawrence Erlbaum Associates.

Akmajian, A., & Heny, F. (1975). *An introduction to the principles of transformational grammar*. Cambridge, MA: MIT Press.

Allen, J. (1981). *A general model of action and time* (Tech. Rep. 97). Rochester, NY: Department of Computer Science, University of Rochester.

Allen, J. (1983). Maintaining knowledge about temporal intervals. *Communications of the ACM, 26*, 832–43. (Also in Brachman and Levesque (1985).)

Allwood, J., Andersson, L., & Dahl, O. (1977). *Logic in linguistics*. Cambridge: Cambridge University Press.

Anderson, J. (1976). *Language, memory and thought*. Hillsdale, NJ: Lawrence Erlbaum Associates.

Anderson, J. (1985). *Cognitive psychology and its implications* (2nd ed.). New York: Freeman.

Anderson, J., & Bower, G. (1973). *Human associative memory*. New York: Holt.

Bartlett, F. (1932). *Remembering*. Cambridge: Cambridge University Press.

Beth, E. (1959). *The foundations of mathematics*. Amsterdam: North Holland.

Bledsoe, W. (1977). Non-resolution theorem proving. *Artificial Intelligence, 9*, 1–35.

Bobrow, D., & Collins, A. (Eds.). (1975). *Representation and understanding: Studies in cognitive science*. New York: Academic Press.

Bobrow, D, Kaplan, R., Kay, M., Norman, D., Thompson, H., & Winograd, T. (1977). GUS, A frame-driven dialog system. *Artificial Intelligence, 8*, 155–73.

Bobrow, D., & Winograd, T. (1977). An overview of KRL, a knowledge representation language. *Cognitive Science, 1*, 3–46.

Bobrow, D., & Winograd, T. (1979). KRL, Another perspective. *Cognitive Science, 3*, 29–42.

Bobrow, D., Winograd, T., & The KRL Research Group. (1977). Experience with KRL-0: One cycle a knowledge representation language. *IJCAI 5*, 213–222.

Boolos, G., & Jeffrey, R. (1980). *Computability and logic* (2nd ed). Cambridge: Cambridge University Press.

Brachman, R. (1977). What's in a concept: Structural foundations for semantic networks. *International Journal of Man-Machine Studies, 9*, 127–52.

Brachman, R. (1979). On the epistemological status of semantic networks. In N. Findler (Ed.), *Associative networks: Representation and use of knowledge by computers*. New York: Academic Press. (Also in Brachman and Levesque (1985).)

Brachman, R. (1985). "I lied about the trees" Or, defaults and definitions in knowledge representation. *AI Magazine, 5*(3), 80–93.

Brachman, R., Fikes, R., & Levesque, H. (1983). KRYPTON: A functional approach to knowledge representation. *IEEE Computer, 16*(10), 67–73. (A longer version appears in Brachman and Levesque (1985).)

Brachman, R., Gilbert, V., & Levesque, H. (1985). An essential hybrid reasoning system: Knowledge and symbol level accounts of KRYPTON. *IJCAI 9*, 532–39.

Brachman, R., & Levesque, H. (Eds.). (1985). *Readings in knowledge representation*. Los Altos, CA: Morgan Kaufmann.

Brachman, R., & Schmolze, J. (1985). An overview of the KL-ONE knowledge representation system. *Cognitive Science, 9*, 171–216.

Breuker, J. (Ed.). (1987). *Model-driven knowledge acquisition interpretation models*. Amsterdam: Dept. of Social Science Informatics, University of Amsterdam.

Brown, F. (Ed.). (1987). *The frame problem in artificial intelligence: Proceedings of the 1987 workshop*. Los Altos, CA: Morgan Kaufmann.

Brown, R. (1973). *A first language: The early stages*. Cambridge, MA: Harvard University Press.

Brownston, L., Farrell, R., Kant, E., & Martin, N. (1985). *Programming expert systems in OPS5*. Reading, MA: Addison-Wesley.

Buchanan, B., Sutherland, G., & Feigenbaum, E. (1969). Heuristic DENDRAL: A program for generating explanatory hypotheses in organic chemistry. In B. Meltzer & D. Michie (Eds.), *Machine Intelligence, 4*. Edinburgh: Edinburgh University Press.

Bundy, A., Byrd, L., Luger, G., Mellish, C., & Palmer, M. (1979). Solving mechanics problems using meta-level inference. *IJCAI 6*, 1017–27. (Also in D. Michie (Ed.). (1979) *Expert systems in the micro electronic age*. Edinburgh: Edinburgh University Press.)

Carlson, N. (1986). *Physiology of behavior* (3rd ed.). Boston: Allyn and Bacon.

Carnap, R. (1947). *Meaning and necessity: A study in semantics and modal logic*. Chicago: University of Chicago Press.

Chandrasekaran, B. (1987). Towards a functional architecture for intelligence based on generic information processing tasks. *IJCAI 10*, 1183–1192.

Chang, C., & Lee, R. (1973). *Symbolic logic and mechanical theorem proving*. New York: Academic Press.

Clancey, W. (1979). *Transfer of rule-based expertise through a tutorial dialogue*. Computer Science doctoral dissertation. (STAN-CS-769.) Stanford University, Stanford, CA.

Clancey, W. (1983). The epistemology of rule-based expert systems: A framework for explanation. *Artificial Intelligence, 20*, 215–51.

Clancey, W. (1984). Classification problem solving. *AAAI 84*, 49–55.

Shoham, Y. (1987). Nonmonotonic logics: Meaning and utility. *IJCAI, 10*, 388–393. (Also in Ginsberg (Ed.). (1987).)

Shortliffe, E. (1976). *Computer-based medical consultation: MYCIN*. New York: American Elsevier.

Shortliffe, E., & Buchanan, B. (1975). A model of inexact reasoning in medicine. *Mathematical Biosciences, 23*, 351–379. (Edited version appears in Buchanan & Shortliffe (Eds.). (1984). Chapter 11.)

Simmons, R, & Bruce, B (1971). Some relations between predicate calculus and semantic network representations. *IJCAI, 2*, 524–29.

Slobin, D. (1971). On the learning of morphological rules: A reply to Palermo and Eberhart. In D. Slobin (Ed.), *The ontogenesis of grammar: A theoretical symposium*. New York: Academic Press.

Sloman, A. (1971). Interactions between philosophy and AI: The role of intuition and non-logical reasoning in AI. *IJCAI, 2*, 270–78.

Sloman, A. (1975). Afterthoughts on analogical representations. *TINLAP, 1*, 178–82. (Also in Brachman and Levesque (Eds.). (1985).)

Sloman, A. (1985). Why we need many knowledge representation formalisms. In M. Bramer (Ed.), *Research and development in expert systems*. Cambridge: Cambridge University Press.

Smith, B. (1982). *Reflection and semantics in a procedural language*. PhD Thesis, MIT, Cambridge, MA. (Prologue reprinted in Brachman & Levesque (1985).)

Smullyan, R. (1968). *First-order logic*. Berlin: Springer.

Sowa, J. (1984). *Conceptual structures: Information processing in mind and machine*. Reading, MA: Addison-Wesley.

Spiegelhalter, D. (1986). A statistical view of uncertainty in expert systems. In W. Gale (Ed.), *Artificial Intelligence and statistics*. Reading, MA: Addison-Wesley.

Stefik, M. (1979). An examination of a frame-structured representation system. *IJCAI, 6*, 845–52.

Stefik, M., & Bobrow, D. (1986). Object-oriented programming: Themes and variations. *AI Magazine, 6*(4), 40–62.

Stickel, M. (1983). Theory resolution: Building-in nonequational theories. *AAAI-83*, pp. 391–397.

Stickel, M. (1987). An introduction to automated deduction. In W. Bibel & Ph. Jorrand (Eds.), *Fundamentals of artificial intelligence: An advanced course*. Berlin: Springer-Verlag.

Stoy, J. (1979). *Denotational semantics: The Scott-Strachey approach to programming language theory*. Cambridge, MA: MIT Press.

Swartout, W. (1981). Explaining and justifying in expert consulting programs. *IJCAI, 7*, 815–23.

Swartout, W. (1983). XPLAIN: A system for creating and explaining expert consulting systems. *Artificial Intelligence, 21*, 285–325.

Tversky, A., & Kahneman, D. (1974). Judgment under uncertainty: Heuristics and biases. *Science, 185*, 1124–1131.

van Benthem, J. (1982). *The logic of time*. Dordrecht: Reidel.

van Harmelen, F. (1989). An overview of meta-level architectures. In P. Jackson, H. Reichgelt, & F. van Harmelen (Eds.), *Logic-based knowledge representation*. Cambridge, MA: MIT Press.

Vilain, M. (1985). The restricted language architecture of a hybrid representation language. *IJCAI, 9*, 547–551.

Wallen, L. (1987). Matrix proof methods for modal logic. *IJCAI, 10*, 917–923.

Waterman, D., & Hayes-Roth, F. (1978). *Pattern-directed inference systems.* New York: Academic Press.

Weyrauch, R. (1980). Prologomena to a theory of mechanized formal reasoning. *Artificial Intelligence, 13*, 133–170.

Wielinga, B., & Breuker, J. (1986). Models of expertise. *ECAI, 7*, 306–18.

Winograd, T. (1975). Frame representations and the declarative/procedural controversy. In D. Bobrow & A. Collins (Eds.), *Representation and understanding: Studies in cognitive science.* New York: Academic Press. (Also in Brachman & Levesque (1985).)

Woods, W. (1975). What's in a link: Foundations of semantic networks. In D. Bobrow & A. Collins (Eds.), *Representation and understanding: Studies in cognitive science.* New York: Academic Press. (Also in Brachman & Levesque (1985).)

Young, R., & O'Shea, T. (1981). Errors in children's subtraction. *Cognitive Science, 5*, 153–77.

Zadeh, L. (1975). Fuzzy logic and approximate reasoning. *Synthese, 30*, 407–28.

Zadeh, L. (1987). Common sense and fuzzy logic. In N. Cercone & G. McCalla (Eds.), *The knowledge frontier: Essays in the representation of knowledge.* Berlin: Springer-Verlag.

Author Index

A

Abadi, M., 58, *230*
Abelson, H., 146, 176, *230*
Abelson, R., *239*
Adams, J., 89, *230*
Aiello, N., 109, *237*
Aikens, J., 174, *230*
Aitkenhead, A., *230*
Akmajiian, A., *230*
Akmakian, A., 119, *230*
Aleliunas, R., 78, *237*
Allen, J., 58, *230*
Allwood, J., 33, *230*
Anderson, J., 16, 116, *230*
Andersson, L., 33, *230*
Asanuma, C., 186, *232*

B

Bartlett, F., 144, *230*
Bates, R., 173, *235*
Beth, E., 39, *230*
Bledsoe, W., 45, *230*
Bobrow, D., 144, 145, 149, 151, 168, *230*, *240*
Boolos, G., 42, 60, *231*
Bower, G., 116, *230*
Brachman, R., 5, 6, 19, 30, 57, 84, 116, 117, 127, 135, 138, 156, 164, 173, 178, 180, 181, *231*, *235*, *236*
Breuker, J., 17, 27, 225, *231*, *241*
Brown, F., 69, *231*
Brown, R., 217, *231*
Brownston, L., 82, *231*
Bruce, B., 119, 141, *240*
Buchanan, B., 2, 27, 80, 88, 101, 102, *231*, *232*, *240*
Bundy, A., *231*
Byrd, L., 26, *231*

C

Carbonell, J., 126, 187, *237*, *239*
Carlson, N., 186, *231*
Carnap, R., 37, *231*
Cercone, N., 125, 133, *239*
Chandrasekaran, B., 225, *231*
Chang, C., 53, *231*
Clancey, W., 17, 27, 103, 104, 111, 225, *231*, *232*, *234*
Clocksin, W., 44, *232*
Cohen, P., 87, 93, *232*
Collins, A., 117, 121, *230*, *232*
Crick, F., 186, *232*
Cullingford, R., 146, *232*

D

Dahl, O., 33, *230*
Davis, R., 26, 27, 81, 99, 100, 101, 102, 106, 107, 114, *232*
de Kleer, J., 73, 75, 76, *232*
Dowty, D., 37, *232*
Doyle, J., 63, 73, 75, 76, *232*, *236*
Duda, R., 129, *232*

E

Elfrink, B., 182, *232*
Elgot-Drapkin, J., 71, *232*
Erman, L., 109, *232*, *233*
Erman, L., 110, *233*
Ernst, G., 2, *233*
Etherington, D., 66, 164, *233*
Eysenck, M., 117, *233*

F

Fahlman, S., 121, *233*
Farrell, R., 82, *231*

243

Subject Index